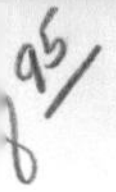

D0986981

THE PUBLIC INTEREST

THE PUBLIC INTEREST

An Essay Concerning the Normative Discourse of Politics

RICHARD E. FLATHMAN

CENTRAL MISSOURI
STATE COLLEGE
Warrensburg

John Wiley & Sons, Inc., New York · London · Sydney

Copyright © 1966 by John Wiley & Sons, Inc.

All rights reserved. This book or any part thereof must not be reproduced in any form without the written permission of the publisher.

Library of Congress Catalog Card Number: 66-15869
Printed in the United States of America

JC507
.F5

For Nancy and Kristen

May they contribute to, and partake of the benefits of, a politics of public interest.

248102

Before proceeding further let us acknowledge that in matters of conduct our theories must be stated inexactly and in outline; for . . . we are to demand only so much of any theory as may be appropriate to its subject matter, and in matters of conduct . . . there are no fixed laws. And if our general theory is thus inexact, its application to particular cases will be all the more so; for these do not come under the head of any specific art or system of rules, but the agent himself must consider on each occasion what the situation requires, just as in medicine or navigation.

Yet while our present theory is thus necesssarily inexact, we must do what we can to help it out.

Aristotle

PREFACE

Man has long believed that he alone among the creatures of the earth is able to distinguish right from wrong and just from unjust and to base his actions on these distinctions. He has also believed that his capacity to reason has made it possible to draw these distinctions and to organize life around them. Hence he has viewed the realm of these distinctions as the realm of reason and thus the realm of the distinctively human. But despite the confidence with which these beliefs have been asserted, they have been subject to recurrent challenge. The affairs of practical men have been disturbed by disagreement and conflict in normative matters, and philosophers, lawgivers, and poets, whose task it has been to clarify them and to guide men concerning them, have fathered an astonishing array of principles and criteria that often mirror rather than clarify the confusions of practical men. Both philosophers and practical men have sometimes concluded that reasoned justification and evaluation are impossible. Few epochs have been more attracted to this conclusion than our own.

Beginning with the powerful analytic efforts of Hume and Kant, modern thinkers have dealt harshly with traditional arguments for the rational basis of moral judgments. Philosophically speaking, these criticisms culminated in the contention of the Logical Positivists that value statements have no cognitive content, cannot be verified or validated, and must be classified as emotive expressions. We can explain the genesis and analyze the behavioral significance of value statements, but the very attempt to justify them rationally involves a philosophical mistake.[1] Now bypassed by the philosophical tradition that produced its most sophisticated formulation, this view has received support from

[1] See the "classic" statement by A. J. Ayer in *Language, Truth, and Logic* (New York: Dover Publications, 1946), Chapter 6, especially pp. 107–112.

a variety of sources—some philosophical, some not—and it commands widespread allegiance.

Nowhere is it more widely accepted than among those who make it their business to study the workings of political life. The student of politics must be aware that political life is value-laden, and it is his task to discover what the values are and to analyze their relationship to other facets of politics. But questions of value are not amenable to rational, transsubjective, scientific analysis, and it is no part of the student's professional task to adjudicate between the values he discovers in political life. If this point of view is valid, it is valid not just for political study but for questions of value wherever they arise. Viewed most broadly, our purpose here is to examine this point of view.

The focal point of the study is a concept that stands at the center of the value dimensions of politics, the concept "public interest." Our aim will be to examine the function of this concept in politics, its relationship to other political concepts such as "rights," "duties," and "authority," the problems that arise in connection with use of the concept, and the merits of some of the solutions that have been advanced for those problems. Since "public interest" is a normative concept, concern with it will lead directly to broad problems of value theory. Hence our particular focus will provide an entry into some of these broader problems.

In addition to standard materials and methods of political study, use has been made of the literature of post-positivistic philosophy (sometimes called "ordinary language philosophy" or "Oxford philosophy"). I have drawn on this body of philosophy in three respects: (1) for an analytic orientation that directs attention to the language ordinarily used in the discourse of politics and morality—an orientation important because it directs attention to a body of evidence about political behavior and practice, (2) for theoretical constructs necessary for the analysis and interpretation of linguistic evidence, and (3) for a body of value theory (especially ethical theory).

The designation "post-positivistic" deserves comment because the belief persists that there is no post-positivistic stage in philosophy, that contemporary philosophy *is* positivistic.[2] This belief is mistaken, and

[2] The designation "positivistic" is extremely crude and could not be sustained in an even moderately detailed discussion of the immediate antecedents of ordinary langauge philosophy, itself a designation of restricted utility. The label is most appropriate in the case of the members of the Vienna Circle and their followers. Extending it to figures such as Russell and the early Wittgenstein—

to dispel it is important to the general issue of the status of value theory in political science and the social sciences generally, to the particular problems of theory about the public interest, and to breaking down the barriers that now separate political science and much of philosophy. Logical Positivism presented powerful arguments for the view that distinctive aspects of value questions are not amenable to reasoned analysis. The belief that contemporary philosophy is positivistic contributes to the continued acceptance of this theory in two ways: it suggests that the theory has the support of those who would be expected to be competent in problems of value theory, and it reduces the likelihood that political and social scientists will grapple with the body of philosophy that has challenged positivism on these questions. The empirically oriented or "scientific" political scientist, whose enterprise has been defined and shaped under the influence of positivism, can believe that his enterprise is built upon firm philosophical foundations. In his case the belief that contemporary philosophy is positivistic impedes communication with philosophy by generating complacency.[3]

The converse case is supplied by those suspicious of a "scientific" political science, those who accept neither the positivistic critique of earlier philosophy nor the closely related critique of earlier political science and political philosophy. As long as this group regards contemporary philosophy as positivistic, it will regard communication with the latter as fruitless. Hence the scientific political scientist holds to the view that value statements are emotive expressions (with most dramatic results in studies of the public interest) without realizing that it has been undermined, whereas the more traditional, philosophically oriented political scientist rejects the view but either does not meet the arguments responsible for much of its popularity or fails to avail himself of findings and reflections most useful in meeting those arguments. Neither group, nor those who occupy positions between them, communicates with philosophy, and the ancient and fruitful ties between philosophy and political science remain broken. It is my hope that use of materials from philosophy will not only be helpful in dealing with the substantive problems of public interest and value

---

better, but still inadequately, described as "logical atomists"—relies upon certain similarities in methodology and in what might be called philosophical inclination, but masks important differences in substantive philosophical position.

[3] See, for example, Herbert Simon, *Administrative Behavior* (New York: Macmillan Co., 1959), especially Chapter 3. See also Simon's remarks in the *American Political Science Review*, **46**, 496 (1952).

theory but will also aid in dispelling the view that Logical Positivism reigns supreme in philosophy.[4]

Concern with language as a source of evidence regarding aspects of human behavior is scarcely a novel development in either philosophy or political science. Aristotle offered the capacity for language as evidence that man is by nature a political animal, and he presented linguistic evidence for his view that justice is the proper end of the Polis. Similarly, much in the theories of Hobbes, Locke, and Rousseau turn on their interpretation of language. This is scarcely surprising. We ordinarily use language not for its own sake but to think and communicate about ourselves, other men, and the world in which we live; that is, our knowledge of and attitudes about ourselves, other men, and the world are available to us primarily if not exclusively through language. Hence, as J. L. Austin said, when we study language "we are looking . . . not *merely* at words . . . but also at the realities we use the words to talk about: we are using a sharpened awareness of words to sharpen our perception of, though not as the final arbiter of, the phenomena."[5]

Note also that we sometimes speak not merely to communicate but to act. Very often speech is not simply a means of describing or communicating some other form of behavior but is *itself* the behavior. To say "I do" when the magistrate has asked, "Do you take this woman to be . . ." is not simply to report a state of mind, make a prediction, or communicate certain expectations to relatives and friends. It is to perform an action in the same sense that throwing a right cross to the jaw, mixing a drink, or casting a ballot is to perform an action. Hence to study speech acts is to study behavior in the same sense that the study of casting ballots is a study of behavior. To the extent that such speech acts are a part of political life, to study them is to study political behavior.

Finally, language is a public, not a private, phenomenon. *You* may have your attitudes, interests, and opinions and *I* mine, and they may

[4] To deal adequately with the place of Logical Positivism in philosophy would require a detailed history of twentieth century philosophy. Introductory accounts are available in G. J. Warnock's *English Philosophy since 1900* (London: Oxford University Press, 1958), and J. O. Urmson, *Philosophical Analysis* (London: Oxford University Press, 1956).

[5] J. L. Austin, *Philosophical Papers* (J. O. Urmson and G. J. Warnock, editors, London: Oxford University Press, 1961), p. 130. For further methodological discussion see V. C. Chappell, editor, *Ordinary Language* (Englewood Cliffs, N. J.: Prentice-Hall, 1964), and Charles E. Caton, editor, *Philosophy and Ordinary Language* (Urbana, Ill.: University of Illinois Press, 1963). Both collections contain useful bibliographies.

or may not coincide in content and consequence. But *we* have a language. If language were not *ours*, it would not be a language because it could not perform the primary function that a language performs—that is, making possible communication between us. It follows that behavior which employs language necessarily takes on a public dimension and becomes subject to certain restraints imposed by the vehicle it utilizes. This is perhaps sufficiently clear regarding the use of language to communicate with others, but it is equally true of behavior that in other respects is entirely private. Even my private thought follows the rules and is subject to the limitations of the language in which I think. Hence, as Clifford Geertz has said, there are respects in which thought is a public activity.[6] The use of language establishes continuity between the public and private realms. This continuity is important to the capacity of men to understand and deal with one another, including the capacity of the student of behavior to analyze and understand behavior. It also provides grounds on which men can question, object to, and offer counterassertions about public performances grounded and justified in terms of private attitudes, opinions, and inclinations. This point is of particular importance to analysis of behavior with value dimensions.

Notice should be taken of a set of distinctions important to ethical theory and basic to much of this book. The distinctions are among (1) questions whether it would be good or right to steal or cheat, whether *X* ought to keep his promise to *Y*, or whether corporal punishment is morally defensible, which are *moral* questions, (2) questions whether a person, group of persons, or society regard it as good or right to steal, cheat, and keep promises, which are questions of *descriptive ethics*, and (3) questions about the structure, logic, and uses of the language employed in moral discourse, which are *ethical* or *metaethical* questions.[7] In this book these distinctions require separations among the studies of "what (policy, decision, action) is in the public interest?" (a *moral* question); "what do the members of society X think is in the public interest?" (a question of *descriptive ethics*); and "when and how do we use the concept 'public interest,'

[6] See Clifford Geertz, "Ideology as a Cultural System," in David Apter, editor, *Ideology and Discontent* (New York: The Free Press of Glencoe, 1964). This point is basic to recent work in the philosophy of mind. I cite Geertz's statement because the paper in which it appears is a splendid example of the fruitfulness of communication between social science and philosophy.

[7] The best short discussion of these distinctions and their significance is in R. M. Hare's article "Ethics," in J. O. Urmson, editor, *The Concise Encyclopedia of Western Philosophy and Philosophers* (New York: Hawthorne Books, 1960).

what force, denotations, and connotations does the concept have in different contexts? How does it relate to other concepts and expressions?" (*metaethical* questions). Our primary concern will be with ethics or metaethics, but it will be impossible to avoid crossing lines from time to time. To cross lines is no transgression: the point of metaethics is to facilitate moral decisions. But to cross lines without being aware that they have been crossed is indeed a transgression.

Richard E. Flathman

Chicago, Illinois
January 1966

Acknowledgments

It is a pleasure to acknowledge the assistance I have received in the course of writing this book. My greatest debt is to the literature on which I have drawn, both the studies mentioned below and the much larger literature from which the cited studies have been selected. I have been somewhat more critical of the literature about public interest than of the body of ethical theory I have utilized, but I have profited greatly from both.

I am grateful to the following publishers and editors for granting me permission to quote passages from books and articles they have published. George Allen and Unwin Ltd. for permission to quote a passage from S. I. Benn and R. S. Peters, *Social Principles and the Democratic State*. Atherton Press for permission to quote a passage from Julius Cohen, "A Lawman's View of the Public Interest," in Carl J. Friedrich, Editor, NOMOS V: *The Public Interest*. The editors of *The Philosophical Review* for permission to quote three passages from John Rawls, "Two Concepts of Rules," *The Philosophical Review*, 64, No. 3 (1955). Little, Brown and Company for permission to quote a passage from Sheldon S. Wolin, *Politics and Vision: Continuity and Innovation in Western Political Thought*. Oxford University Press for permission to quote passages from R. M. Hare, *The Language of Morals* and a passage from R. M. Hare, *Freedom and Reason*. Penguin Books Ltd. for permission to quote a passage from P. H. Nowell-Smith's *Ethics*. The University of Washington Press for permission to quote a passage from H. L. A. Hart, "Legal and Moral Obligation," in A. I. Melden, Editor, *Essays in Moral Philosophy*. Full references to the quoted passages are provided in the appropriate footnotes.

A number of colleagues have read all or part of the manuscript and have improved it more than I care to remember. For their stimulation and generosity my thanks to Professors Hugo Bedau, Malcolm Brown, Maure Goldschmidt, Marvin Levich, Grant McConnell, James Nyman, and Yosal Rogat. I have also learned much of relevance to this study from my many discussions with Professors Sylvain Bromberger and J. David Greenstone. Finally, I would like to record my long-standing and many-faceted indebtedness to my teacher, Professor Norman Jacobson. If my capacities were closer to the level of his teaching, this would be a much better book.

Research grants from Reed College, the Social Science Research Committee of the Division of Social Science, University of Chicago, and the Faculty Research Fund, The College, University of Chicago, have facilitated the completion of the work, as has the editorial assistance of Mrs. Ruth Grodzins and Mr. William Gum. Responsibility for the study is entirely mine, although I could never have completed it without the encouragement and support of my wife Nancy.

R. E. F.

CONTENTS

PART ONE

Reason, Politics, and Public Interest

Chapter One

PUBLIC INTEREST AND POLITICAL DISCOURSE

I

Congressman Jones, in a speech to the American Medical Association, says "The Medicare Bill is in the public interest." What is the force of his statement? His audience might respond that the statement demonstrates Jones's lack of the necessary qualifications for public office. The President of the United Americans for the Defense of Senior Citizens might regard it as evidence of Jones's deep understanding of social problems, his compassion for his fellow man, and the high priority to be assigned to his request for campaign assistance. The sophisticated political analyst is likely to interpret the statement as evidence that Jones is beholden to the President, who ranks the bill first on his legislative program, or that Jones has a large populace of senior citizens in his constituency. But there are two points on which all of these respondents agree: the force of Jones's statement is to express, however sincerely, approval, approbation, or commendation of the measure in question; and his approval carries the special force of commending the measure as one that could properly be made the law of the land. They would agree that "public interest" is employed to express approval of public policy or proposed public policy.

It could be contended that these respondents are mistaken, that "public interest" is not, or is not always, employed to commend. Perhaps Jones is using it as a purely descriptive category. It is perfectly good English for Jones to say "The public interest in this matter is *A*, but my interest is *B*, and I am doing everything I can to bring *B* about." As a matter of fact, we do not always approve of everything that is in the public interest, and our language allows us to state that this is the case. But if behavior contrary to the public interest is common enough, statements announcing such behavior are rare indeed—and positively unheard of from congressmen. The reason is precisely that "public interest" is a term ordinarily used to commend or approve; the primary function of the concept in our language is to convey approval or commendation of public policy. Hence, if an English-speaker applies it to a measure or policy, thereby conveying to other English-speakers that he believes the measure is deserving of approval, but then expresses personal disapproval of it, his behavior is odd if not contradictory. What is more, his behavior will carry a strong suggestion of immorality.[1]

At a minimum, then, we can say that "public interest" is used to express approval or commendation of policies adopted or proposed by government. Starting from this rudimentary position, we can investigate what philosophers call the "logic" of the discourse of commendation in the area of politics. A beginning can be made by asking why it is that we utilize a specialized vocabulary in political discourse. We speak not of the satisfaction or service of "interest," but of service of the "public interest"; not of "good," but of the "common good"; not of

[1] These remarks do not mean that "public interest" can be employed only to express approval. Consider the following. "It is widely believed that X is in the public interest." "Is X in the public interest?" "At first I was persuaded that X is in the public interest, but now I'm not so sure." None of these locutions would make sense to a person who did not understand that "public interest" is most commonly used to express approval or commendation. It should also be noted that "public interest" performs a number of more specialized functions. The Federal Comunications Commission, for example, is charged by Congress to regulate broadcasting as the "public convenience, interest, or necessity requires." And the Commission itself has said, "The public interest to be served under the Communications Act is the interest of the listening public in the larger and more effective use of radio." (The examples are taken from Arthur S. Miller, "The Public Interest Undefined," *Journal of Public Law,* Vol. X, p. 184, 1961. See the Symposium of which this article is a part for a variety of examples of uses of the concept.) In these examples, the concept performs a somewhat special function defined by the legislation or context in question, but the specialized function depends upon the general commendatory use of the concept and would be incomprehensible without it.

welfare, but of the "general welfare." [2] A partial explanation for the presence of the adjectives lies in a fact concerning the political order. In political life, one agent, government, acts in the name and on the behalf of all of the members of the system, and its actions apply to all. The actions of government are in principle universal (within the system) in application.[3] The concepts we use to express our evaluations of these actions are adapted from more general commendatory language in recognition of this fact.

We can explore this question further by examining the relationship between "public interest" and other major concepts of political discourse. A good starting point is the concept of "rights." This concept and the concept of "duties" are correlative. No one can have a right unless other persons have corollary duties.[4] If I claim that I have a right to strike against my employer, I *mean that* the other members of the political system in question have a duty not to interfere with my efforts to strike. Furthermore, rights and duties together imply a system of sanctions which supports rights and enforces duties. If I claim the right to strike as a legal right, I mean that the exercise of my right is guaranteed by law and others will be prevented from or punished for violating their duty to respect that right. If I claim this right as a moral right, I mean that other individuals have a moral duty not to interfere and that it will be proper to apply moral sanctions, for example the expression of moral disapproval, against those who do not perform that duty.

The relevant aspects of this argument can be summarized by saying that rights are relational in character and create new interdependencies

[2] "Public interest" is now the most common of these locutions, although all three remain in use. (We use the term "national interest" in discussing foreign affairs.) We will discuss the rise to prominence of "public interest" in the next chapter, but we will treat the first three expressions as synonymous.

[3] In practice we regularly use classifications that restrict the force of laws to classes of people with specific characteristics. But we insist that the laws apply to any and all members of the system who have or come to have the characteristics which define the classification. What is more, we are particular about the principles of classification used. This is the problem of "permissible classification" within the framework of the rule of law.

[4] This relationship has received considerable attention. See, for example, T. H. Green, *Principles of Political Obligation* (London: Longmans, Green, revised edition, 1941); Wesley N. Hohfeld, *Fundamental Legal Conceptions* (New Haven: Yale University Press, 1923); H. L. A. Hart, "Are There Any Natural Rights," *The Philosophical Review*, Vol. 64, No. 2 (April, 1955).

and extend existing ones. By definition, granting a right to an individual or class of individuals has consequences for others. The worker's right to strike means that his employer has a duty not to prevent him from striking; the employer has a duty not to prevent the worker from bringing the conduct of his business to a halt.

The key concepts used in this brief discussion of "rights" and duties are normative. If I say "I have the [legal] right to strike," I am not merely stating a fact concerning the legal order under which I live. Even if this were the case, or more obviously if I were claiming that such a legal right were my due, I would also be saying that I ought to be allowed to strike and others ought not be allowed to prevent me from striking. Consider the challenges my claim might have to meet. If my employer says, "I am aware that present legislation establishes your right to strike, but the legislation ought to be repealed or altered for the following reasons . . . ," I must be prepared to offer warrants in defense of the legislation which exists (or which I contend should exist). If I am not prepared to do so, I place myself in the position of seeking benefits under a law which I tacitly concede to be indefensible. Since this law has a marked impact upon others, the warrants I offer must take that impact into account; they must be normative warrants.

This is the point at which the concept of public interest becomes important. If my assertion of a right is successful, it will affect, in principle, all members of the system in which I live. A law will be enforced against any and all members of the system who interfere with my efforts to strike. It might be agreed that the benefits to the individuals with the accorded right are a consideration in deciding whether the law in question *ought* to be enforced, but this consideration is an insufficient warrant for the law. It does nothing to take into account the restrictions placed upon individuals prevented from interfering with strikes and the very real harm strikes might do them. The criteria used to evaluate actions of government must take account of the full range of the effects of those actions. The adjectives "public," "common" and "general" reflect recognition of these effects. This means that we can properly apply "public interest" to a measure only when we have considered the full impact of the measure and have marshaled normative considerations relevant to justifying that impact.[5]

[5] The discussion of rights supports an additional conclusion, the importance of which will emerge below. As far as legal rights are concerned, the logic of our

These remarks can be broadened by examining the relationship between "public interest" and a second characteristic feature of modern political systems, representation. The members of the representative's constituency will make conflicting demands which he will be unable to reconcile completely. Yet he will often be required to reach a single decision which must apply to all of his constituents, hence he will be forced to choose among the demands of his constituents and use the power of government to support some of them and frustrate others. If he does so simply because he has a personal preference for one part of his constituency, he will be rightly accused of partiality. This might make it difficult to justify demanding compliance from those who opposed the policy. But avoiding partiality is only one precondition of properly demanding compliance. The representative must justify his decisions in light of his position as an agent whose decisions will be enforced against all of the members of the system. He certifies that he is able to do so when he states that the measure is in the public interest.[6] Since this is the function of the concept, the representative is required to offer considerations of the type discussed in connection with rights. If he applies "public interest" to a measure without marshaling such considerations, he has violated the logic of the concept.

The represented also need the concept, and they too must respect its logic. They must decide how to cast their ballots and what to ask of their representatives. It may be that most individuals formulate their decisions and demands on the basis of purely self-serving considerations. A number of problems would be created if all political activity took this form. Recall the position of Thomas Hobbes. In his system individual citizens pursue their interests as vigorously as possible, and it is the responsibility of the sovereign to care for the institutions and conditions which are shared by the members of society. The individual, in other words, has no need of "public interest" and is obligated to discipline his political activity in the name of public interest only as he is commanded to do so by the sovereign. This position might be expected to lead to ineffective government because of the constant conflict be-

---

use of the concept "rights" requires the presence of a more general commendatory concept such as "public interest." It is only when we are prepared to say "establishing this right and these duties is in the public interest" that we can justifiably assign the right.

[6] Hence it is difficult to imagine how the representative could function if he had no such concept at his disposal.

tween government and the citizenry. The position also suggests that the individual, group, or corporation ought simply to consume the benefits of life in a political order and make no conscious effort to contribute to them. No degree of clarity concerning "public interest" will prevent men from behaving in this manner. Clarity about the concept, however, will help us appreciate the consequences of such behavior.

This discussion suggests the following generalizations concerning the function of "public interest" in political discourse. The concept relates closely to the problem of the one and the many.[7] The "many" are the great diversity of individuals and groups found in any political system. Their interests, demands, and needs regularly conflict, but geography and biology, if not more, force them to live together and create extensive interdependencies. Interdependence makes necessary an authoritative agent to control conflicts and tend to interrelationships. This agent is the "one," or government. It is a public agent; it exists not merely for the sake of single individuals or groups, but for the many. Its actions are directed to all the members of society, and they are enforceable against all. This means that government will not be justified in acting partially. Yet the very fact of diversity in society means that government cannot assign rights and duties or make any authoritative decision without serving some interests, demands, and needs, and restricting others. The individual citizen may be obligated to obey governmental actions that conflict with his interests, but government is expected to justify its decisions and actions in terms of a standard appropriate to the position which requires those decisions, its position as a public agent. The function of the concept "public interest" is to provide such a standard, and its logic corresponds to that function.

II

Our findings to this point place "public interest" squarely within the boundaries of the larger controversies noted in the Preface. "Public interest" is used to express evaluations of public policies, and the logic of the concept requires assessment of the consequences of policies for

[7] See J. Roland Pennock, "The One and the Many: a Note on the Concept," in Carl Friedrich, editor, *The Public Interest* (Nomos V) (New York: Atherton Press, 1962).

the members of the public. This means that the general difficulties of evaluation, as well as problems peculiar to politics, arise in connection with use of "public interest." Hence it comes as no surprise that a number of writers have reached very pessimistic conclusions concerning the concept. These writers concede that the concept is widely used in political discourse. It is a political "datum" of which the political scientist must take cognizance. But because of its function the concept can never be given "operational meaning," either by political actors or by political scientists. Once we have begun to answer the question "What is the status, significance, and function of 'public interest'," we will see that there can be no rationally defensible answer to the question "What (policy, decision, action) is in the public interest?" Since the concept is used to commend, it can only be used to express personal (or group) preferences.

The argument, it should be stressed, is not simply that the concept is sometimes, often, or even always used to express preferences or for purely propagandist purposes. The misuse of the concept (and its ancestors) is as old as politics and requires little documentation.[8] The argument takes a more radical form: the concept *can only be* used to express subjective preference or as an honorific label. The nature or character or essence of the concept excludes the possibility of its having any trans-subjective content. These commentators urge political scientists not to attempt to determine "what is in the public interest"; indeed, they argue that political scientists should banish the concept from their analytic vocabularies.[9] Assessment of the validity of these conclusions will be a secondary concern throughout the remainder of this book.

III

Since "public interest" is used to express commendations and justifications, the analysis that has been done of other commendatory terms, whether political or not, is likely to be useful to understanding

[8] Thucydides, for example, noted that, "Leaders of parties in cities had programs which appeared admirable . . . but in professing to serve the public interest they were seeking to win prizes for themselves." *The Peloponnesian War* (Rex Warner, translator, Penguin Classics, Baltimore, Md.: Penguin Books, Inc.,) III, 5, p. 210.

[9] See especially David Truman, *The Governmental Process* (New York: Alfred A. Knopf, Inc., 1951), pp. 50–51, Glendon Schubert, *The Public Interest* (New

it. In his analysis of the word "good" R. M. Hare has drawn a distinction between the "primary" or "commendatory" force of the term and its "secondary" or "descriptive" force. Whenever we say that something is "good" our primary purpose is to convey commendation. This is true whether we are speaking of a fountain pen as good because it writes smoothly or of a man as good because he is virtuous, kind, and altruistic. What is more, we are able to understand the commendatory force of "good" even when we know nothing of its descriptive meaning in a specific case.

> To teach what makes a member of any class a good member of the class is a . . . new lesson for each class of objects; but nevertheless the word "good" has a constant meaning which, once learnt, can be understood no matter what class of objects is being discussed. We have . . . to make a distinction between the meaning of the word "good" and the criteria for its application.[10]

Hare's distinction is clarified by the reasons he offers for terming the commendatory meaning primary. First, the commendatory meaning is constant despite great variation in the descriptive meaning. We commend fountain pens for very different reasons than we commend men, automobiles for reasons other than television sets; yet we can use the word "good" in all cases, and our listeners or readers will be able to understand that we are using it in part to commend. The second is that

> . . . we can use the evaluative force of the word ["good"] in order to *change* the descriptive meaning for any class of objects. This is what the moral reformer often does in morals; but the same process occurs outside morals. It may happen that motor-cars will in the near future change considerably in design. . . . It may be that then we shall cease giving the name "a good motor-car" to a car that now would rightly and with the concurrence of all be allowed that name. How, linguistically speaking, would this have happened? At present, we are roughly agreed . . . on the necessary and

York: The Free Press of Glencoe, 1960), *passim;* Glendon Schubert, "Is There a Public Interest Theory," and Frank Sorauf, "The Conceptual Muddle," in Friedrich, *op. cit.*, pp. 162, 183.

[10] R. M. Hare, *The Language of Morals*, p. 102. (London: Oxford University Press, 1952). See Part 2 of this work for a full discussion of the distinction in question. For an alternative analysis of "good" see Paul Ziff, *Semantic Analysis* (Ithaca, N. Y.: Cornell University Press, 1960), Part VI. The two analyses conflict in important respects, but I do not find that Ziff has upset Hare's conclusions. (Ziff does not mention Hare's work.)

sufficient criteria for calling a motor-car a good one. If what I have described takes place, we may begin to say "No cars of the nineteen-fifties were really good; there weren't any good ones till 1960." Now here we cannot be using "good" with the same descriptive meaning as it is now generally used with; for some of the cars of 1950 do indubitably have those characteristics which entitle them to the name "good motor-car" in the 1950 descriptive sense of the word. What is happening is that the evaluative meaning of the word is being used in order to shift the descriptive meaning; we are doing what would be called, if "good" were a purely descriptive word, redefining it. But we cannot call it that, for the evaluative meaning remains constant; we are rather altering the standard.[11]

This analysis might appear to support the view that commendatory expressions are employed in a highly subjective, nonrational manner. It would appear that we can commend anything without failing to communicate. Regardless of what we call good, our audience will always understand the force of our expression—even if it has no idea why we are commending. Partly for this reason, some commentators have classified Hare's ethical theory as "emotivist," as a theory holding that moral statements have no cognitive content and are best understood as expressions of emotive states or attitudes.[12] This interpretation misconstrues the (admittedly difficult) relationship between the primary and secondary meanings of "good".

The logic of the word "good," that is the logic of the manner in which "good" is actually used in ordinary language, is such that we misuse the word if we commend when we are unable to supply a descriptive meaning in support of the commendation. To see this we have only to construct an appropriate response to a commendation. "It always makes sense, after someone has said 'That is a good motorcar,' to ask, 'What is good about it?' or 'Why do you call it good?' " [13] If the commender responds, "Well, I just like it, that's all," he demonstrates that his first statement was simply an expression of preference. It would then be appropriate to say that the commender had misused the word good. He should have *begun* by using, "I like that motorcar" or "That motorcar suits my fancy" or some other typically preferential locution. But it he responds, "It handles well at high speeds, gets 30 miles to the gal-

[11] Hare, *op. cit.*, p. 119.

[12] See, for example, Richard Brandt, *Ethical Theory* (Englewood Cliffs, N. J.: Prentice-Hall, Inc., 1959), pp. 221–5.

[13] Hare, *op. cit.*, p. 130.

lon of gas, and requires a minimum of maintenance," he has supplied a descriptive meaning which supports the commendation. To answer the question "Why do you call it good?" is "to give the properties in virtue of which we call it good." [14]

This account raises some extremely thorny questions. Most important, the "in virtue of which" in the last sentence quoted from Hare involves us in the problem of "naturalism," the problem of the relationship between statements of fact and statements of value. It might be unproblematical to call a motorcar good "in virtue of" the *fact* that it can deliver 30 miles to a gallon of gasoline. But if we make comparable statements such as, "X is a good father in virtue of the fact that he sends his children to Sunday school" or "measure X is in the public interest in virtue of the fact that it will serve to increase GNP," it becomes apparent that we are in the throes of the hoary problem of moving logically from the "is" to the "ought."

But Hare's account does solve some problems. He shows that use of commendatory expressions does not necessarily bring reasoned discourse to an immediate halt or reduce us to an exchange on the "I like it—Well I don't" model. The fact that the logic of "good" requires a descriptive meaning opens the way for, indeed renders mandatory, some discussion of why "good" was applied. The content of this exchange will vary according to the subject matter in question—the descriptive meaning varies while the primary meaning holds constant. But the fact that providing a descriptive meaning is a requirement of the proper use of "good" distinguishes moral discourse from discussions of the merits of peppermints versus chocolate creams.

Hare's distinction applies directly to "public interest." The primary function of the concept is to commend, and it is primary for the reasons indicated by Hare in connection with "good." The requirement that a descriptive meaning be supplied corresponds to the demands of the logic of "public interest." The descriptive meaning will vary in content from case to case, but the characteristics of political life discussed above establish general criteria which any descriptive meaning must satisfy. Hare's terminology provides an economical means of discussing these features of "public interest," and we will utilize it.

Hare's analysis is also enlightening concerning the question, "What is in the public interest." It shows that this question *cannot* be properly answered by an unsupported statement of preference. It also teaches

[14] *Ibid.*, p. 130.

us not to expect any single, all-inclusive, once-for-all-time answer. The content of the descriptive meaning, to repeat, will vary. Finally, when combined with the earlier analysis, it suggests the possibility of defining general criteria which any answer to the question, "What is in the public interest?" must satisfy.

IV

We have emphasized the commendatory function of "public interest," but the significance of the concept is not exhausted when this aspect of its use has been analyzed. Some men take justification seriously, and their behavior cannot be understood unless this is recognized. Similarly, the political landscape is crowded with institutional arrangements which reflect concern with justification and which cannot be comprehended if their relationship to the problems of justification is not observed. Hence even those willing to forgo evaluation and justification in politics must recognize that others do not do so. Perhaps this is what Frank Sorauf intends when he concedes that "public interest" must be recognized as a political datum.[15] But it is difficult to grasp what it can mean to "recognize" the concept if not that political scientists must understand the manner in which it functions and concern themselves with the problems that surround it.

The analysis thus far indicates why the concept presents such puzzling difficulties. Public interest is a normative standard, and it raises the whole panoply of problems associated with standards in general. The history of moral philosophy testifies that problems of standards are not easily solved. There is no reason to think that they will be easily solved in the case of public interest. But difficulty of analysis is not ordinarily considered a valid reason for abandoning a problem. The problems associated with "public interest" are among the crucial problems of politics. Determining justifiable governmental policy in the face of conflict and diversity is central to the political order; it is a problem which is never solved in any final sense but which we are constantly trying to solve. The much discussed difficulties with the concept are difficulties with morals and politics. We are free to abandon the *concept*, but if we do so we will simply have to wrestle with the *problems* under some other heading.

[15] Friedrich, *op. cit.*, p. 190.

Chapter Two

THE CONCEPT OF INTEREST AND THE PUBLIC INTEREST

I

"Public interest" is now a commonplace in political discourse, but it is a relatively recent innovation, earlier writers having preferred formulas such as "public good" or "commonweal." The replacement of "good" or "weal" with "interest" is of more than linguistic importance. In significant respects allying "public" with "interest" rather than with "good" reflects substantive changes in political thinking which alter the problems surrounding the selection and justification of public policy.

The term "interest" carries individualist and subjective connotations which, until twentieth century ethical theory, have rarely been associated with the concept of "good." It was not until the satisfaction of subjective, even idiosyncratic, individual interests came to be considered a prime object of politics that "interest" could replace "good" as the primary commendatory concept of political life. The political importance of individual interests had long been recognized, but it was not until the seventeenth and eighteenth centuries that satisfaction of interest came to be considered the foremost objective of politics. In this period politics began to be thought of as "significant only insofar as it impinged upon men's interests." [1]

If satisfaction of individual interest was to be the objective of politics, public policy had to be formulated and judged according to the

[1] S. S. Wolin, *Politics and Vision* (Boston: Little, Brown and Company, 1960), p. 280. See this work generally for an acute analysis of the transition in question.

demands and standards of the individual members of society. The age-old quest for more stable and elevated criteria, the long-standing belief that there is a body of political wisdom that transcends time, place, and individual idiosyncracy and without which good public policy, could not be made—these and other beliefs had to be set aside in deference to the all-encompassing demands of interest. Appropriately, writers such as Jeremy Bentham adopted "public interest" as the standard of public policy and drew the predictable inference concerning its content. "The interest of the community then is, what?—the sum of the interests of the several members who compose it."[2] From this point of view there is little in political life that does not revolve around the concept of interest.

The oversimplifications of this formula were bound to create difficulties. If each man were to define his own interest—and Bentham and his followers held that it was best for each man to do so—and if men were different from one another in politically significant respects, the summation in question was likely to be difficult. To that extent it was necessary either to abandon interest as a standard or to shift its meaning to modify its extremely subjective connotations. This difficulty led to the gradual development of a wide variety of uses of "interest," each of which carried quite different political consequences. Today there are few terms in political discourse used in a more diverse and shifting manner.[3] The fact that use of "interest" is a relatively recent development which reflects basic changes in political thought, together with the diverse and often confusing uses of the term, suggests the desirability of looking critically at the noun in isolation from the adjective.

II

In most of its uses the noun "interest" denotes a two-termed relationship between someone or something (for example, a collectivity

[2] Jeremy Bentham, *A Fragment on Government* and *Principles of Morals and Legislation* (Oxford: Basil Blackwell, 1948), p. 126.

[3] For a helpful analysis of "interest" and the confusions that often attend its use, see Hannah Pitkin, *The Theory of Political Representation*, especially Chapter 14. (Unpublished doctoral dissertation, University of California, Berkeley,

such as a labor union) and a substantive in which that person or thing "has an interest." When we see "an interest in," we typically ask, "Who has an interest in what?"[4] Ordinarily the relationship is such that the substantive, the thing in which one has an interest, affects the situation, desires, wants, or needs of the person who has an interest in it. The first of the sixteen uses of "interest" delineated by the *OED* reads: "The relation of being objectively concerned in something, by having a right or title to, a claim upon, share in." An example would be ownership of shares of stock in a corporation. The relationship, however, need not be as legalistic as the language of this entry suggests in order to warrant use of "interest." A person (or a collectivity) might have an interest in the weather, the price of beans, or a pending legislative measure and yet have no right or title to or claim on them in any legal sense.

We also use "interest" to mean "on behalf of" or "as a means to." "In the interest of world peace" means simply "as a means to" world peace. We can use this language with only the most distant and loosely specified reference to the second term of the relationship, that is, without specifying *what* is a means to world peace. We can say, "Congressman *X* always acts in the interest of world peace." When such a statement is challenged, the speaker is expected to adduce specific actions and to detail the manner in which those actions advanced world peace (or might have advanced world peace). We might be tempted to say that the speaker was forced to specify "what" world peace had an interest in. Such an analysis would be misleading; interest is "two-termed" when we are concerned with a "who" (or with a collectivity consisting of several persons). It is the latter type of case that is of greatest concern here. Public policies that are a means to world peace or justice are sometimes in the public interest. When this is so, it is because members of the public have an interest in world peace or justice.

The relationship between person and substantive (*who* has the interest in *what*) varies along a continuum moving from "subjective" to "objective" (that is, we use "interest" to denote a considerable variety of relationships between persons and things). At the "subjec-

---

1962.) I would also like to record my particular indebtedness to Professor Hugo Bedau for his assistance with this chapter.

[4] The etymology of the word is suggestive in this respect. Interest derives, via French, from the Latin *interesse* which meant in part "to be between." See *Oxford English Dictionary* (hereafter *OED*), and Pitkin, *op. cit.*, p. 388.

tive" end of the continuum the relationship consists entirely of a psychological or intellectual attitude or curiosity toward or about the substantive. When that attitude changes or terminates, the relationship is modified or brought to an end. (It is in this sense that the relationship can be termed subjective.) This sense of "interest" is conveyed by the adjectival form "interesting"; my relationship to, that is, my interest in, antique pencil sharpeners consists in the fact that I find them "interesting." At the "objective" end of the scale the relationship obtains, the substantive affects the person, whether he is aware of the effect or not. It is in this sense that we say that a child has an interest in a diet which provides a certain quantity of protein. (Or do we say "it is in the child's interest" to have such a diet? Although I am not certain of the point, the latter locution rests more comfortably with assertions at the objective end of the continuum under discussion.)

III

The self-regarding and potentially evanescent character of interests in the subjective sense has suggested to some that they are of little or no political significance. Consider the following passage from Bentham.

> . . . the action of a thinking being is the act either of the body or only of the mind: and an act of the mind is an act either of the intellectual faculty, or of the will. Acts of the intellectual faculty will sometimes rest in the understanding merely, without exerting any influence in the production of any acts of the will. Motives, which are not of a nature to influence any other acts than those, may be styled purely speculative motives, . . .

Bentham does not use the word interest, but his description of the phenomenon in question is in close accord with that denoted by the sense of "interest" under consideration. He continues:

> But as to these acts, neither do they exercise any influence over external acts, or over their consequences, nor consequently over any pain or any pleasure that may be in the number of such consequences. Now it is only on account of their tendency to produce either pain or pleasure, that any acts can be material. With the acts, therefore, that rest purely in the understanding, we have not here any concern.[5]

[5] Bentham, *op. cit.*, p. 214.

Bentham's statement applies much more widely than to the trivial curiosity of our earlier example, and it is characteristic of his psychology. The force of his argument is that purely subjective and self-regarding "intellectual acts," motives, or interests do not have sufficient consequences to become matters of public concern. It would follow that "interests" in this sense can be ignored safely when the public interest is discussed.

We must be cautious in accepting such a conclusion. Interests in this sense regularly lead to the development of interests in the sense of having "a material stake in." If my curiosity concerning antique pencil sharpeners becomes sufficiently intense, it may lead me to make material demands which involve "external acts" and "pain and pleasure" both for myself and others. A host of recreational interests have such effects, and they have prompted some of the most vigorous public disputes of our century.

Now Bentham might concede this point. But it is not true that only the material demand, not the curiosity, has significance for public interest questions. Surely the public ought not to favor the satisfaction of any and every psychological or intellectual interest that happens to gain currency. The development of public attitudes should be preceded by an assessment of the acceptability of the interest as such. Cock-fighting and bear-baiting are properly outlawed not because of their material costs but because the "curiosities" in question are unacceptable. Since interests of this kind become matters of public concern, there can be cases in which determination of the descriptive meaning of "public interest" requires that the interests be examined and evaluated. There could also be cases in which the descriptive meaning of "public interest" corresponds more or less exactly with what people "find interesting."

The next stage on the continuum involves a combination of subjective awareness *and* effect of the substantive (the "what") independent of awareness on the part of the subject (the "who"). The state of the wholesale beef market affects the individual consumer of beef whether he is aware of the existence of that market. Yet, whether he is or not, it is good English to say that he "has an interest in" that market (or that developments in the market are "in the interest of" the individual consumer). But the possibility of independent effect (of the "what" on the "who") scarcely rules out or hampers development of awareness and concern. Many writers in the Anglo-American tradition of political thought have argued that it is precisely the presence of "objective interests" which prompts the emergence of subjective awareness and even intellectual curiosity.

Bentham went further in this respect than any other thinker, but views similar to his are available in Hobbes, Locke, Madison, and both of the Mills. The following excerpts from Bentham's writings make the point very directly.

> Consider the backwardness there is in most men, unless . . . spurred by personal interests.
>
> . . . by what motives, or, which comes to the same thing, by what obligations can . . . (a man) be bound to obey the dictates of probity and beneficence? In answer to this, it cannot but be admitted, that the only interests which a man at all times and upon all occasions is sure to find adequate motives for consulting, are his own.[6]
>
> It is an old observation how Interest smooths the road to Faith.[7]
>
> Experience, it has been said of old, is the Mother of Wisdom: be it so;—but then Interest is the Father. There is even an Interest that is the Father of Experience.[8]

In Bentham's view it is the presence of interests of the material kind that spurs men to act and triggers the operation of the psychological and intellectual mechanisms which allow them to act resolutely and effectively. In the absence of such interests, men are either dull and torpid or engage in insignificant speculation. It follows that interests which combine subjective and objective dimensions will be of the greatest political significance.

Bentham marks the independent material effect of the substantive as the initial agent in the sequence leading to political action. But it cannot be said that the subjective aspect of the relationship is undervalued or devalued in his theory. If the individual's awareness of and concern with the substantive are not the initiating agents, Bentham suggests that they stimulate the "will" and provide the direction without which there would be no effective action. What is more significant, they eval-

[6] *Ibid.*, p. 413.
[7] *Ibid.*, p. 52.
[8] *Ibid.*, p. 77.

uate the importance of the interest to the individual. This evaluation, in some passages at least, is held to be virtually immune to challenge. As Bentham put it in a discussion of punishment:

> Cases in which punishment is groundless. . . . Of this number are those in which the act was such as might, on some occasions, be mischievous or disagreeable, but the person whose interest it concerns gave his consent to the performance of it. This consent, provided it be free, and fairly obtained, is the best proof that can be produced, that, to the person who gives it, no mischief, at least no immediate mischief, upon the whole is done. For no man can be so good a judge as the man himself, what it is gives him pleasure or displeasure.[9]

Objective considerations and the judgment of independent observers must give way to the individual's assessment of what is in his interest. We have already noted the conclusion Bentham drew regarding the proper criterion of public policy.

Bentham brings three senses of interest together into a single use. To be psychologically or intellectually curious about, to be affected by, and to be benefited by (which stands farther toward the objective end of the continuum) are all dimensions of his use of the term. The Benthamite position has several important implications. First, Bentham's argument lies near the root of present conceptions of "interest-oriented" and "interest-group" politics. Political life centers about tangible, material realities, not insubstantial and evanescent ideas, curiosities, or other products of the intellect or imagination. Since interests are rooted in material aspects of man's environment and do not depend upon the idiosyncracies of intellectual or psychological processes, they are likely to be shared by men in homologous situations. This in turn provides a material basis which allows such men, when awareness of the interest has developed, to band together in "interest groups" and to act politically to serve that interest. Because different collections of men relate to their material environment in different ways, there is a material basis for different interests, different interest groups, and a politics which consists of competition between such groups.[10] Second, owing to its emphasis upon the sanctity of the individual's evaluation

[9] *Ibid.*, p. 282.

[10] There can also be "potential groups" (to borrow the terminology of David Truman), that is, groups of men who are affected in common by a substantive but who are not aware of that effect or not aware that others are so affected as well.

of his interest, Bentham's position forms an important part of the liberal democratic tradition. It opposes theories which contend that few individuals understand what affects them or what is good for them and that those decisions ought to be made for them by men who understand and are able to make intelligent judgments. This aspect of the Benthamite position prompted a political theory which stressed that the individual be left to pursue his own interests with a minimum of interference from centralized authority and that when centralized authority is necessary it ought to be as responsive as possible to individual demands and claims. Later writers placed more emphasis on the degree to which groups of men share the objective aspect of interests and are able to pool their efforts by acting in groups. Central authority, in this view, must be responsive to *group* demands and claims, which, of course, requires that the subjective evaluations of men with common objective interests be made to coincide and that the members of interest groups be united in outlook and understanding as well as in objective relation to their material environment. This, in turn, means that the whole set of questions concerning leader-follower relationships rises anew on the intragroup level. It is in part for these reasons that a great debate concerning intragroup democracy has raged throughout the twentieth century.

Whether individuals or groups are the basic units in the political process, the Benthamite position created some obvious dangers and difficulties. It led inevitably to the view that the descriptive meaning of "public interest" ought to be determined by making a summation of individual interests in the community. When combined with an insistence upon the universality of governmental action and with social and political conflict, this summation was not merely difficult but (if we take the word summation literally) logically impossible.

One answer was to substitute the formula "the greatest good of the greatest number" for "the sum of the interests of the several members" of the community. The details of Bentham's view of the relationship between these two formulas are outside the scope of present concerns. Whatever his view, the second formula could not solve the problem without giving up the distinctive elements of the theory as a whole. If the emphasis upon satisfaction of individual interest is retained, it remains necessary to "add up" a majority—which is neither logically nor practically any easier than adding up *all* of the disparate interests. A more recent "answer" is that government does not sum up anything, indeed that government does not *do* much of anything about policy formulation. Public policy is made by establishing an arena in which interests clash. And to the victors go the spoils.

In addition to the forgoing difficulties, the Benthamite view has no consistent way to handle the possibility that the individual might be mistaken concerning his interest and that the interference of an authority might in fact be beneficial to him. Also, Bentham's identification of motives and obligations implies that interests and duties are equivalent. If this is the case, there can be no *legitimate* ground for compelling an individual to act contrary to his interest as he understands it. This would seem to leave only two possibilities: either governmental decisions must be arbitrarily imposed upon those whose interests are not part of the "summation," or the scope of governmental action must be limited to areas in which there is unanimity. On neither view could "public interest" have any role to play in politics. This outcome can be traced directly to the view that there are no trans-subjective standards for evaluating an action based on an individual's own interests. The individual must judge for himself, and anyone who disagrees with him is wrong, by hypothesis.

IV

The ordinary uses of "interest" do not restrict us to the Benthamite position. The pertinent dictionary entry reads: "That which is to or for the advantage of any one; good, benefit, profit, advantage." On this definition "interest in" can be used interchangeably with "benefited by," and "good for" can be substituted for "in the interest of." Since "good" connotes a (descriptive) meaning which transcends the idiosyncracies of individual views, when "interest" is equated with "good" it readily absorbs the more objective connotations of the latter. This use of "interest" minimizes the individual's own evaluation of his interests and emphasizes factors and considerations accessible to other observers.

Instructive examples of this use of "interest" are found in the writings of Edmund Burke. In 1788 Burke's position on British policy concerning Irish trade won him the hostility of his merchant constituents in Bristol. With their sharply stated disapproval of his position before him, Burke wrote his constituents as follows:

You will be so good as to present my best respects to the society [of Merchant Adventurers of Bristol], and to assure them that it was altogether unnecessary to remind me of the interest of the constituents. I have never regarded anything else, since I had a seat in Parliament. Having frequently and maturely considered that interest, and stated it to myself in almost every point of view, I am persuaded that, under the present circumstances, I cannot more effectually pursue it, than by giving all the support in my power to the propositions which I lately transmitted to the hall.[11]

Burke then presented a lengthy discussion of the general principles which he believed should govern commercial relations and offered further assurances.

I have written this long letter, in order to give all possible satisfaction to my constituents with regard to the part I have taken in this affair. It gave me inexpressible concern to find, that my conduct had been a cause of uneasiness to any of them. . . . However, I had much rather run the risk of displeasing them than of injuring them.[12]

It is for you, and for your interest, . . . that I have taken my share in this question. You do not, you cannot suffer by it.[13]

"Interest" is considered objective in character, and the individual's evaluation of his own interest is no more than one piece of evidence among many which the qualified observer ought to consider. More important are the facts and the general principles necessary for the judgment.

Burke's discussion of interest provides a solution to the difficulties of Bentham's theory, but it also complicates some of the questions to which Bentham's theory offers a cogent answer. Having rejected subjectivism, Burke could accommodate the possibility that lack of involvement and concern on the part of the citizenry might require those in political authority to define and act on behalf of the interests of the citizens—that is if interests are to be served by the political process. The existence of an interest-type relationship between governmental policies and the individual's situation, for example, does not guarantee the development of awareness of that relationship on the part of the individual. To assume that such awareness will develop if the interest is a significant one is to run the risk that interests will go

[11] *The Works of Edmund Burke* (London: F. and C. Rivington, 1803) Vol. III, p. 209.

[12] *Ibid.*, pp. 219–20.

[13] *Ibid.*, p. 223.

uncared for. Nor does the development of awareness in itself guarantee the capacity to take effective political action in the service of the interest. Inequalities in position, resources, and many other factors will give some individuals and groups great advantages. Hence there is no necessary incompatibility between the view that individual and group interests ought to be served and the view that those in authority must sometimes define, evaluate, and act on behalf of the interests of other members of the system. Burke also holds that individuals and groups, although aware of an objective interest, might mistakenly evaluate it or misjudge what is necessary to serve it; hence the intervention of authority with superior information and understanding might be genuinely beneficial.

Finally, and most important here, Burke rejects Bentham's identification of duty and interest; he thereby lays the foundation for a view of "public interest" which allows the policy maker to consider factors other than individual interest and which is compatible with the belief that public interest can be given a descriptive meaning which can be defended on rational, trans-subjective grounds. Hence it is consistent for Burke to argue that men might be morally obligated to act in accordance with policies found to be in the public interest and that it might be proper to compel them to act morally even if they choose not to. Such compulsion would be proper whether the men in question regard the policies to be in their interest. Both views, that men are morally obligated to act in accordance with the public interest and that it is proper to compel them to do so, are commonplaces of our political life.[14] It is of some importance that a theory of "public interest" be able to account for them.

Burke's theory also provides an alternative view concerning questions Bentham seemed to have answered. In contrast with the thoroughgoing "objectivist" theory of Plato, Burke insists that the representative consult his constituents about their conception of their interests and what would serve them. He also supports democracy to

[14] The above remarks ignore the place of authority in the obligation-public interest relationship. It would be better to say, "Men are morally obligated to obey commands which are promulgated by a properly constituted authority and which are in the public interest, and it is proper to compel them to do so." But even this formula is incomplete. This is a good example of the manner in which the family of normative concepts interrelates. Unfortunately, it is impossible to analyze them all at one time.

the extent of favoring (narrowly restricted) elections to select representatives and to hold them accountable. He favors elections specifically on the ground that the individual's evaluation of his interest (what Burke tends to call "opinion") should be obtained whether the individual has any understanding of the objective situation (what he calls the "interest"). Yet he argues that government might (using what he calls "reason") properly define and pursue a policy which no citizen believes to be in his interest, and that in such a case the citizen might be wrong about his interest as well as his duty.[15]

Burke's position recommends a very different kind of politics than does the Benthamite argument. Specifically, the procedures used to determine the descriptive meaning of "public interest" will vary substantially between the two positions. Burke's theories clash with Bentham's egalitarian precepts—precepts that are sometimes thought to underlie political life in the Western democracies. However this may be, his theory of public interest does not violate the logic of that concept's function in democratic systems. The crux of the differences between the two views lies in their estimate of the individual's evaluation of his interests and what would serve them. However much we might like to agree with Bentham's emphasis on this evaluation, our use of "public interest" does not give private individuals or groups a veto power concerning its proper descriptive meaning. Individuals or groups may regularly exercise such a veto, and the label "in the public interest" may be claimed for the resultant policy. But the logic of the concept will always allow us to ask, "Why is that policy in the public interest?" The answer, "Because individual or group X regards it as in his or its interest," will never be responsive to that question. In this respect, Burke's position, with all of its implications for "a politics of public interest,"[16] is much more faithful to the logic of "public interest" than is Bentham's.

It is true that in some cases, the authority to define the descriptive

[15] In addition to the passages quoted above, for Burke's view of "opinion," "interest," and "reason," see especially *The Works of Edmund Burke, op. cit.,* Vol. III, pp. 18–21. On "opinion" see also Vol. II, pp. 61, 218–19, 224, 265; Vol. III, pp. 179–80, 236, 373–4. On "interest" see Vol. II, pp. 161–2, 224, 229, 265, 320–3; Vol. III, pp. 121, 249–50, 373–4; Vol. V, pp. 183 ff; Vol. VII, pp. 383–5. On reason see Vol. II, pp. 180, 196–7; Vol. III, pp. 236, 249–50, 373–4; Vol. V, pp. 183 ff; Vol. VII, p. 236.

[16] By this expression we intend a political practice in which the participants appreciate and attempt to behave in accordance with the logic of "public interest,"

meaning of "public interest" is placed directly in the hands of the general citizenry. Burke would prefer to restrict this practice by contrast with Bentham and with the practice of democratic countries in and after the lifetimes of the two theorists. But granting authority to make a decision is not to be confused with establishing the criteria for judging whether that authority has been exercised in a justifiable manner. When the question of standards is raised, Burke's position is again closer to the logic of "public interest" than is Bentham's.[17]

V

Two uses of "interest," both tangential to the subjective-objective continuum, remain to be discussed. The dictionary defines the first, "self-interest," as follows: "Regard to one's own profit or advantage; selfish pursuit of one's own welfare." "Selfish" self-interest is explicitly distinguished because there are individual interests which are not selfish. To avoid the pejorative adjective "selfish," the individual must give consideration to the profit, advantage, or welfare of others. Hence we can utilize the following breakdown:

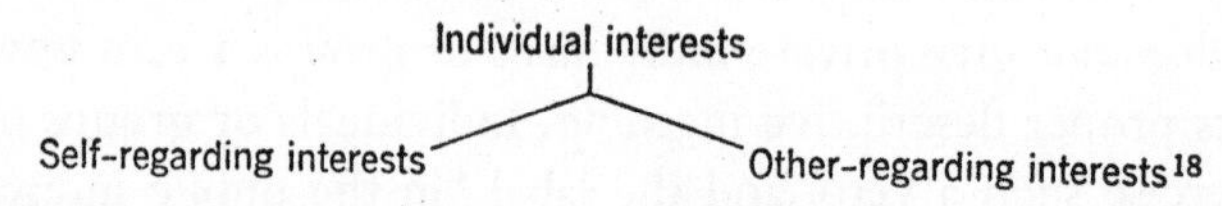

Where the adjective "selfish" is employed, "self-interest'" must contain a subjective dimension. We also speak of objective interests which, while not "selfish self-interests," relate strictly to the profit, advantage, or welfare of the individuals whose interests they are imputed to be.

[17] These comments deal somewhat brusquely with a rather tricky question. It might be argued that if all of the members of a political system hold that policy *X* is in the public interest—for whatever reason, that policy is in the public interest. Or at least if one is a democrat one must agree that the policy is in the public interest. The proper reply to this view may be evident from what has been said so far, but the question will be taken up again in the following chapter.

[18] It has been argued that "other-regarding interests" is a reference to a psychological impossibility, that all individual interests are self-interests. This position is known as egoism. This theory has been thoroughly demolished several times, and it would be pointless to go over the ground in a systematic manner. See, for example, C. D. Broad, "Egoism As a Theory of Human Motives," in C. D. Broad, *Ethics and the History of Philosophy* (London: Routledge and Kegan Paul, 1952); and P. H. Nowell-Smith, *Ethics* (Baltimore, Md.: Penguin Books, Inc., 1954), Chapter 10.

Other-regarding individual interests are somewhat more complex in this respect. If I have an other-regarding interest, it is *my* interest, but my interest is *in* the profit, advantage, or welfare of *others*. The "who" is myself, the "what" is the profit, and so forth, of another man or other men. Contrary to egoism, my interest is satisfied by serving the other man, not by any reward, pleasure, or satisfaction which I obtain as a consequence of serving that man. If the latter were the case, we would properly say, "My interest is my pleasure, satisfaction, etc. . . ." We simply must take seriously the words, "My interest is the profit, advantage, etc., of X."

This fact raises the question whether other-regarding interests must be subjectively defined. It would seem to be possible for an observer to discover that I have an other-regarding interest in the profit of another man before I am aware of it, especially if the observer knows me well, if he knows that I am an altruistic person. But because other-regarding interests ordinarily involve altruism or benevolence and because altruism and benevolence, like selfishness, involve motives that are highly personal, it is odd to speak of them as having an "objective" status. This does not mean that other-regarding behavior is a purely subjective matter with which observers have no concern. When observers speak of such behavior, they ordinarily use the language of obligation or duty, not of interest. It is not odd for an observer to say that I have a duty to serve the welfare of another man—whether I am aware of the duty and whether I profit from the other man's welfare, but it is odd for an observer to say that I have an (other-regarding) interest in the welfare of another man when I am not aware of it. If he knows me well, he might expect me to develop an other-regarding interest in certain situations. But for the prediction to become a description, I would have to develop awareness. Hence we can expand our classification as follows:

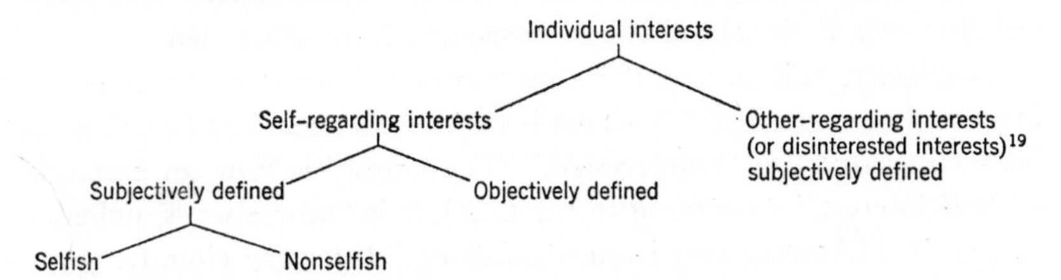

[19] The term "disinterested" will be discussed immediately below. I insert it here because it is convenient to present a complete classification at this point.

The prevalence of the notion "selfish interest" is relevant to the questions discussed in connection with Bentham and Burke. The use of the word selfish is pejorative. It allows other men to express adverse judgments about my conception of my self-regarding interests and how they should be served. To avoid the pejorative adjective I must take account of the situations and interests of other men. *Mutatis mutandis,* when other men judge my (self-regarding) interests to be selfish, they must make a judgment about the relationship between my self-regarding interests and the interests of other men. This fact does not call into question the distinction between self-regarding and other-regarding interests; the object of the interest (the "what") might be entirely self-regarding. But action taken to satisfy my self-regarding interest might have consequences for other men which ought to be considered. As Nowell-Smith says:

> To be selfish is not to do what one wants to do or enjoys doing [or is in one's self-interest], but to be hostile or indifferent to the welfare of others. It comes out in two ways. (A) A man whose dominant desires were for his own pleasures . . . and who seldom or never wanted to do good to others would be a selfish man. (B) [which is the relevant category here] A man who does what he wants to do or what he likes, *when he does it at the expense of others,* is a selfish man, even if what he does is not in itself selfish. To eat when one is hungry is certainly not altruistic: but it is not selfish either. What is selfish is to eat the last biscuit when others are hungry.[20]

The prevalence of the usage does not reflect rejection of the notion that a man is or should be regarded as the best or final judge of his self-regarding interests. But one man's pursuit of his interest often has consequences for others, which means that he has a *duty* to evaluate those consequences. It is perhaps for this reason that the notion of "selfish interest," with its implication of a violation of duty, is important to political discourse. Political action has consequences for other men.

Originally, "disinterested" meant "without interest or concern; not interested or concerned." This use is now obsolete, and its function has been taken over by "uninterested." "Disinterest" is now an antonym of "self-interest." According to the *OED,* it is "now always, unbiased by personal interests; free from self-seeking." It is very close to, if not

[20] Nowell-Smith, *op. cit.,* pp. 142–3. The italics are in the original.

identical with, other-regarding individual interests.[21] It denotes the absence of a self-regarding stake (whether material or otherwise and whether subjectively or objectively defined), but the presence of psychological and/or intellectual concern or commitment. It also suggests that another individual has a material stake in a substantive and that the disinterested individual involves himself in order to assist the former in serving his interests. It is close to "altruistic."

Owing in part to the appeal of egoism, much modern political thought has argued that disinterested political behavior is rare, ineffective, and unreliable. We have seen Bentham's view on this subject ("Consider the backwardness there is in most men, unless . . . spurred by personal interests"), and much contemporary political science agrees that political behavior is "interested" behavior. The most plausible foundation for this view is egoism. If egoism could be substantiated, we would be obliged to abandon the notion of disinterested behavior; but it cannot be substantiated. We should add that there is reason to believe "plain men" do not agree with the view. The notion of disinterested behavior appears widely in political discussion and self-interested behavior is regularly criticized.

These linguistic facts suggest a belief that disinterested behavior is possible and that self-interested behavior can be avoided or minimized. We do not urge men to do things that are impossible for them to do or condemn them for doing things they have to do. "Ought" implies "can." [22] Whatever the empirical incidence of disinterested behavior might be, then, one task which lies before the student of politics is to understand the potential significance of such behavior. If we learn that such behavior is potentially significant and valuable but empirically rare and insignificant, we might better understand some of the characteristics of our politics. We might then be moved to take measures to increase the incidence of disinterested behavior. The empirical finding that disinterested political behavior is rare and insignificant does not warrant the conclusion that political life must do without such behavior or that it would be improved if it did.

[21] *OED*'s phrase, "unbiased by personal interests," is imprecise in that it fails to distinguish between self- and other-regarding interests. The disinterested person has a personal or individual interest, but it is *in* the profit, etc., of another person or persons.

[22] On this point see William Frankena, "Obligation and Ability," in Max Black, editor, *Philosophical Analysis* (Ithaca: Cornell University Press, 1950).

The question of the significance of disinterested political behavior recalls an old and still influential tradition which insists that such behavior is indispensable to a functioning political system. From Plato's philosopher-king through the medieval conception of the monarchy and the Burkean notion of the representative, it has been insisted that a political system which lacks disinterested leadership will degenerate into tyranny and disintegrate into civil war. Although many of the conceptions that had supported this view were rejected by modern political theorists (nowhere more clearly than in *The Federalist*), we continue to give them verbal service and sometimes more. We insist that our judges be unbiased, and that our cabinet members divest themselves of material interests which might influence their decisions; we sometimes become mildly excited concerning the "connections" of our legislators. With all of our sophistication concerning "interest-group politics," we occasionally become disgusted with the spectacle of a politics blatantly dominated by special interests. Few will contest the proposition that these requirements often receive little more than verbal service and are sometimes a rhetorical facade for a politics of unmitigated self-interest.[23] The extent to which this has been the case in any system at any period of time is a matter for empirical research. The tradition to which we have referred would lead us to expect that diminution of serious concern with these requirements would cause normative and practical difficulties. We have merely mentioned, not explored, that tradition, and hence cannot discuss this question here. It can be said that a "politics of public interest" would be impossible in a system in which disinterested political behavior was unknown and unmourned.

VI

The following conclusions emerge from our survey of the uses of "interest." (1) The uses of the term are diverse and complexly related, and it is important to recognize and respect the differences be-

[23] They could not be used exclusively for propaganda purposes or as a rhetorical facade and remain effective. If there were no genuine concern with these requirements there would be no point in hiding behind them. This point applies equally to the view that "public interest" is nothing more than a propaganda device. See Bertrand de Jouvenel, *The Pure Theory of Politics* (New Haven: Yale University Press, 1963), p. 188.

tween them. (It might be argued that the uses ought to be "cleaned up" and confined much more narrowly. This is an inappropriate response. The diversity of use reflects the complex reality to which the concept relates [why else would there be a diversity of uses?], and recognition of this fact and sensitivity to it can facilitate and enrich communication.) (2) In some contexts, "interest" is equivalent to "good" or "welfare." When it is joined with the word "public," ordinary usage does not require the result to differ significantly from that obtained when "good" is joined with "public." In some of its uses, "interest" retains the denotations it carried when "public interest" was first adopted as a general commendatory concept in politics. Hence "public interest" can be significantly different from "common good." (3) The intellectual and institutional procedures used to determine the descriptive meaning of "public interest" will vary according to the conception of the word "interest" in the minds of those making the determination. Particularly significant is the "subjective-objective" distinction. Where "interest" is used in the sense we have designated "subjectively defined self-interest" (whether "selfish" or not), the public interest would consist of that policy on which unanimity is perceived and expressed among the members of the public. Hence, institutional arrangements capable of canvassing and implementing the wishes of the public would be appropriate. Conversely, where "interest" is used to denote an objectively determined relationship between a person and a substantive, the emphasis would fall on the ascertainment of reliable information about the consequences of alternative policies and the development of trans-subjective criteria of value. The issues between these positions cannot be adjudicated on the basis of an analysis of "interest" alone. The following chapter will place them in somewhat broader perspective.

Chapter Three

INDIVIDUAL INTEREST AND THE PUBLIC INTEREST

I

The view that subjectively defined individual interests ought to be served forms an important part of modern political thought and exercises considerable sway upon political practice. Many have lamented an alleged erosion of the commitment to this idea, but the merest glance at Western political thought and practice demonstrates that it remains one of the dominant political ideas of the twentieth century. The view implies that the individual should be allowed not only to define and evaluate but to pursue and satisfy his interests with a minimum of interference from the state. To appreciate the degree to which this view continues to prevail, we need only consider the number of fundamental human decisions which, so far as public policy is concerned, are left almost exclusively to the individual: vocation, place and mode of residence, political and religious belief, association, avocation, possession or not of most types of property, marital status, family size, diet and a host of others. Decisions concerning these matters are only minimally regulated by public policy, and such regulation as exists is justified on the grounds that it controls factors external to the individual and hence maximizes his self-determination. However present practice compares with other historical periods, contemporary Western societies continue to value the subjective definition and pursuit of individual interest very highly.

Strictly speaking, these practices imply that the question of "public interest" has not arisen or, at best, that the descriptive meaning of "public interest" lies in governmental inaction. But refusal to regulate denotes that private practices are acceptable if not beneficial; it implies a public judgment that the totality of individual interests in society constitutes the descriptive meaning of the "public interest." When such practices are challenged, the challenge must be met on the grounds that the practices are in the public interest. This suggests that in large areas of national life a "sum" of the self-interests of the individual members of society is considered identical with the public interest. There is continual dispute concerning particular aspects of the policy of self-determination, but few advocate abandoning it. As long as this continues to be the case, satisfaction of subjectively defined individual interests will be a part of the operative criteria for determining the descriptive meaning of "public interest."

Despite the foregoing, the difficult questions concerning the relation of individual interest and public interest arise in connection with the determination of positive public policy. Here problems arise which have led many thinkers to argue that the expressed self-interest of the individual members of the public and the public interest are, and ought to be kept, entirely distinct.[1] The general issue breaks down into three subquestions, the answers to which divide thinkers into a considerable array of positions on the overall problem. (1) What value should be placed on the satisfaction of the various types of individual interests? (2) Who should define what individual interests are? (3) Who should define the descriptive meaning of "public interest" and the place of individual interests within it?

We shall begin examination of these questions with a further look at the position which maximizes the place of subjectively defined interest in the public interest—the position of the individualist democrat. Argued by Bentham and much of liberal democratic thought from the seventeenth century forward, the position involves the contentions that maximizing the satisfaction of individual self-interests is the basic purpose of the body politic, that the individual is the best judge of his own interests, and that allowing the individual members of society to define public policy achieves the greatest possible degree of identity

[1] For recent statements see, for example, Bertrand de Jouvenel, *Sovereignty* (Chicago: University of Chicago Press, 1957), Chapter 7, and C. W. Cassinelli, "Some Reflections on the Concept of the Public Interest," *Ethics*, Vol. 69, pp. 48 ff (1958–1959).

between public policy and the totality of individual interests. The descriptive meaning of "public interest" consists of expressed individual interests, and it is defined by the individuals who possess those interests.

Some of the essentials of the psychology which underlies this argument have been described in Chapter 2. Self-interest is the only sure springboard to thought and action, and it is only when the individual is allowed to pursue his interests that his abilities will be fully developed and utilized. To allow the individual to define and satisfy his interests is the most efficient means of releasing energies and "getting things done." Furthermore, interests well up from springs deep within the individual and hidden from the view of other men, thus making it impossible for one man to know another man's interest sufficiently to assist him in satisfying it. Wolin summarizes this aspect of Benthamite individualism.

> . . . the exclusive nature of interest rendered it impossible that anyone could really advance the interest of another: impossible not merely because each individual acted primarily from motives of self-interest, but also because an interest existed in the closest possible intimacy to the individual holding it. No outsider, not even one prompted by altruistic motives, could ever know enough to act benevolently. Nor was it a crushing rejoinder to protest that the individual might still be mistaken about where his true interests or happiness lay. What was important was not any supposed "objective" status of interest but what each individual believed to be his interest. As John Stuart Mill later pointed out, the test of what is desirable is whether in fact men do desire it, and hence it would be inherently self-defeating to impose a "truer" interest on men who stubbornly refused to recognize it as such.[2]

Acceptance of this psychology, however, neither entails an identification of self-interest and the public interest nor requires a particular set of procedures for defining the descriptive meaning of the latter. For there remains the crucial question whether, or why, individual development, the release of energy and activity, and "getting things done" *ought* to be valued and accepted as a goal of public policy. A

[2] S. S. Wolin, *Politics and Vision* (Boston: Little, Brown and Company, 1960), p. 339. In general, see Wolin's illuminating comparisions between liberal conceptions of interest and Protestant notions of conscience. It should be added, however, that the citation of John Stuart Mill is somewhat misleading. Mill struggles fruitfully if unsuccessfully with the problems surrounding the equation of desired and desirable throughout his *Utilitarianism,* and this struggle is symptomatic of his discomfort with a number of aspects of the Benthamite doctrine.

number of thinkers have accepted aspects of Bentham's psychology but have reached very different conclusions concerning the public interest. To that psychology was added the basic article of faith of English liberal thought from Hobbes through James Mill, the notion that the individual is to be valued, and that his development, satisfaction, and happiness, as the individual sees them, will be the ultimate goal of the body politic. Although these thinkers were not *atomistic* individualists,[3] they did hold that the social and political order exists for the sake of the individual and must be judged on the basis of how well it serves him. This view is the foundation of the notion of the "felicific calculus" as a means of arriving at a morally defensible decision, and it is the basis of the idea of determining the descriptive meaning of "public interest" by summing up the interests of discrete individuals.[4] A passage or two from Bentham will reinforce the point.

> But if the whole assemblage of any number of individuals be considered as constituting an imaginary compound *body*, a community or political state; any act that is detrimental to any one or more of those *members* is, as to so much of its effects, detrimental to the *state*.

> An act cannot be detrimental to a *state*, but by being detrimental to some one or more of the individuals that compose it.[5]

When this normative position is added to the psychology discussed above, the rationale for the theory of public interest is complete. Individual interest satisfaction is the most efficient means of fostering individual development, and individual development, morally speaking, ought to be the goal of the body politic. Hence for the descriptive meaning of "public interest" to consist of a summation of individual self-interests (and for it to be defined by the individuals possessing those interests), meets the requirements of morally defensible practice as well as sound practical politics.

[3] Wolin, *op. cit.*, pp. 338 ff. Hobbes is an exception. Although he wanted a highly integrated society for certain very limited purposes, the integration he desired was to be achieved by command flowing from a determinate authority directly to each individual, and not by communication or influence flowing from private individual to private individual.

[4] It is not a necessary part of either utilitarianism or hedonism. See G. E. Moore's remark in *Principia Ethica* (Cambridge: Cambridge University Press, 1959), Chapter 3, paragraph 64, p. 107 of the paperback edition.

[5] Jeremy Bentham, *Op. cit.*, p. 313.

The Benthamite position is subject to ready attack on a variety of basic points, but it does contain merits and insights of continuing significance. Bentham's relentless insistence upon the satisfaction of individual interest is a position that ought to be abandoned with caution. The point is in part a logical one. However much we may insist upon disinterested or benevolent behavior and avoiding selfish pursuit of personal interest, at some point we must return to Bentham's willingness to value the individual and his development. The "others" for whom the individual is asked to show concern are, after all, individuals, and the public whose good the individual is expected to seek consists of individuals. If we refuse to value individual self-determination and satisfaction, exhortation to other-regarding behavior threatens to become baseless if not vacuous.[6]

Our findings suggest that it would be a mistake to hold that subjectively defined self-interest has no legitimate place in the descriptive meaning of "public interest." The large realm of behavior which the public chooses not to regulate, together with the valid aspects of Benthamism, require this conclusion. The conclusion is reinforced (albeit with the introduction of important reservations) by examination of a number of writers of a very different philosophic orientation.

A considerable number of nonutilitarian thinkers, both before and after Bentham, have appreciated that the pursuit and satisfaction of self-interest are effective means of stimulating the will and the intellect and releasing productive energies. The fact that the resultant energies would be put to uses other than those prescribed by the utilitarians neither made these psychological principles less useful nor altered the fact that public policy must take account of expressed individual interests and allow for their satisfaction. This understanding underlies Machiavelli's belief that free republics are most likely to generate the energy and power necessary for territorial expansion. James Harrington relied heavily on Machiavelli's idea in prescribing how England could dominate the world. In the view of both Machiavelli and Harrington, the individual citizens are to be allowed to define and pursue their interests, while those in political authority channel the resulant energies and abilities in order to strengthen and benefit the collec-

[6] For a related analysis in a somewhat different context, see Marcus George Singer, *Generalization in Ethics* (New York: Alfred A. Knopf, Inc., 1960), pp. 224–5.

tivity.[7] One of the most explicit statements of this view by a modern thinker occurs in Hegel's *Philosophy of Right*. "The principle of modern states has prodigious strength and depth because it allows the principle of subjectivity to progress to its culmination in the extreme of self-subsistent personal particularity." [8] Hegel insists, as do Burke, Harrington, and Machiavelli, that the pursuit of particular interests must be controlled by public authority. Where subjectivity conflicts with the universal, to use Hegel's suggestive terminology, the latter must triumph. But subjectivity is indispensable to the universal, and if the universal disregards it, restricts it excessively, or crushes it, the universal weakens and destroys itself. Individual (or group) pursuit of subjectively defined interest, if not an end in itself as with Hobbes and Bentham, is to be highly valued, fostered, and protected as a means of strengthening the body politic. The public interest is not likely to be regarded as a sum of individual interests, but individual interests will be considered a legitimate and important part of it.

II

For a number of reasons, then, the expressed self-interest of the members of the citizenry has been considered necessary to defining the descriptive meaning of "public interest." But an adequate theory of "public interest" must encompass and account for a number of other considerations as well. It is characteristic of politics and public policy that they deal with situations involving conflict between subjectively defined interests, with situations in which satisfying the interest of individual or group *A* renders impossible or minimizes the extent to which it is possible to satisfy the interest of individual or group *B*. to value interest satisfaction and self-determination provides no assistance in deciding which of two or more competing interests ought to be satisfied. or does it provide justification for expecting *B* to consider himself obligated to comply with a decision which satisfies *A* but

[7] For Machiavelli's view, see *Discourses*, I, 1; and II, 2. Harrington asserts this view again and again, but see especially "The Introduction or Order of the Work," and "Part I. The Preliminaries," in *The Commonwealth of Oceana*.

[8] G. W. F. Hegel, *Philosophy of Right*, translated with notes by T. M. Knox (London: Oxford University Press, 1942), p. 161. Very similar views are to be found in the writings of Burke. See *Works*, *op. cit.*, Vol. II, pp. 229, 338, 341.

precludes the satisfaction of *B*, or for an authority to compel *B* to comply with such a decision. It is sometimes helpful to think of these questions from the standpoint of the hanged and the hangman. Reliance upon individualism as a basis for political decisions stumbles against the root facts of interdependence and social conflict. It is true that self-interest has a legitimate place in the public interest, but deciding whose self-interest and to what extent requires the utilization of values and principles which transcend such interests.

The first consequence of interdependence and conflict is that perceived or expressed self-interest *as such* cannot define the public interest. The *mere* fact that an individual perceives X to be in his interest cannot create imperatives concerning the content of the public interest. Aside from the practical problems this position would create,[9] it violates the maxim that no individual should be judge in his own case, and it releases the individual from all duties to other men in the area of public policy. As long as individual interest is all that is offered to justify X, the fact that another man perceives X to be contrary to *his* interest will be of equal moral weight.

These difficulties, contrary to Bentham, are not overcome if the individual's perceived interest coincides with the perceived interest of many, a majority, or all but one of the members of his society. The concept of public interest functions to *justify* the demand that members of the society regard themselves as obligated (not merely forced) to obey particular commands and to conform to particular policies which they regard as contrary to their personal interests. The concept, in other words, is a moral concept, and moral considerations are part of properly defining its descriptive meaning in any given case. If no moral warrant can be provided for a claim when it is presented by an individual, the fact that many individuals present it scarcely alters the case. Number—that is, force—is not a criterion of right. This is the timeless message of Rousseau's distinction between the will of all and the general will. Those who regard this distinction as antidemocratic or antiliberal simply equate democracy or liberalism with the rule of force and demonstrate that they either have not read or have not understood the first four chapters of Rousseau's *Social Contract*.[10]

[9] For a cogent summary of these, see Bertrand de Jouvenal, *Sovereignty*, pp. 110–11.

[10] See also de Tocqueville, *Democracy in America* (New York: Vintage Books, 1957), Vol. I, p. 269. It might be added that the "but one" could be eliminated

If we take seriously the view that the members of the citizenry are *unable* to act except in a narrowly self-interested manner, these considerations would disqualify them from a voice in determining the descriptive meaning of "public interest." Procedures might be established which would make the demands of the citizenry known to those in authority, but the information acquired would be of no greater normative significance than the Gross National Product or the Dow Jones Averages.

Whatever the role of central authority, and whatever the facts concerning the behavior of the citizenry, the individual citizen will not be relieved of his responsibilities in regard to the public interest. Individual interest demands constitute a part of the political life of a nation; they affect other citizens and have to be taken into account by them. If individuals judge their personal interests and formulate their political demands without considering the requirements of a politics of public interest, the possibility of other individuals satisfying their interests will be reduced, and determination and implementation of the descriptive meaning of "public interest" will be rendered extremely difficult.[11] In a narrower sense, to be supported by public authority the individual's demands must be judged compatible with the public interest. Hence whatever the individual's duties may be, he will have a stake in attempting to conform his demands to the public interest.

These considerations raise the question of the requirements of a politics of public interest for the individual. In part this question is simply an aspect of the more general problem of moral behavior: the individual must consider the consequences of his behavior for others and attempt to fashion his behavior to be consistent with moral principles and rules which are more than rationalizations tailor-made to justify a specific action. But the public interest poses special problems and special requirements; it makes demands which are both more and less exacting than those we make on nonpolitical behavior.

Like moral decisions generally, specific decisions concerning political behavior demand consideration of contextual factors which no set of moral principles or rules can include. No general theory can provide

from the third sentence in the paragraph above. Had each of the Roman citizens believed it to be in his personal interest to annihilate the Carthaginians, the policy would not thereby have been justified.

[11] This is the force of Rousseau's discussion of the question which the citizen must ask when making political decisions. *Social Contract*, IV, 1.

"recipes" for particular decisions. But this does not mean that such decisions are purely *ad hoc* in character, that no principles or rules apply. Part of the *definition* of a moral decision is that it be based upon principles and stated in the form of a principle.[12] This is true of political behavior as well. The requirement stems from the fact that a decision is a moral decision, and moral decisions can arise in politics, business, athletics, or any other realm of behavior. Without entering deeply into the problems of ethical theory at this point, we will consider the basic principles relevant to the range of decisions in question.

The first principle to be discussed has been called the "universalizability" or "generalization" principle.[13] It is close to Kant's categorical imperative, although recent thinkers have amended, or perhaps only clarified, Kant's formulation in an attempt to meet the long train of objections against it. One of the most thorough of the recent students of the principle states it as follows: "What is right (or wrong) for one person must be right (or wrong) for any similar person in similar circumstances."[14] This principle is "formal" in the sense that it entails no substantive moral rule[15] and will not, taken alone, answer any moral question. As Hare says, "No moral judgment . . . of substance follows from the thesis [of universalizability] alone."[16] But this does not mean, as Hegel and others have argued, that the principle is vacuous or trivial. If the principle does not entail substantive answers to moral questions, it does provide a logical test which any substantive answer must meet. Somewhat more specifically, the principle relentlessly exposes attempts to impose rules or decisions on others when the individual is not or would not be disposed to apply them to himself.[17]

[12] For a discussion of recent conceptions of the distinction between moral and nonmoral (as opposed to immoral), see William Frankena, "Recent Conceptions of Morality," in H. Castenada and G. Nakhnikian, editors, *Morality and the Language of Conduct* (Detroit: Wayne State University Press, 1963).

[13] It is important to distinguish between the *requirement* or *principle* of universalizability or universalization and the *fact* of the universality of application of governmental decisions. As we will see, the two are related in important respects. But logically speaking they are quite different.

[14] Singer, *op. cit.*, p. 5.

[15] For the distinction between principles and rules, see *Ibid.*, Chapter 5, and in this book, Chapters 5 and 8.

[16] R. M. Hare, *Freedom and Reason* (London: Oxford University Press, 1963), p. 32. In citing Singer and Hare together we are ignoring for the moment the very extensive differences between them. These will be examined in Chapter 8.

[17] These are assertions. For a more thoroughgoing analysis of universalizability see Chapter 8.

The principle is peculiarly relevant to political behavior. When an individual demands that the state act in a certain manner, he demands that the action be imposed upon all of the members of the society. To demand state action is to insist upon the universal (in terms of the society) application of the policy in question. Hence it is appropriate to ask: "Would that policy be right (or wrong) when imposed upon all similar persons in similar circumstances in this society?" The relevance of the universalizability principle to political behavior stems in part from the fact that in the politics which we know universality is not speculative but a fact of life.

Stated less formally, the universalizability principle requires that political actors consider the impact of their actions and demands on the other members of society, reduce idiosyncratic demands, and seek constantly to find common ground with other men. They must perform the difficult task of thinking of themselves as members of a class of people.[18] Through this process they subsume their interests under a larger precept or maxim and thereby begin to transform them into "claims" which can legitimately be pressed in the public forum.[19] The point here is not that interests should never be pressed or satisfied if they do not coincide with the interests of all other men in society. Such a requirement would make unanimity the precondition of a justifiable policy and would reduce politics and state action to trivial proportions. The concept "public interest" functions to justify action in the face of disagreement. To contend that the requirements of "public interest" are such that individuals may press only those demands about which there is unanimity is to fly in the face of elementary facts concerning the concept and political life generally.

At this point the qualification "similar persons in similar circumstances" becomes important. We have described state action as, "in principle," universal in application. But the principles which lie behind state action, the demand for the rule of law and equality before the law, are interpreted to allow the use of "permissible classifications"; to allow the legislature to treat different people differently as long as similar persons in similar circumstances are treated alike. Thus conscription laws utilize a complex system of classification as a basis for requiring

[18] See the brilliant discussion by Rousseau, *Social Contract*, II, 4.

[19] See S. I. Benn, "Interests in Politics," *Proceedings of the Aristotelian Association*, New Series, Vol. LX, pp. 123 ff (1959–1960), and Charles Fried, "Two Concepts of Interest," *Harvard Law Review*, Vol. 76, pp. 755 ff (February, 1963).

some men to take enormous risks and make great sacrifices while excusing other men from those risks and sacrifices. We do not object when healthy men over eighteen but under twenty-six years of age are asked to take such risks, while healthy men under eighteen and over twenty-six are not so asked. This is because we believe that men under and men over twenty-six are not similar persons in similar circumstances. Sometimes we permit classifications that involve very small numbers. The highest brackets used by our income tax laws would be an example. But the person who proposes such a law must be prepared to universalize it, to apply the law to all of the members of the class, including himself. In pressing interests and demands, therefore, the individual or group is not obligated to find common ground with an entire population; but it is his (or their) duty to test the classifications he proposes in the light of this principle.

Because of its formal character, the universalizability principle cannot provide complete guidance for political behavior, and adherence to it cannot exhaust the duties which a public interest politics imposes upon the citizen. Consider the case of assigning punishments according to the classification "All those who have commited murder in the first degree." We first have to agree that the classification is defensible in terms of the "similar persons similarly situated" requirement. If we agree to this and we treat all such persons the same, we have satisfied the demands of one part of the principle.[20] But application of the principle also presupposes an answer to the question: "Is it right (or wrong) to treat *X* (who has commited murder in the first degree) in manner *Y?*" This depends upon the consequences of so treating him. Universalizability is relevant in that it teaches that *if Y* is right for *X* it must be right for *A, B, C,* and *D if* they are similar persons similarly situated. But universalizing alone cannot determine whether the consequences are good or bad, the policy right or wrong. This does not mean that the principle is trivial. If we do not or cannot universalize, the policy fails. The principle is necessary but not sufficient.

[20] The question of what constitutes significant differences and similarities must be in part a contexual matter about which it is difficult to generalize. We will see below that it depends primarily upon whether the consequences of treating the persons involved are the same. But Singer presents an illuminating discussion of *types* of differences which can never be significant. His discussion disposes of many of the stock objections to the generalization principle. See *op. cit.*, especially Chapter 4; also Kurt Baier, *The Moral Point of View* (Ithaca: Cornell University Press, 1958), especially Chapter 8.

We must now ask whether we can identify any general principles concerning the manner in which consequences are properly assessed. A number of philosophers believed that very elaborate and definitive requirements could be established in this regard—for example, Bentham's felicific calculus. But this question involves the whole range of controversy among "naturalists," "intuitionists," "noncognitivists," "formalists," and others. We are not yet in a position to examine these questions and positions, and for the moment we will rest with a slight extension of the previous argument.

We have argued that a politics of public interest requires the individual to consider the impact of his behavior upon others and to conform to the demands of the universalizability principle. Both requirements force him to move beyond the idiosyncratic and subjective and support his decisions and demands with considerations of a publicly exchangeable type. This requirement suggests the most general answer to the question of how to evaluate the consequences of a demand or policy. Since the evaluation is a matter of public significance, the grounds on which it rests must be exchangeable in a public, that is a trans-subjective or intersubjective, manner. Stated negatively, they cannot rest solely upon "I like." The generic term for such considerations is "reasons," and the generic descriptive of the behavior which the public interest requires is giving reasons or being reasonable or resting conclusions upon reasons. The validity of reasons depends upon rules of inference and the existence of evidence, not upon purely personal interests and preferences. This means that reasons provide grounds upon which agreement can be reached despite differences of the latter kind. In most general and formal terms, then, a "politics of public interest" requires that political actors rest their assessment of the consequences of proposed policies on reasons.

III

To summarize, a politics of public interest requires that citizens shape their political behavior according to the principles of universalizability and the canons of reason. Since decisions concerning the public interest are moral ones, it might be said that fulfilling these requirements is simply a duty which needs no further justification. The type of behavior described is a duty because of its consequences, because its nonperformance creates problems for others, and its performance solves problems that are shared by the members of society. It remains to specify more closely the problems which would be solved.

We argued that the satisfaction of subjectively defined individual and group interests can be a legitimate part of the public interest, and also that "public interest" is a normative concept, the descriptive meaning of which might differ from the expressed interests on any particular issue. To the extent that the first criterion is emphasized, the root of the problem of the public interest is interest diversity and conflict in society. The greater the range of expressed interests on any question, the more difficult it will be to find a policy that will satisfy all or any substantial proportion of them. Individual behavior of the kind discussed would contribute to the solution of this problem by narrowing the range of demand and conflict. Purely idiosyncratic and self-serving demands which could not meet the principle of universalizability and the canons of reason would be reduced or eliminated. In the jargon of contemporary political science, the task of "interest aggregation" and refinement would be performed to a greater degree at the individual and group level, thereby reducing the burden on semipublic aggregative agencies, such as political parties, and on authority itself. Or in more traditional language, the degree of "community" would be enhanced. (These points are at the heart of Rousseau's argument in *The Social Contract.*)

Such behavior would also contribute to meeting the second criterion. Although diversity of opinion and expression can contribute to understanding and the ascertainment of truth, to do so the opinion must be directed to the issue or question about which understanding or truth is desired. Since "public interest" is a normative standard, discussion and expression that is nothing more than a parade of individual interests will be irrelevant except as data to be evaluated. On the other hand, to the extent that individuals and groups conform to the requirements discussed, their expressions and views will be relevant to defining the descriptive meaning of "public interest," and the task of defining it will be facilitated by a plurality of relevant views and understandings. This is in contrast to a situation in which only those in authority are expected to concern themselves with the normative problem.

It might be objected that these arguments conflict with basic aspects of the creed underlying liberal-democratic societies and that if accepted they would eliminate the rich pluralism of political life. A partial answer to this criticism has already been presented, but there are a number of points to be added. The requirements which have been posited are by no means narrow or cramping. The universalizability principle is formal in character, and in a particular case it might be satisfied by a number of policies, especially if the "similar persons in similar circumstances" qualification is understood. Again, to insist that reasons must be given in support of an assessment of consequences is scarcely to rule out the possibility of a plurality of views. A variety of policies might have desirable consequences on most issues of social policy. Given the complex implications of such policies, a great variety of reasons might be relevant to proving them desirable or undesirable. Nor does the present argument rule out *discussion* of an enormous array of demands, policies, or courses of action. Contrary to Rousseau's view that the citizenry must "think their own thoughts," it is through discussion that arguments for policies can be tested. But it is one thing to discuss, another to insist, demand, threaten, or bring pressures to bear.

Finally, we have spoken of the requirements of a politics of public interest, not the public interest itself. There is an important difference between the conditions that maximize the possibility of defining and implementing the descriptive meaning of "public interest," and the act of defining it authoritatively; between the questions, "Would satisfying this claim be in the public interest?" and "Would advancing this claim contribute to a politics of public interest?" It would be consistent to argue that private individuals ought to behave politically in the manner described and yet to exclude them entirely from the process of authoritatively defining the public interest. Individual political behavior of the kind described is a necessary, not a sufficient, condition of a public interest politics. This at once relaxes the demands on the citizenry and raises the question of the role of authority—to which we will return.[21]

Yet the requirements suggested would reduce the range of demands presented as opposed to a situation in which those requirements were not adhered to. If this were not the case, there would be no point in insisting upon the requirements. If they run counter to certain postu-

[21] It might be added by way of emphasis that the entire discussion of the requirements a politics of public interest creates for individual political behavior has been concerned with moral, not legal, imperatives.

lates or practices, those postulates and practices are untenable and ought to be abandoned or modified. If these requirements are not accepted and met to an appreciable degree, a Hobbesean system in which the responsibility for the public interest is placed exclusively in the hands of central authority would be the only means of achieving justifiable public policy. Thinking about the difficulties of Hobbesean politics, as Rousseau understood so well, is an effective way of appreciating the significance of the requirements we have been discussing.

The preceding discussion justifies the earlier statement that a politics of public interest creates more exacting requirements than moral requirements outside of the realm of politics. Owing to the fact of universality in politics, the task of the citizen in determining and assessing the other-regarding consequences of his political behavior is gargantuan in its proportions. But the very scope of the task suggests two senses in which the requirements of political behavior are less exacting than those of nonpolitical life. The very fact of universality, first of all, renders inescapable the use of broad, even crude categories in formulating public policy. The sensitive distinctions expected within the comparatively limited confines of individual and small-group relations are seldom practicable when dealing with whole populations. Since public policies must deal in comprehensive categories, it would be unrealistic and perhaps debilitating to expect individual political behavior to reflect the sensitivities expected in more intimate dimensions of life. The standards by which individual behavior is judged must be appropriate to the conditions in which that behavior must take place.

Second, and more important, the information necessary to an assessment and evaluation of the consequences of a political demand is enormous in bulk and difficult to obtain. Consider the case of the farmer who urges the government to institute or maintain a system of farm price supports. The economic ramifications of such a policy are extraordinarily complex and difficult to evaluate. This does not relieve the farmer of his duty to base his demand upon the best judgment his situation allows. It does indicate, once again, that his behavior must be judged by standards appropriate to his situation. It is perhaps in recognition of these facts that societies have been unwilling to emphasize or hold their members to the requirements we have discussed. More accurately, these facts provide the most generous possible explanation for the permissiveness of societies in this regard. But fitting the canons of responsibility to the circumstances of behavior should not be confused with abandoning requirements.

IV

If the difficulties we have been discussing affect the canons of individual responsibility, they also do much to account for the function of central authority in defining the descriptive meaning of "public interest." Assuming that the foregoing arguments are tenable, a citizenry which meets the requirements of a politics of public interest can contribute to defining the descriptive meaning of "public interest" and thereby relieve the burden on those in authority. They can never take over that burden entirely. A society that takes "public interest" seriously will require the assistance of central authority devoted to the service of the public interest. This is true in part because men do not meet the requirements of a public interest politics in anything like a perfect manner. To reject egoism is not to deny the prevalence of selfish behavior. And few of us, steeped as we are in Hobbes, Bentham, *The Federalist,* and their descendants, expect such behavior to disappear entirely. As long as selfish behavior continues, a determinate authority, which exists to promote the public interest, will be needed to control the effects of such behavior and to assert the public interest in the face of selfish demands.

This Augustinian view of authority is true but incomplete. To it must be added the ancient understanding that a complex and interdependent society of men, even if they are good men, requires a determinate central authority with its energies and capacities devoted exclusively to the problems and potentialities of those men in their life together. This conclusion follows from the extraordinary difficulties of political judgments, of judgments which affect all of the members of a society. These difficulties and complexities underline the necessity of obtaining information and understanding from throughout the body politic. The importance of a citizenry that will contribute such information and understanding in a usable form is clear. But these difficulties also create a need for a central agent to bring the information and understanding together and decide which policies will best serve the community. When the citizenry have transformed their interests into claims which can legitimately be pressed in the public forum, authority must canvass those claims, supplement them by considering interests which have not been pressed, and adjudicate between them. Defining the descriptive meaning of "public interest" requires not only good will, which in principle is as likely to be found among private citizens as in authority,[22] but also knowledge, information, and the judgment which only wide knowledge and information make possible. We establish central authority not merely to enforce decisions against recalcitrant citizens, but in order to build institutions which facilitate the gathering and assessment of the complex information necessary to proper judgments concerning public policy.[23]

These considerations lead to the rather commonplace conclusion that on most issues of public policy the descriptive meaning of "public interest" should be defined by a determinate central authority.[24] However commonplace this may be, it has important implications concerning the place of self-interest in the public interest. Since we have insisted that the descriptive meaning of "public interest" consists at least in part of individual interests, the argument concerning authority commits us to some form of the view that those in authority are able to define the individual's personal interests for him; it commits us to some form of an objective view of interest. Although the procedural implications of our conclusion are commonplace, this latter view will cer-

[22] There is a sense in which institutionalizing authority is an attempt to guarantee disinterested behavior. The individual who accepts authority must swear to divest himself of personal concerns and devote his efforts to the public interest. In the modern era, however, this very practice exposes the lack of faith in disinterested behavior. Modern man multiplies oaths and professions profusely, but he clearly has little faith in them. For he surrounds those in authority with devices designed to insure that they recognize it is in their interest to act disinterestedly.

[23] After completing the present book, I learned of Charles Lindblom's analysis of the comparative merits of centralized and decentralized systems of coordination and adjustment. (*The Intelligence of Democracy*, New York: The Free Press of Glencoe, 1965.) Lindblom's distinctions between various processes of coordination and adjustment would make it possible to refine the above discussion of authority. But his criticisms of centralized coordination and adjustment are unconvincing because they are leveled against a model which posits a single decision maker acting in splendid isolation and hence bears little relation to either the theory or the practice of centralized authority and decision making. See especially Chapter 9 and Part 5.

[24] The conclusion militates against extensive use of popular decision-making procedures such as the referendum. Although contrary to the practices of some systems, this would scarcely be controversial in terms of the literature of contemporary political science.

tainly provoke objections, and not only from the Benthamites. Bertrand de Jouvenel, for example, writes of this view.

We are repelled at the outset. To know each man's good [good and interest are used synonymously] better than he knows it himself is something within the competence of God alone. It is the duty of a father, ruler in his tiny realm, to perceive wherein the good of each of his sons consists and to set the feet of each in his proper path while making the others help him in the task; yet with how many blunders does even a father exercise this function! Clearly it cannot be exercised over a large population, for the indispensable adjuncts of a jurisdiction of this kind are personal knowledge of each single subject and unceasing vigilance in his regard. . . . The infirmity of the human intelligence makes it impossible for the ruler to consider individual goods particularly; he can only conceive of them in general terms.[25]

This is a case of being misled by an analogy. When we recognize wherein the analogy is inappropriate, a more adequate view is immediately suggested. The language of "paternalism" is misleading when applied to the ruler. He does not deal with those intensely personal matters that concern only the individual or his family. He deals with the individual in his situation as a member of a society, as a person affecting and affected by an enormous range of individuals, many of whom he does not and may never know. It is true that the ruler "can only conceive of" the individual's good "in general terms"; but this is exactly as it should be.[26] And the fact that the individual's good or interest must be generalized scarcely makes it any the less important to him.

Can it be said that the individual will be able to protect himself adequately from the impact of those multitudes upon him, to take advantage of the opportunities which life in association with those multitudes makes available to him? Granting that he must be treated as one of a large and diverse body of men, is it not more reasonable to assume that a central authority, with sources of information concerning the entire society, will be able to aid him in the pursuit of those interests which are bound up with his social being? And if the individual believes that he can pursue his own interests without assistance, can he confidently claim that he will not interfere unjustifiably with the simi-

[25] De Jouvenel, *Sovereignty*, pp. 111–12.

[26] See Aristotle, *Politics*, especially Book I.

lar pursuits of other men? These, after all, are the propositions in question.

It is of course true that a central authority will never understand individual interests perfectly, and it is true that it will be in constant danger of perversion; hence the importance of respect for private judgments, the need for a variety of safeguards and mechanisms for enforcing responsibility, and the insistence that the citizenry decide who should occupy the positions of authority. But the difficulties and dangers of the exercise of authority in this area must be weighed not against the capabilities of God but against the difficulties of men attempting to live together without the assistance of authority.

V

It is time to summarize and draw conclusions concerning the place of individual interest in the public interest. Much of Western tradition has assigned individual interest a legitimate and dominant place in the descriptive meaning of "public interest." We have modified but by no means abandoned this view. We have not challenged the policy of inaction, the policy of identifying the totality of self-defined individual interests and the public interest. Our discussion of interdependence, conflict, and the role of authority suggests that this policy is not sacrosanct. Nothing argued here implies that any specific aspect of this policy is mistaken. Rather, the present emphasis upon the value of individual self-determination and development suggests that this policy ought to be continued except where it is self-defeating in allowing some individuals unjustifiably to hamper and interfere with the freedom and development of others.

We also argued that it is important to a politics of public interest that the citizenry assert their interests and demands and contribute to the process of determining what is in the public interest. This argument was qualified by the view that the citizens must transform their interests into justifiable claims by considering the impact of these interests on other men and on society generally. Considering the claims and interests of others does not imply ignoring the individual's own. "Our" can never be exclusively "mine," but it includes the latter by definition. Again, we have emphasized the difficulties which the individual or group faces in making judgments concerning the public interest and the consequent necessity of fitting the canons of responsibility to the formidable character of the task. When combined with the importance of informing those in authority of the situation of the individual or group, and with the distinction between meeting the requirements of a politics of the public interest and the descriptive meaning of the "public interest" itself, the discussion suggests significant but by no means narrow limitations upon individual interest assertion.[27]

The argument concerning the role of authority undercuts aspects of the radical individualist position; it also supports that position in important respects. If private individuals were responsible for the authoritative determination of the public interest, we would have to abandon the distinction between what is in the public interest and the requirements of a politics of the public interest. As Rousseau's theory indicates, this would require marked reduction of the freedom allowed to individual interest assertion. With authority goes responsibility.

When authority defines the public interest it cannot "sum up" perceived individual interests as Bentham urged, but it should seek to serve and satisfy them. It should do so in part because satisfaction of individual interest is productive of stability, energy, and creativity in the citizenry, and because the satisfaction and development of human beings is the fundamental *raison d'être* of the body politic.

Because it must deal with large classifications and owing to the practical and moral problems flowing from interdependence, complexity, and conflict, authority cannot restrict itself to the service of subjectively defined interests. It must serve individual interests and promote respect for objectively defined duties. But this does not alter the fact that it is individual interests that authority attempts to serve. Therefore individual interests retain a place in the public interest. This is important because it is the foundation on which rests the right of the populace to select and judge the performance of those in authority. Although private citizens cannot authoritatively define the public interest, they are preeminently able to judge the results of that definition as those results impinge upon them and their fellow men. If it is assumed that the descriptive meaning of "public interest" should not include and serve individual interests, there would be little justifi-

[27] These are the grounds on which we would differ with Cassinelli's argument that viewing individual interests as part of the public interest leads to antidemocratic results. Cassinelli, *op. cit.*, pp. 49, 54.

cation for authorizing individuals to judge the performance of those who define the public interest. Many democratic practices, from holding open the channels of political expression and communication to elections themselves, rest on the assumption that public policy ought to serve individual interests and that individuals are capable of judging, if only after the fact and in an overall manner, whether it has done so. If this assumption is dropped, much of democratic practice is undercut.

In all of these respects individual interest has an integral place in the determination and content of public interest. In insisting upon this interpretation, however, we must remember that individual interests *as such*, whether subjectively or objectively defined, and regardless of the force, influence, or number that can be marshaled in their support, can never create imperatives concerning the public interest. The most elementary aspects of life together require that all interests for which public protection or support is requested be examined, first by the individual or group and then by an authority, in order to determine their impact upon society, and protection or support must never be provided unless that impact, as reinforced and extended by the force of government, can be justified in a reasoned, trans-subjective manner. Evaluation in terms of standards applied in common to all interests distinguishes the determination of the public interest from a "summation" of idiosyncratic individual interests and justifies the imposition of a policy on all interests. In Chapters 4 and 5 an attempt will be made to deal more fully with the characteristics of such justifications and the manner in which they must be developed, that is, with the characteristics and means of defining the descriptive meaning of the "public interest" in specific cases.

Chapter Four

THE PUBLIC INTEREST: DESCRIPTIVE MEANING (I)

We now turn from the requirements of a "politics of public interest" to further discussion of the decision criteria appropriate to the determination of the descriptive meaning of "public interest." We shall begin by surveying a sample of the many theories which have been advanced concerning this question. Examination of these theories will provide an efficient vehicle for identifying and clarifying issues and a means of establishing some basic propositions.

A good starting point is a type of theory that is as old as serious concern with the moral and political problems which lie behind "public interest." This theory, which was argued with unequaled force and beauty by Plato, holds that the words "public interest" (or "common good," as Plato would prefer it) refer to or stand for a body of substantive truths or principles. These truths or principles are not formal tests that any public policy must meet; however general they may be and however much skill may be required to apply them in particular cases, they provide substantive guidance to the proper content of public policy. They are akin to what some philosophers now call "rules" as opposed to "principles." [1] The problem of determining what

[1] "Do not say what is false" is a rule. It is "substantive" in the sense that it indicates what one should or should not do in cases to which it is relevant. "What is right (or wrong) for one person must be right (or wrong) for any similar person similarly situated" is a principle. It is "formal" in the sense that it does not prescribe particular behaviors, but merely establishes a test which any proposed form of behavior must meet.

is in the public interest is first and foremost a problem of attaining knowledge of this body of supreme truth. One who does not have such knowledge could only stumble onto the right policy as a blind man might stumble onto the right road at a junction.[2] One who truly has such knowledge will always find the right policy, because there is a sense (difficult to define) in which the right policy is "contained in" the body of supreme truth.

> . . . the Sun not only makes the things we see visible, but also brings them into existence and gives them growth and nourishment; . . . so with the objects of knowledge: these derive from the Good not only their power of being known, but their very being and reality . . .[3]

Plato's position minimizes the "contextual" dimension of the descriptive meaning of "public interest."[4] The justifiability of a particular public policy turns not upon the relationship between that policy and features peculiar to the problem or circumstances to which or in which the policy is to be applied. It turns upon its relationship to a truth or body of truths which exists and has been discovered antecedent to the emergence of the problem, circumstances, or policy. It is the fact that the statesman has been trained to know this timeless "Good" which equips him to decide questions of common concern. This view raises questions about the relationship between the particular policy enacted *now*, which is held to be in the public interest, and the timeless truth or truths which the philosopher-king must know. Whether we ever speak of *the* public interest in the sense of a body of substantive truths such as those Plato denominates *the* Good, we do say, "This policy is in the public interest." When we do so we are saying that *this* policy, in *these* circumstances, is a justifiable or commendable public policy—because of its relationship to the Good or for some other reason. A theory of "public interest" that is to account for the manner in which the concept functions must be able to account

[2] Plato, *Meno* 97; *Republic*, 506, Francis M. Cornford, translator (London: Oxford University Press, 1941).

[3] Plato, *Republic*, 508, p. 220.

[4] If the metaphysical and epistemological substructure of Plato's theory is set aside, it becomes clear that many theories of "public interest" are closely akin to Plato's. Whenever it is argued that "public interest" stands for a body of substantive truths or propositions about public policy, the theory can be likened, however enormous the other differences may be, to Plato's theory. For this reason, conclusions reached about Plato will prove to be applicable to a large number of other theories as well.

for the manner in which we justify *this* policy, not a set of highly abstract metaphysical or moral truths.

It is difficult to see how such a justification could be constructed without detailed examination of the facts and circumstances surrounding the specific policy in question. Assume that it has been proposed that country *X* enact legislation to conscript men for military service. It might be urged that the legislation is in the public interest because military protection is necessary to the security of the nation. Few would disagree with the abstract proposition that maintaining national security is an activity in the public interest. Yet the simple assertion that conscription is in the public interest because it serves security is going to convince very few—least of all those to be conscripted.

One can imagine a variety of contexts in which such an argument would be vigorously and properly challenged. The relationship between security and the policy in question must be defined and demonstrated. What are the threats to security that require conscription? What concrete problems will the proposed form of conscription solve? What problems will conscription create, and how will they be handled? When relationship between security and conscription has been established, there will remain the question of determining the impact of the latter on other values such as freedom, equality, and justice, and of making a judgment as to which of these, in the circumstances in question, ought to be favored. In the absence of detailed contextual evidence and arguments, the assertion that conscription is in the public interest will be arbitrary and unconvincing, regardless of how highly we value security.

The point is not that the Platonic-type theory has nothing to teach us. It is Plato's argument that justifying a public policy decision requires standards and criteria which are more than rationalizations tailored to the exact shape of the decision or policy in question. This requirement is a part of the very definition of a moral decision. Plato is also correct in arguing that we must appeal to a body of high-order and substantive norms and rules to decide public policy questions. The contextual facts do not carry labels assigning normative character and standing. We assign such standing by relating the facts to general propositions and values (such as "maintain national security"). For these reasons, the Platonic-type theory must be accepted as partially true.

Having conceded this it might be thought that the objection against this type of theory, that it ignores or underemphasizes contextual factors, is trivial. Not so. This objection is important because it combats the view that "public interest" has, or ought to have, *a* descriptive meaning which can be stated in general terms and which, taken alone, will determine proper public policy (and that if no such general descriptive meaning can be stated the concept is meaningless or vacuous). The concept has a commendatory meaning about which we can generalize. We learn from Plato and others that there are principles, criteria, and standards of a general nature which will be relevant to determining what its descriptive meaning should be in any case. These "decision criteria" can be discussed in general terms, but the descriptive meaning of "public interest" will always be in part contextual. We will never be able to say, "This policy is in the public interest," unless we have examined the policy and circumstances in detail and related them to general standards and criteria. To the extent that theories of the Platonic type deny or minimize this fact, they violate the logic of "public interest." To the extent that pessimistic conclusions concerning "public interest" stem from the inability to discover a general descriptive meaning for the concept, they stem from a misunderstanding.[5]

[5] The foregoing deals with Plato's theory as representative of a major type of approach to "public interest." Hence it ignores many of the features special to Plato's argument. These are of great interest, and it will be useful to consider them briefly.

Perhaps for the reasons offered in the Seventh Letter (especially 341c) and suggested by Socrates in *The Republic* (It "would call for an effort too ambitious for an enquiry like ours" [506a, Cornford, *op. cit.*, p. 217]. "I will not leave out anything that can be said on this occasion" [509c Cornford, *op cit.*, p. 220].) Plato refuses to specify the content of the Good (or at least refuses explicitly to label any of the positions which he takes as constitutive of the Good) and says little about the manner in which the philosopher-kings will put it to use. This makes it difficult to define the relationship between the Good and a specific policy; it makes it difficult to specify the grounds on which it is held that a policy constitutes the descriptive meaning of "public interest." Yet Plato insists that knowledge of the Good is essential and, what is more, that it can be attained only by a very select few. This has the momentous consequence that decisions about matters of common concern must be the exclusive prerogative of the philosopher-kings. Plato's conclusion is that "public interest" and "common good" are concepts which would be appropriately employed only by philosopher-kings in discussion with other philosopher-kings. If it is true that "public interest" functions to commend and justify public policy, and if only the philosopher-kings are capable of fully understanding the justifications and commendations, it follows that there would be no occasion to use the concepts outside of the circle of philosopher-kings.

This conclusion can be restated in yet another manner. Plato teaches that the

Plato sought objectivity and timelessness of content for "public interest" through transcendence of the particular, through expanding the concept of common good to equivalence with ultimate truths about man and the universe. There have also been attempts to achieve a related kind of result, reduction of the ambiguity and uncertainties of the concept through a very different technique, through narrowing "public interest" to equivalence with a single value or standard which can be defined with relative precision. Such an attempt is made by S. I. Benn and Richard Peters in *Social Principles and the Democratic State.*[6] Benn and Peters argue that "public interest" is not a substantive concept at all, not a goal of public policy, but simply a procedural principle or requirement which is one of a number of conditions that a justifiable public policy must satisfy. In their words:

> . . . the prescription "seek the common good" is not of the same type as "maintain full employment." Whereas the latter is a counsel of substance,

standard of proper public policy is no less than the most timeless and profound truths about man and the universe. But the result of that teaching is that the only public justification which can be offered for a policy is that it has been decided upon by men who know these truths, by men who are *properly* in positions of public authority. If "public interest" was to retain currency outside of the circle of philosopher-kings, it would have one fixed descriptive meaning, "passed (or promulgated) by those in authority." Whenever this statement could be made about a policy, that policy would be fully justified.

Whatever one might think about the philosophical position that underlies this conclusion, the result is at variance with the manner in which "public interest" is employed in our discourse. It is in part because the statement, "It was made by a properly constituted authority," is not regarded as a sufficient justification for public policy that we use "public interest." Until the question of authority has been settled, the question of public interest does not arise. When it does arise, it is as a demand for justification going beyond the demonstration of authority. (This argument does not demonstrate that Plato was "wrong." His purpose was in part to criticize existing practices and to replace them with what he thought to be more adequate ones. Hence it is scarcely surprising that the language in which his recommendations were cast conflicts in some respects with linguistic uses that reflect political practices of which he would disapprove. One cannot agree or disagree with Plato's political philosophy on the basis of the analysis offered here. One might achieve a greater appreciation of what is at stake in such an agreement or disagreement.)

It should also be said that the foregoing oversimplifies the authority-public interest relationship somewhat. We sometimes decide whether authority exists *by* determining whether the action in question is in the public interest. The point above, however, is that we would not decide that an action is in the public interest on the ground that it is within the authority of the agent who takes it.

[6] (London: Allen and Unwin, 1959.)

the former is one of procedure. We may have different ideas about the way to maintain employment, but we are clear what the world would be like with it and without it. "Seek the common good" is different, not because it is vague or more general, but because it does not describe a determinate goal at all. It is an instruction to approach policy-making in a certain spirit, not to adopt a determinate policy. To say that the state should seek it is to say only that political decisions should attend to the interests of its members in a spirit of impartiality.[7]

On this view, the English sentence "Policy X is in the public interest" is equivalent to "Policy X is commendable because it was passed in a spirit of impartiality." It will be noticed that there are important similarities between this position and some of the arguments advanced in the previous chapters. "Impartiality" is not equivalent to "disinterestedness," lacking as it does the latter's connotations of intellectual or psychological commitment. Neither are its demands identical with those of the universalizability principle, since "absence of bias" does not necessarily imply the equal treatment of equals (one might treat them unequally unwittingly or for some other reason not related to bias). But there is a close "family relationship" between these terms;[8] one who is partial or biased cannot be disinterested and is not likely to meet the requirements of the universalizability principle. Therefore we are in no position to reject this position entirely.

But to notice these similarities is to begin to see the difficulties with the position of Benn and Peters. The argument above is that the logic of "public interest" requires disinterested service of the public interest and demands adherence to the universalizability principle. It is not contended that these are the only requirements of "public interest" or of a "politics of public interest." To reduce the requirements of "public interest" to disinterestedness, the universalizability principle, or impartiality would be to violate the manner in which the concept is actually used in political discourse. There are surely policies which, although "not prompted by a purely sectional concern,"[9] would receive the accolade "in the public interest" from few other than Benn and Peters themselves. If I poison the air breathed by every human being in the United States, including that which I breathe, I have acted in an

[7] *Ibid.*, p. 273.

[8] Recall Wittgenstein, *Philosophical Investigations*, G. E. M. Anscombe, translator (New York: Macmillan Co., 1953), I, pars. 65–76.

[9] Benn and Peters, *op. cit.*, p. 273.

entirely impartial and disinterested manner, and I have satisfied the formal dictates of the universalizability principle. But would we say that my action was in the public interest? Benn and Peters would strip "public interest" of all substantive considerations and dimensions, reducing it to equivalence with a single formal requirement. The concept might be more manageable if we performed this bit of linguistic reduction, but that is not how the concept is employed—which is exactly what Benn and Peters are contending.

There are good reasons for assuming that ordinary linguistic uses reflect a nonlinguistic reality which will not be disposed of by the simple expedient of changing our language. This assumption is supported by the present case. "Public interest" is a general commendatory concept used to express evaluations of public policy. It is not equivalent to "impartiality" because impartiality, as important as it is, is by no means the only standard we expect public policy to meet. The reduction of "public interest" to impartiality would simply require us to devise some other terminology in order to talk about the other standards we want to apply. Such a term would have the same difficulties as "public interest," and we would have accomplished little indeed. (If we make the suggested reduction solely in our function as analysts, the only significant result would be to create a disjunction between ordinary and scientific or philosophical uses.)

The difficulties with the position of Benn and Peters suggest a larger generalization concerning "public interest." They serve first to reinforce the understandings obtained from Plato, namely that substantive considerations will ordinarily be required to give descriptive meaning to "public interest." They also call into question any attempt to reduce "public interest" to a single consideration, whether substantive or procedural. We use "public interest" to express evaluations of a great variety of types of policy; hence, the concept must be able to accommodate the diverse considerations necessary for evaluating a wide range of policies. Also, public policy decisions involve reconciling and adjusting conflicts of value. If we equate the descriptive meaning of our general commendatory concept with any single value, we eliminate the possibility of using that concept as a framework within which to carry on discourse concerning conflicting values. In doing so we imply that any conflict between values must be decided in favor of that one value with which we had equated the general commendatory concept. Jouvenel, for example, argues that the descriptive meaning of "common good" consists in what he calls the "social tie."[10]

If this is justified, any conflict between freedom or justice and the "social tie" must be decided in favor of the latter—or else we must alter the commendatory force of "common good." Jouvenel defines the "social tie" broadly enough to win wide agreement about its importance. However important it may be, it does violence to the highly pluralistic value system of Western societies to suggest that service of the "social tie" will always take precedence. Determination of the descriptive meaning of "public interest" will involve examination of substantive considerations of a highly general sort—norms, values, precepts—but its meaning cannot be equated with a single norm, value, or precept.

These conclusions lead to the theory of "public interest" argued by Peter Drucker. Drucker suggests that "public interest" is purely "an organizing concept," a concept that provides a framework within which substantive values and procedural norms are related to one another and to the contextual considerations peculiar to specific policy decisions.[11] Once again, this view has much to recommend it. "Public interest" does not *supply* the values, formal principles, and contextual facts relevant to determining its descriptive meaning in particular cases; it provides a heading or category under which values, *etc.*, can be brought together and evaluated. To this extent it is enlightening to think of "public interest" as an organizing concept.

But this view is incomplete and misleading. Owing to the purposes for which "public interest" is employed, the framework it provides serves to shape and limit the facts and values brought to it. Mere expressions of individual self-interest, for example, are of restricted significance in determining the descriptive meaning of the concept. This shows that the framework will not admit any and all of the phenomena of the political world. Again, the logic of the concept requires satisfaction of the universalizability principle. Hence the proper use of the concept serves to *add* dimensions to the political process as well as to organize those features and dimensions that would be present whether "public

[10] Bertrand de Jouvenel, *Sovereignty*, Chapter 7 (Chicago, University of Chicago Press, 1957).

[11] Drucker's view is reported in Wayne Leys and C. M. Perry, *Philosophy and the Public Interest* (Committee to Advance Original Work in Philosophy, Chicago, 1959), p. 31.

interest" were employed. "Public interest" is not simply a rubric or category under which certain aspects of political life can be grouped and discussed. It stands for a distinct dimension of political life, the attempt to evaluate and justify public policy. This dimension possesses characteristics and features peculiar to itself.

Two theories remain to be considered. The first, akin in some respects to the Platonic position, argues that the descriptive meaning of "public interest" is determined by examining the generally accepted norms and values of the community or society. To the extent that this view simply substitutes "community values" for a Platonic "Good," it involves the same insights and difficulties noted earlier, and we need say no more about it. But the argument can be made in a form that adds understandings and creates problems not yet discussed. Julius Cohen offers a persuasive version of this kind of argument. "Public interest," he suggests is

> . . . used in a dual sense; first in a logical sense—i.e., to explicate the *meaning* of the established basic values of the community. Thus it would be in the public interest to pursue a certain goal because it would be consistent with the *meaning* of a basic community value. Second, it is used in an instrumental sense—i.e., that a policy would be in the public interest if its consequences would implement one or more of the established basic values of the community.[12]

Cohen recognizes that general norms and standards are necessary to determine the descriptive meaning of "public interest"; he also asserts that we look to "community values" to find those norms and standards—as opposed, perhaps, to the laws of nature, the products of an autonomous reason, or the patterns of history.

There are persuasive considerations that support Cohen's view. Defining the descriptive meaning of "public interest" ordinarily involves a reconciliation of conflicts among the values to which the individuals and groups in the society are commited. Accepted values, along with the facts of the matter in question, provide the "givens" on the basis of which a decision must be reached. The individuals involved in the political process will import such values into the process, and those values will influence the determination. Owing to environmental and educa-

[12] Julius Cohen, "A Lawman's View of the Public Interest," in Carl Friedrich, editor, *The Public Interest* (Nomos V) (New York: Atherton Press, 1962), pp. 155–6.

tional influences, it can be expected that the values of those in authority will comport in considerable degree with "general community values."[13] An understanding of community values will be necessary in order to define the public interest in a politically acceptable manner. If those in authority think the community values are objectionable, they will either have to alter those values through education and persuasion or simply override them through the use of sanctions. The degree to which and the pace at which either procedure is possible are narrowly limited, especially in democratic societies.

For these reasons Cohen's view must be incorporated into any adequate theory of public interest. But there are difficulties with the position. There is a cluster of problems, first of all, centering around identifying and "explicating the meaning" of community values. Identifying such values is a difficult practical problem. When they have been identified, they are likely to be general in character, and there is likely to be conflict and diversity among them, especially about their "meaning" vis-à-vis any specific question. This means that there will have to be men with the authority to "speak for" the community. Burke understood this, and the understanding lies at the heart of that aspect of his position discussed above. Cohen recognizes facets of the problem when he says that the "basic values . . . spring from the more articulate and influential" members of a community and that they receive general standing through "acquiescence," either "overtly, implicitly, reluctantly, or by default." [14] Greater emphasis should be placed on this problem. To the degree that community values are difficult or impossible to discover, authority does not merely "explicate their meaning," it defines and establishes.

Similar implications flow from value diversity and conflict. Cohen is careful to avoid a simple identity between the descriptive meaning of "public interest" and community values. This allows him to accommodate value diversity and the need to "translate" or explicate community values in concrete cases. This is extremely important. If these qualifications are not entered, the "community values" approach to "public interest" leads readily to a dismissal of the latter concept as vacuous. David Truman, for example, equates "public interest" with

[13] Where they consistently fail to do so, again as a practical matter, one would expect the decision makers to lose their authority.

[14] Cohen, *op. cit.*, pp. 156–7.

social unanimity, and, finding no issue on which the latter prevails, dismisses "public interest" as a mere "datum" of politics.[15] But this difficulty deserves greater emphasis than Cohen gives it. To say that the descriptive meaning of "public interest" is determined by "explicating the meaning" of community values suggests that the descriptive meaning is somehow *in* the values and can be discovered by examining them closely. But if the values are in conflict, it is difficult to see how their meaning for the public interest can be found within them. Descriptive meaning will have to be given to "public interest" through a creative process of adjudication between values, a process which produces a result not "contained *in*" any of the values taken alone. This process deserves great emphasis since much of public policymaking is concerned with it. It is one of the reasons why leadership or statesmanship, as well as authority, is important to a political system.

The foregoing remarks add emphasis to aspects of Cohen's argument, but there is one important problem with the "community-values" approach that Cohen does not mention. A policy which is in the public interest is a policy which is justifiable in terms of a normative standard. It is by no means obvious that every policy which accords with the meaning of community values will satisfy such a standard. Communities have been known, as the men of this century should be well aware, to be committed to (or to acquiesce in) values that are entirely objectionable. To identify public interest and the meaning of community values is to suggest that whatever those values support as right or proper is right or proper. In the absence of an argument as to why "right" should be so defined, this is simply to commit the logical error of identifying the "is" with the "ought."

Recognition of this difficulty does not invalidate Cohen's argument. As a practical matter it is difficult to imagine a definition of the descriptive meaning of "public interest" not heavily influenced by community values. Neither is there any prima facie reason for thinking that this ought not to be the case. The fact that community values can fail to meet normative standards does not support the inference that they always do or that they must. But if we are to take seriously the notion that "public interest" expresses a moral evaluation, we must accept the possibility that societies as well as individuals will sometimes be mistaken in their evaluations.

[15] Truman, *op. cit.*, pp. 50–51, 358–9.

One theory remains to be considered—that associated with the "group theory" of politics. We have already noted that the proponents of this theory tend to dismiss "public interest" as a standard and to regard it as a mere datum of politics. Indeed, the most influential contemporary proponent of the theory has urged political scientists to forgo concern with the problem of standards and evaluation generally.[16] Yet the group theory purports to explain the process by which a public policy is selected and made acceptable to the conflicting groups concerned with it. Hence, although it urges that political scientists abandon "public interest," it purports to account for at least some of the phenomena which fall under the rubric of "public interest."

In its baldest form the group theory suggests that public policy on any given issue is the outcome of the interaction of the interest groups concerned with that issue. The groups subject the agencies of government to "pressures," and the policy which emerges is that demanded by the strongest group as modified by the counterpressures generated by less powerful groups. In Latham's words:

> The legislative vote on any issue thus tends to represent the composition of strength, i.e., the balance of power among the contending groups at the moment of voting. What may be called public policy is actually the equilibrium reached in the group struggle at any given moment, and it represents a balance which the contending factions or groups constantly strive to weight in their favor.[17]

Government, it is conceded, is not an "inert cash register," a "mindless balance," [18] or a "steel ball in a pinball game, bumping passively from post to post down an inclined plane." [19] Governmental agencies are "groups like any other" and have group norms which the factions must respect. Or, more generously, "in a sense one may think of the principle governmental leaders . . . as the leaders of . . . [the] unorganized groups" by whom societies' "notions of fair play are represented." [20] Within the very broad limits of these notions of fair play the theory regards policy as made by the extragovernmental interest

[16] See Truman, *op. cit.*, p. 38.

[17] Earl Latham, "The Group Basis of Politics," *American Political Science Review*, Vol. 46, p. 390 (June, 1952).

[18] *Ibid.*, p. 391.

[19] Truman, *op. cit.*, p. 332.

[20] *Ibid.*, p. 449.

groups and merely "ratified" and "recorded" by government.[21] What is more, the metaphors and analogies that the group theorists select to explicate their position are almost uniformly physical metaphors, that is, metaphors of force.

Despite its rejection of "public interest," the similarities between this theory and the theories of Benn and Peters, on the one hand, and of Cohen, on the other, are striking. Having groped through the misleading analogies, it becomes clear that the primary test of legitimate (in this case accepted) public policy is procedural. Whatever emerges from the "group struggle" is automatically stamped "approved." The proper procedures, moreover, are defined as "notions of fair play." As with Benn and Peters, procedural fairness is the only standard public policy must meet. Moreover, these very broad limits are defined, as with Cohen, by the "prevailing values" [22] of the community.

Thus the theory suffers from many of the difficulties noted in connection with Cohen and Benn and Peters. Two of these deserve further mention. The theory excludes the possibility of distinguishing between "is" and "ought." Societal norms, as reflected in the outcome of the group struggle, are the only possible criteria for evaluating public policy. What is more, the theory so stresses the environmentally determined character of thinking that it becomes difficult to imagine an individual capable of questioning the prevailing values.[23] The theory, of course, disclaims concern with "ought," and perhaps it is inappropriate to tax it on this ground. But leaving aside the persuasiveness of the disclaimer, it is imperative that those who retain interest in normative questions be aware of the implications of the group theory in this regard.

The theory also creates a difficulty similar to one noted in connection with Cohen. Although aiming above all at an adequate account of the rich pluralism and complexity of group life and the political process, the group theory in fact minimizes one of the consequences of that pluralism. With an array of conflicting groups surrounding every significant political issue, it will seldom if ever be easy to find a policy that satisfies a significant number of the contending groups (to say nothing of evaluating those demands against the background of prevail-

[21] Latham, *op. cit.*, p. 390.
[22] Truman, *op. cit.*, p. 348.
[23] *Ibid.*, Chapter 2 and *passim*.

ing conditions and making a judgment as to what a *proper* policy would be). Conflict resolution will be a constant problem. Compromises between groups must do a part of this job, and in practice single interests may sometimes impose all of their demands upon their competitors. But these possibilities scarcely provide an adequate account of the policy-making process in pluralistic societies. To a greater degree than Cohen, the group theory underestimates the need for arbitration, leadership, and imposition from government. Admitting that government officials are not "mindless," the group theorists rarely if ever attribute a genuinely positive role to them.[24]

We argued that a politics of public interest is impossible without the positive exercise of governmental authority and without disinterested service of the public interest by those in authority and by members of the citizenry. The group theory allows for very little of either; if the theory is correct the societies to which it is applicable do not have such a politics. The correctness of the theory in this respect is beyond the scope of this book. But it is a fact that certain concepts loom large in political discourse and that these concepts have a function and a logic for which the group theory is unable to account and which it serves to distort. We would expect that the logic of "public interest" would alter if there was nothing in the political behavior of men which corresponded to its demands. Together with questions raised from other quarters,[25] these considerations create serious doubts concerning the adequacy of the theory.

It is time to summarize the results of our survey of other theories. Our most general finding is that "public interest" has no general, all-embracing, descriptive meaning. It is not equivalent to an all-inclusive

[24] There is one exception to this. It is occasionally suggested that members of government are extremely positive in defending the norms of group life within the confines of government itself, that is, the norms of the "official groups." See especially Latham, *op. cit.*, pp. 392–6. There is an interesting parallel between this theory of the state and Marx's theory about all states in the pre-Communist era. Both theories deny or minimize the possibility that the state can act on behalf of the entire society. Both theories treat the state as a special interest group.

[25] See, for example, Harry Eckstein, *Pressure Group Politics* (Stanford: Stanford University Press, 1960), especially pp. 150–55; R. Macridis, "Interest Groups in Comparative Analysis," *Journal of Politics*, Vol. 23, No. 1 (February, 1961); S. I. Benn, "Interests in Politics," *loc. cit.;* Frank Sorauf, in Friedrich, *op. cit.;* Allan Gewirth, "Political Justice," in Richard Brandt, editor, *Social Justice* (Englewood Cliffs, N.J.: Prentice-Hall, Inc., 1962), pp. 160 ff.

truth about the universe or to some very general body of propositions concerning which there is a consensus or unanimity in any particular society. Its descriptive meaning is partly contextual, and to search for a more general meaning that will decide all questions of public policy is to misunderstand the concept and to pursue a will-o'-the-wisp. But this does not mean that it is impossible to generalize about the descriptive meaning of the concept. We cannot generalize about what that meaning is, but we can generalize concerning the principles and procedures necessary for determining what it should be. We can generalize about the decision criteria relevant to assigning descriptive meaning in any individual case.

Several generalizations emerge from the survey. Since "public interest" is a normative concept, normative considerations are necessary to determine its descriptive meaning. The facts about and consequences of specific policies (the contextual factors) must be uncovered, for they are what must be evaluated. But to evaluate we must examine their relation to and impact on normative criteria. These criteria will consist partly of substantive values and moral rules or precepts (such as "maximize human freedom," "promote justice," or "preserve stability"). The service of any single value may constitute the descriptive meaning of "public interest" in a specific case, but, because of its general commendatory function, the descriptive meaning of the concept cannot be made equivalent to any single substantive value. (This is simply a corollary of the finding that it is impossible to generalize about its descriptive meaning.) Community values will be a major source of these substantive criteria, but such values are general and diverse, and a simple identification between them and the descriptive meaning of "public interest" would create both practical and normative problems.

Chapter Five

THE PUBLIC INTEREST: DESCRIPTIVE MEANING (II)

I

In order to illustrate and extend the points discussed in the previous chapter, we will apply them to a common type of public policy decision. The issue is whether to build an expressway to serve intraurban traffic in a middle-sized city in the United States. It would be a joint project involving federal, state, and municipal funds.

Such an issue is likely to involve interests of every type identified in Chapter 2. There will be road-building buffs who find the construction of expressways "interesting"; commuters and property owners who have a personal material stake in the expressway and who are very much aware of it; taxpayers in distant parts of the country who may be unaware of the proposal but who are nevertheless compelled to help pay for it; members of groups such as the Council to Promote Road Safety who might have another regarding or disinterested concern. Some of these individuals and groups will be for the proposal, some against; some for one route and some another; some for an elevated-type construction, some for a subway or a depressed roadway. All will insist that their position represents the public interest.

The issue, of course, will allow a certain degree of horse-trading: an elevated construction in one area, a subway in others, passage through area X but with no accesses in that area, a route inconvenient for one group but with a commitment to improve the existing arteries that group utilizes. But there is a decision whether to build an expressway, and this decision and all its consequences will be imposed upon all of the interests by the force of government. How do the stewards of the public interest decide what ought to be done?

The interests and objectives of the individuals and groups affected will prompt the emergence of the issue and provide a starting point for public consideration of it. Since the issue is whether the expressway is in the public interest, the expression of these interests and objectives must be generalized. The person whose concern has been aroused by the slow and dangerous character of his drive to work must transform this into a concern with problems of all commuters, and he must state this concern in terms of the high economic and human price of an inefficient transportation network. The property owner threatened by the construction of the expressway must attempt to see his problem as a part of the general desirability of maintaining stable residential neighborhoods or avoiding unnecessary interference with property acquisition and maintenance.

The process of generalization will take place in part because of the tactical importance of finding allies in the controversy. Positions that cannot be subsumed under a rule applicable to large numbers are likely to be disadvantaged. This consideration is a partial explanation for the fact that we rarely hear: "I'm against this expressway because I don't want my house condemned." Rather, such issues prompt the formation of associations such as the Azure Hills Friends of the Family Neighborhood or the Citizens League for Progress. But whatever the explanation for these facts, the reason generalization ought to take place is that a politics of public interest requires it. If the citizenry does not transform its interests into claims in this manner, the burden will fall entirely on those in authority. If those in authority are not equal to it, it will be impossible to offer justifications for public policy.

Interests are generalized under a rule or maxim, and the rules under which they are subsumed will ordinarily be community values. This is close to a truism. The individual will want to identify his interest with those things valued by large numbers of the members of the community, and those things so valued are, by hypothesis, community values. Hence the process of expression and generalization of interest will identify many of the community values relevant to the decision. (It may not identify all of the relevant values if only because some interests may not be expressed or generalized. Again, this is one of the reasons that authority is necessary.) Without this step, further proceedings would be impossible. Contextual factors must be investigated in order to discover the consequences of the policy or policies under consideration. But in the absence of a specification of relevant values, it would be impossible to know which factors to examine. An investigation presupposes criteria of relevance and principles of judgment.

But it is equally the case that the values, taken alone, will not provide a basis for a decision concerning the merits of the proposal. For the question is not whether fast and safe traffic flow or preservation of family neighborhoods is in the public interest. The question is whether building *this* expressway is in the public interest. The latter question would never arise if the former questions were not of concern to members of the society. But abstract answers to the former questions only raise, they do not properly answer, the latter. Before a decision can be made as to whether building *this* expressway would be in the public interest, we must know whether (or to what extent) this expressway would in fact contribute to a safe and speedy flow of traffic, disrupt neighborhood life, raise or lower taxes. Detailed studies would have to be made of existing traffic flow and accident rate, factors likely to increase or decrease them in the future, types of construction feasible in the area, and availability of property for relocation of facilities the expressway would destroy.

On occasion these steps, the expression and generalization of interest, assertation of relevant values, and the examination of the contextual considerations, will be conclusive in regard to the descriptive meaning of "public interest." Let us say that the interests have been fully expressed and appropriately generalized; that investigation shows, first, that there is a serious traffic problem which is costly in time, money, and human lives and that construction of an expressway will greatly relieve this problem; and, second, that a route is available which will minimize neighborhood disruption and other disadvantages sometimes associated with expressways. Conversely, suppose studies demonstrate that an expressway will make no appreciable dent in a traffic problem which can be solved only by a public transit system and that it will require scarce land resources, divide and demean stable residential districts, and deplete tax rolls. In such cases the public interest will have been determined.

This might appear to be an unwarranted conclusion. Dispute and disagreement will continue and adoption of the indicated policy will create dissatisfaction on the part of some. In the case of the decision to build the expressway, it is apt to be impossible to implement the policy without resort to sanctions or the threat of sanctions. Recall, however, that it is in part because disagreement is rarely if ever eliminated that we have the concept "public interest." When we say, "X is in the public interest," one of the things we are saying, to put it harshly, is that "X can justifiably be imposed on all of the members of society—whether they like it or not." [1] And "justifiably imposed" means "X can be imposed because it meets the best available standards for judging public policy." This in turn is why the descriptive meaning of "public interest" has been determined in the hypothetical cases in question. Strongly felt objections might remain, but if those objections do not alter the fact that the policies in question meet the best available tests or criteria of a justifiable public policy, they do not upset the judgment concerning the public interest.[2]

Cases of this type are perhaps unusual. It is rare to find all of the contextual facts on one side of a public policy issue. Or more precisely, it is rare for such a matter to become an *issue*. Yet the unusual case enlightens the ordinary or commonplace. The point of the foregoing discussion is that the descriptive meaning of "public interest" can sometimes be determined without making a ranking, either permanent or temporary, of the values involved in or affected by the policy or policies in question. The decision to build the expressway in the first of the above instances need not reflect a preference for fast and safe traffic flow over neighborhood stability. It might simply reflect the fact that the expressway in question would serve the former and not damage the latter appreciably. If it is rare for the evidence to be as overwhelming as is posited in the example, this evidence is often sufficiently conclusive to allow a decision to be reached without ranking

[1] This does not mean that X can be imposed in any manner whatever. "Expressway X is in the public interest" justifies the state in taking *A*'s property if it is a necessary part of building the expressway. But it does not relieve the state of the obligation to use justifiable procedures—for example, paying a fair compensation arrived at through a due process—when it takes that property.

[2] There is one suppressed premise in this argument which will be discussed below.

values. It is in part because this is the case that contextual factors are a necessary consideration in determining the descriptive meaning of "public interest." [8]

These conclusions bear upon two larger topics. They are important in connection with the nature of the value structure of society. Community values are general in character, and there are sometimes conflicts between them. We have heard a great deal, for example, about the conflict between liberty and equality and the difficulties created by that conflict. To the extent that this is a genuine issue, the discussion of the expressway offers a partial answer. It suggests the possibility of valuing both liberty and equality in the abstract and of deciding some policy questions on the basis of the evidence of which value will be most effectively served in the situation at hand. If this were not possible, it is unlikely that a society could maintain a genuinely pluralistic value system for long. If each particular decision demanded a ranking of conflicting values, the value structure would become hierarchical.

Second, our findings concerning the expressway are important to the question of the degree to which public policy decisions are amenable to reasoned analysis and adjudication. Some decisions concerning the public interest can be made on the basis of "instrumental" rationality. Even if it were true that ends or goals or values are unamenable to reasoned analysis and adjudication, reason would still have a place in determining the instrumental relationship between values and particular policies designed to serve them. Therefore, it cannot be said that reason has no place in making public policy decisions. This may be a trivial point, but it has real implications for the view that "public interest" can never be made operational and hence ought to be "abandoned."

II

There are cases in which a full investigation of the contextual facts proves to be inconclusive, in which it is possible to serve competing values equally well, or in which the comparative importance of the

[8] These arguments do not support the view that the descriptive meaning of the public interest can be determined on the basis of the facts alone. It is because a policy serves a value or set of values that it is justifiable or not.

values in question is properly in dispute. In such cases the decision hinges in part upon an estimate of the relative importance of the competing values as served or disserved in the case at hand. Decisions of this kind raise the question whether, to what extent, or how it is possible to find trans-subjective grounds on which to adjudicate value conflicts.

Three observations will be offered as preliminaries. We have rejected the notion that "public interest" has any single, all-inclusive descriptive meaning. We must also reject the notion that "public interest" has one and only one descriptive meaning in every decision-making situation. To say that a policy is in the public interest is to say that it meets standards and satisfies principles. There is no reason to think that there is one and only one policy which will meet those standards in each of the myriad policy-making situations which arise in a modern polity. Perhaps several routes or types of construction, for example, meet the tests we have discussed. This does not mean that the selection of one of the policies will be simply arbitrary; it will be possible to justify the imposition of the policy selected with reasoned argument. But it might be true that the arguments for the policy selected would not be conclusive arguments against the other policies which had survived earlier tests. To this degree an element of arbitrariness—in a very loose sense of that word—would enter. This is a secondary, or perhaps tertiary, reason for authority. When some decision is necessary and a number of policies satisfy the best available tests of a justifiable policy, the dilemma is resolved by the principle of authority.

It is important to see the question that remains in proper perspective. If all of the policies seriously considered serve values and interests which have been generalized in the manner indicated, it is difficult to imagine them leading to serious consequences for the system. This is not to deny the importance of decisions which require a ranking of values. They are likely to involve matters of great concern to the members of society, and they are likely to influence value commitments which in turn influence many later decisions.

A full discussion of the means of adjudicating between values requires a detailed analysis of many of the basic questions of value theory. Such an analysis will be attempted in Part 2, and it will only be then that the question presently before us will be fully answered.

What follows in this chapter will be some of the basic propositions of an argument which will be more fully developed and defended below.

So far we have appealed, albeit without much attention to labeling, to two formal moral principles and a substantive moral rule. The principles are the universalizability principle and a general utilitarian principle (discover the consequences!) which we will call the Principle of Consequences (PC).[4] The rule is: "Serve community values except when doing so violates the universalizability principle [hereafter "U" or "GP" for generalization principle], PC, or other formal principles." These criteria are anything but irrelevant to deciding issues requiring adjudication between values. But there are limits built into the very structure of arguments grounded upon such criteria. These limits stem from the fact that we can avoid an untenable identification of "is" and "ought" only if community values are tested by GP and PC. However, the fact that GP and PC are formal means that neither has any force until its particular premises have been established. There are two such premises in GP. They are of the form: "This *X* is right for this *A*," and "This *A* and this *B* are similar persons similarly situated." PC contains one particular premise: "The consequences of this *A* doing this *X* are undesirable." Neither principle can itself aid us in establishing these premises in any particular instance.

This appears to produce an insoluble dilemma. Substantive rules must be tested by formal principles, but there are issues which cannot be decided by reference to formal principles without antecedent decisions concerning substantive rules. One solution is to posit basic substantive principles which require no testing either by formal principles or by lesser substantive rules. Such principles would provide the criteria by which all lesser rules and decisions could properly be judged. Platonic forms perform this function. But one does not have to be a Platonist to adopt a view of this type. Hedonistic utilitarianism, in most respects worlds apart from Platonism, depends on an argument very similar to Platonism. Bentham accepts something like PC, but he argues that the particular premise of PC is always properly given content by calculating which action produces the greatest quantity of

[4] Stated formally, this principle reads, "If the consequences of *A*'s doing *X* are undesirable, *A* ought not to do *X*." Or, in positive terms, "If the consequences of *A*'s not doing *X* would be undesirable, *A* ought to do *X*." I take the language from Marcus George Singer, *Generalization in Ethics* (New York: Alfred A. Knopf, Inc., 1960), pp. 63 ff. The logical features of the principle and its relationship to universalizability are examined in Chapter 8.

pleasure and the least quantity of pain. "Maximize pleasure and minimize pain" is a substantive moral rule which is not subject to question. The felicific calculus is a means of solving the practical problems of implementing the rule in particular cases.

Bentham's position allows us to restate the problem before us. We accept the formal basis of the utilitarian position, PC, but reject as incomplete the classical utilitarian solution to the problem of establishing the particular premise of that principle, namely hedonism. No substantive rule or value (or set of rules or values) whether pleasure, freedom, justice, the social tie, or whatever, is itself beyond question in particular cases, and therefore no such value can constitute an adequate final criterion for all other decisions. But this leaves a serious gap in our theory. Arguments already presented [5] show that this gap cannot be filled with a substantive rule. We require a principle or criterion that is not substantive but is less restricted than GP and PC. To meet this need we turn to the principle on which all principles, and hence all nonarbitrary decisions, rest, the principle "give reasons." If the tests suggested above prove to be inconclusive, if it is necessary to decide which of two or more competing values is to be served, the choice is to be made and defended by *giving reasons.*

To ask what is gained by requiring that we "give reasons" is in part to ask how the English words "give reasons" (and cognate expressions) are used. (To suggest that the requirement is meaningless or vacuous is to suggest that these words have no accepted use, that English speakers do not communicate anything when they use these words.) We can begin with the dictionary, which indicates that a "reason" is "a fact or circumstance forming, or alleged as forming, a ground or motive [6] leading, or sufficient to lead, a person to adopt or reject some course of action or procedure, belief," etc. To give reasons is to ad-

[5] The reference is to the argument that equating public interest with a single substantive principle (or set of principles) violates its function as a general commendatory concept. This argument rests upon the logic of language and it is a complete answer to the Platonic or Benthamite position only if the purpose at hand is to account for the logic of language. Additional arguments for the position will be offered in Chapters 9 and 10.

[6] The use of "motive" in this entry is misleading. We do use "reason" in the sense of motive, but this refers to a psychological process, not a proposition which is verifiable or supportable. The present use of "reason" will be exclusively in the latter sense. See Stanley Cavell and A. Senonske, "Moral Theory, Ethical Judgments and Empiricism," *Mind*, Vol. 61, p. 551, New Series, 1952. See part 2 of this article for an argument similar to that presented here.

duce facts or circumstances as grounds for doing or believing something. To require that we decide by giving reasons is to require that we not decide without a ground, "for no reason at all." But giving reasons involves more. To give reasons is to engage in the act of reasoning, it is "to reason," "to employ reasoning or argument with a person in order to influence his conduct or opinion." It is "to think in a connected, sensible, or logical manner," and it is to be "reasonable," which is to be "sensible, sane . . . : not irrational, absurd, or ridiculous." To require that decisions be made by giving reasons is to require that the decision-making process be governed by the canons of logic and evidence.[7] It is to rule out "I want" as a basis for a decision and insist upon "I want because . . . "; to forswear "you must" and require "you must because. . . ." It is to insist that criteria be met in filling in the ellipses in any particular case.

Although general, these requirements are not vacuous. To require that the grounds of a decision meet the canons of reason is to require something which we all understand and without which we could not live together. The generic character of these requirements is a virtue, not a vice. It means that the requirements will be relevant to judging all aspects of all types of decisions. GP and PC are specific principles, whose formulation and application must meet the general requirement of reasonableness. But they provide a more detailed test which can be applied to particular aspects of a decision. Once these principles have been validated, we can use them instead of the generic requirement in the area of their applicability. But where we have no specific principle, we fall back on the general requirement.[8]

The foregoing remarks are an unfortunately abstract statement of a position that is quite straightforward and not likely to be questioned in most contexts. Notice that the requirement, "give reasons," is assumed in the earlier discussion of "instrumental rationality." (It is the suppressed premise referred to at the end of that discussion.) Contextual

[7] As will emerge more fully below, we are using "logic" in the general sense of orderly thinking, not in the technical sense in which professional logicians use it to refer to their subject matter.

[8] For an excellent discussion of "reason" and its place in practical discourse, see John Ladd, "The Desire To Do One's Duty," in H. Castenada and G. Nakhnikian, editors, *Morality and the Language of Conduct* (Detroit: Wayne State University Press, 1963), especially pp. 325–42. Ladd treats reason as a motive, but the substance of his discussion indicates that this involves no more than a terminological difference with the present argument.

considerations sometimes lead us to conclude that one value will be served and another not disserved by a policy. But this is possible only because there are standards or criteria which can be used to determine what the contextual considerations show and what they do not. If asked to describe these criteria, we might well respond that they are the "canons of reason," that arguments of this type require that we support our interpretation of the evidence by giving reasons to show that a particular conclusion is justified. Evidence does not speak for itself. We might go on to explicate, "give reasons," in terms of canons of logic and avoidance of irrational or absurd conclusions. We would be likely to respond in this manner for the *good reason* that this is the vocabulary we all use as a matter of course in referring to the standards employed to judge the validity of arguments and conclusions.

But there appears to be an important difference between the "instrumental" reasoning of our earlier example and reasoning in defense of value rankings. In the former, the content or substance of the "grounds" to be tested by the canons of reason is not in doubt. The "grounds" consist of the facts and predictions concerning the policy in question. The canons of reason are necessary to judge whether those facts have been marshaled and interpreted in a defensible manner. But in the latter case, by hypothesis, the facts are inconclusive, and the values are in conflict. To return to the example, the expressway will greatly facilitate traffic flow and safety, but it will seriously divide and disrupt stable residential neighborhoods with a predominance of single family dwellings (SRNPSFD), reduce property values substantially, and force large numbers of people to move to less desirable areas. Policy *A* (building the expressway), in other words, will serve one value or set of values and disserve another. The effects of *B* (not building the expressway) will be the converse of *A*. How can a justifiable decision be reached? [9]

[9] One decision strategy might be to adopt some variant of the view that "Value decisions are matters of personal preference and are unamenable to reasoned analysis." This would have the virtue of simplifying the process of decision making. If asked why decision *X* had been reached, those in authority would reply, "because it accords with our personal preferences." They would then hope that their preferences coincided with the preferences of a substantial part of the citizenry. They would also hope that those whose preferences led them to disagree with *X* would be led by other preferences to decide not to resist implementation of *X*. Finally, they would hope that a substantial number of the citizenry would have preferences such that they would be prepared to support the decision makers

If those in authority attempt to follow the dictates of a politics of public interest, the first step would be to make the most fully reasoned case for each of the values in question. How does one make a reasoned case for a value commitment, that is for "valuing" or "considering of worth or importance" (*OED*) a particular condition or phenomenon? What could be said in defense of valuing SRNPSFD's?

B might offer the following argument:

> Such neighborhoods are conducive to friendship and community interaction, which foster the development of the individual. Crime and delinquency rates are lower. Schools and other community activities are better because people have roots in the community and are willing to work and sacrifice to improve them. Property values tend to be steadier, making it possible for families to invest in a home with confidence, which in turn contributes to stability.

B's strategy is to list the major consequences of maintaining such neighborhoods and to attach value to those consequences by demonstrating a positive relationship between them and conditions he values and believes to be valued by others. He attempts to show as fully as possible what is involved in maintaining stable neighborhoods; in so doing, he tries to show that to refuse to value stable neighborhoods is to refuse to value friendship, community, and low crime rates. He tries to win appreciation for the fact that a substantial price must be paid for disagreement with his position. Would we say that *B*'s argument was a reasoned one? If we found that his facts were correct and that there were no logical flaws in the conclusions he drew from them, surely we would.

How can such an argument be tested or attacked? How does *A* respond when faced with this argument for preserving SRNPSFD's? His most likely strategy, aside from making an argument in favor of his value, is to attempt to show that *B* is mistaken in his assessment of the consequences that follow when SRNPSFD's are maintained.

> People just stick to their own yards. There is less community interaction than in apartment-house districts where everyone must make use of common facilities. In point of fact the crime rates are not any lower. And

---

in the application of sanctions against those whose preferences led them to reject X and to resist its implementation. There are two related things which this strategy would not require: the first would be to give reasons in justification of X, and the second would be to say that X was in the public interest.

the schools are worse because such neighborhoods soon come to have a majority of people whose children have finished school. These people refuse to support tax increases and bond issues. Rather, they have their own little nests and will not contribute to or participate in community projects of any kind. Show me a city full of SRNPSFD's and chances are you've shown me a city with a starved public sector.

A contends that *B*'s reasons are not good reasons because the facts on which they rest are faulty. To do this he must go beyond the contextual considerations special to the policy issue in question and examine available evidence concerning the general consequences of serving *B*'s value. If that evidence disproves *B*'s contentions, *B*'s reasons for considering SRNPSFD's of worth or importance will be undercut, and the canons of reason will require that *B* produce new reasons or cease to value SRNPSFD's.

A might also take the more radical course and agree with *B*'s estimate of the consequences of maintaining SRNPSFD's, but argue that those consequences ought not to be valued.

All of this emphasis on community interaction is a mistake. It leads to the mass conformism which is stifling our society. Where is the personal and family privacy in the neighborhood you want to preserve? The neighborhood replaces the family as the basic unit of life; the children are educated and learn their morals in the streets rather than from their parents; and everything is reduced to the lowest common denominator. It is no surprise to hear you extolling the merits of stable property values. This is just a facet of the cult of the material which flourishes in the type of neighborhood you admire. The fact that this expressway will divide some of these neighborhoods and force people into other types of areas is not much of an argument against it.

A indicates his willingness to pay the price *B* had tried to attach to the rejection of his value. Again, *A* has reasons for doing so. His reasons consist of considerations designed to demonstrate that *B* had not fully considered the implications of community, friendship, and stability. Although often thought valuable, *A* in effect says, SRNPSFD's undermine more important aspects of life such as individualism, family solidarity, rigorous moral training, and appreciation of the nonmaterial dimensions of life.

At this point, *B* would be obliged to show either that *A* is wrong in holding that friendship and community require a sacrifice of individualism and family solidarity or that the former are more valuable than the latter, and to give his reasons for thinking so. A new exchange would begin, with both *A* and *B* attempting to offer evidence for thinking that community did or did not undermine individualism, that individualism did or did not lead to certain other consequences. In short, *A* and *B* would be forced to look ever more deeply into human relationships, attempting to specify the grounds on which they were commited to certain views and to support those views with the evidence which, perhaps in a not very systematic manner, led them to adopt those views to begin with. At every stage of the discussion the range of relevant experience would enlarge, and the difficulties of gathering and marshaling it would increase. *A* and *B* would be driven from the particular problem of the expressway to the problems of political philosophy.

Attention must be given to a number of problems (for example, "infinite regress" and "circularity") thought to be raised by these arguments. For our immediate purposes, two points will suffice to conclude the discussion.

1. The major purpose of the example is to show that reasons can be offered in support of and in opposition to value positions. Although we might disagree with the remarks of *A* and *B*, they would not fall into the category of "ridiculous" or "absurd" statements. To offer such arguments in support of a proposed policy would be to meet the requirement of "giving reasons." Moreover, the arguments presented can be tested by the canons of reason. Factual assertions which can be checked into are presented, and conclusions are drawn from the facts in a manner which can be tested by logical criteria. By moving outside the considerations peculiar to the particular policy decision, the problem of producing "grounds" which can be put to intersubjective tests can be overcome.

2. Reasoning of this kind will only rarely produce unanimity among those concerned. But this does not mean that the reasoning has been inconclusive vis-à-vis the public interest. Since reasoning is relevant to supporting and attacking value choices and positions, there is no reason to believe that it will always be inconclusive. If *B* opposed the expressway because SRNPSFD's gave people ample space to wash their cars on Sunday afternoons, we would have no doubt that *A*'s arguments were superior. If he rested his view on the fact that children

in such neighborhoods generally had better suntans in the summer, we would still have few if any doubts. If he could show a slightly lower incidence of serious illness, we would at least give him a serious hearing. At some point it might become very difficult or impossible to be sure. But must we construct out entire theory around that "some point"? Must we throw out the host of cases in which we can decide value questions in a rational manner because of the possibility (a question yet to be examined) that there are some cases in which we cannot? We know that decisions which involve value choices are made. We know that the values of individuals, groups, and societies are implemented, modified, and sometimes transformed. Once we know that reasons are logically relevant to value choices, is there anything but blind prejudice to make us think that arational or irrational considerations alone influence this process?

But let us assume cases in which reasoning is genuinely inconclusive. *A* and *B* debate at great length and "ultimately" reach a point at which they are reduced to an irreducible or unanalyzable statement of preference. Such an outcome does not demonstrate that the process of reasoning which preceded it was meaningless or insignificant. *A*, *B*, and their audience are in a better position to make a judgment after the exchange than before it. If a governmental body chooses policy *A*, *A*'s reasons put it in a preferable position vis-à-vis *B* than it would be without them. Remembering that "arbitrary" means "based on mere opinion . . . ; capricious," it would be inappropriate to say that the decision was entirely arbitrary.

Value decisions are properly made by giving reasons. All who know the language know in a rough way what reasons are, and no one could act effectively without them. Furthermore, we all believe—and our lives sometimes depend on our being right—that we can distinguish valid from invalid reasons. But our judgments often differ substantially. This is true of reasons in support of descriptive generalizations as well as those justifying decisions with a value dimension. It is not to be expected that disagreement concerning the descriptive meaning of "public interest," including disagreement based upon careful use of the decision procedures discussed here, will be entirely eliminated. But if such reasoning is not as conclusive as the deductions of a geometer, it is surely preferable to "I want" or "I like." It does provide trans-subjective considerations which minimize if they do not eliminate the element of whim and caprice to which we are otherwise reduced. It is because exclusive reliance upon whim and caprice is incompatible with the manner in which "public interest" is employed in our discourse that the procedures discussed here are required by the logic of "public interest." More important, it is because whim and caprice have such destructive consequences in the public realm that we have the concept "public interest" and that we employ it in the way we do.

III

We conclude that "public interest" is a general commendatory concept used in selecting and justifying public policy. It has no general, unchanging, descriptive meaning applicable to all policy decisions, but a nonarbitrary descriptive meaning can be determined for it in particular cases. This descriptive meaning is properly found through reasoned discourse which attempts to relate the anticipated effects of a policy to community values and to test that relation by formal principles. We also conclude that the concept is neither a vacuous phrase nor a verbal device useful only for propaganda purposes. It performs a function in political discourse, and it has a logic which, if taken seriously, will influence the kinds of policies adopted and rejected and the character of the political process utilized to adopt and reject those policies. A politics which takes the logic of the concept seriously, a politics of public interest, will differ in a significant and predictable manner from a politics which misunderstands or "abandons" the concept.

At the risk of concluding Part 1 in a minor key, let me add a word concerning the argument that *political scientists* should abandon the concept (except to observe it as a political datum). It may not be entirely clear that the foregoing conclusions meet that argument squarely. "Public interest" does not provide a divining rod or philosopher's stone for determining proper public policy. There will be cases in which the most conscientious efforts will not eliminate legitimate disagreement. This is apparently what is meant by the charge that the concept cannot be rendered "operational."

The question is whether the appropriate conclusions are drawn from the facts in question. Absolute certainty and unanimity concerning the descriptive meaning of "public interest" may sometimes be unattainable. But does it follow that we should *therefore* abandon the attempt to achieve justifiable policy? Certainly no logic would support such an inference. (How many questions would remain if we applied this test, that is, the possibility of achieving absolute certainty, to the subject matter of political science?) But if we do not abandon the attempt to justify policy, what is to be achieved by abandoning the concept which we use to communicate about the problems of justification? (We might substitute some other verbal formula, but the problems are with morals and politics, not with the concept, and verbal substitutions would solve nothing.)

There is a temptation to explain the argument for abandonment in terms of substantive attitudes toward politics. The uncertainty, inconclusiveness, and occasional inefficacy of rational deliberation and discourse are upsetting, and observers throw up their hands in despair at a crucial part of the process. It might be contended that lurking behind the abandonment argument is an urge for irrefragable answers. Having been disabused of hope in this respect, these observers over-react and argue for giving up the entire enterprise of evaluation and justification.

But this explanation misses the mark. The "abandon public interest" school of thought is not concerned with politics or justification at all, but with a more tender growth known as political science. Desiring to turn political science into a hard science on *their* model of the natural sciences, these writers wish to cut away all concepts, questions, and concerns which, in their view, hold political science back from this goal. *Political science* ought to eschew value judgments and cut away all concepts stricken with the cancer of ambiguity and imprecision generated by value judgments. If politicians, journalists, or citizens wish to concern themselves with the public interest, political science will not object. But the discipline itself must remain pure and exclude from its conceptual apparatus such prescientific curiosities.

This approach rests upon a fundamental confusion concerning the concept itself. "Public interest" is not a tool developed by political science for analytic purposes; it is a part of political discourse. The decision to abandon or retain the concept is to be made not according to standards which the academic discipline sets for its analytic vocabulary, but according to the facts concerning and the problems involved in understanding the political order. If political scientists conclude that the concept has no meaning and serves no function in politics, they will justifiably decide not to pay attention to it. But if the concept performs a function in politics, political scientists will be obliged to become as clear as possible concerning it—simply because it is the task of political science to achieve clarity and understanding concerning the political order. The fact that dispute over the descriptive meaning of "public interest" cannot be completely eliminated is irrelevant to whether political science should deal with the concept.

PART TWO

Reason and Value

Chapter Six

REASON, INTEREST, AND MORALITY

The argument of Part 1 raises two major types of questions. First, a set of questions concerning the relevance of that argument to an understanding of the manner in which politics "really" works. Do the decision criteria we have discussed play any role in politics? Are people aware of them, and do they take them seriously? Much of contemporary political science urges a negative answer. The bulk of the modern citizenry is held to be uninterested in and ill informed and irrational about politics. The more knowledgeable remainder operates from self-interest of the narrowest kind and is rational only in a very restricted sense. To argue for a politics of "giving reasons" is to demonstrate hopeless naïveté. This contention is not a major concern, and we will do no more than indicate the manner in which it relates to or bears upon the arguments we have presented.

Second, there are a number of philosophical problems which must be faced. Whatever the psychological, sociological, or anthropological characteristics of particular populations, is it logically appropriate to argue that reasons should be given concerning the political problems which arise in connection with the public interest? Are reasons relevant to the reconciliation or adjudication of conflicts of interest? Public policy decisions rest in part upon value choices and commitments. Can it be said that reasons are relevant to making and justifying such choices? It might be contended that the foregoing arguments beg the very questions at issue. We have suggested that interest and value conflicts are properly adjudicated by giving reasons. But is not the very question whether reason is logically relevant to such conflicts and decisions? Concern with explicating the logic of "public interest" has forced us to hurry past a host of difficulties. If the position developed above is to be sustained, attention must be given to these. Part 2 will cover much of the ground traversed in Chapters 3, 4, and 5, this time leaving "public interest" in the background and concentrating upon the philosophical questions raised by the foregoing arguments.

I. REASON AND INTEREST

It has often been held that political activity is motivated primarily if not exclusively by considerations of subjectively defined self-interest. It has also been held that "interests" are extremely private in source, that they well up from springs deep within the individual which he himself cannot alter and which are inaccessible to the observation and the influence of other men. Taken together, these interpretations go far to suggest that the fundamental bases of political activity are subrational or arational in character. The concept of "reason" and its cognates is many-sided and difficult to pin down precisely. In addition to the observations presented earlier, however, there are some generalizations which can be made concerning the concept. Thinking of it in psychological terms (as seventeenth and eighteenth century philosophers tended to think of it—the "faculty" of reason), it is distinguished from passions, impulses, and emotions. Since Bradley's attack on psychologism in epistemology, philosophers have tended to think of it as a process or activity rather than as a faculty. From either standpoint, the concept denotes something which is "public" in two senses: first, that it (or its workings) can be made accessible to other men through the vehicle which allows men to communicate with one another—that is, language; second, that it is subject to test and control by standards applicable to the workings of the faculty or process irrespective of the person whose faculty it is or who is engaged in the process.[1]

[1] Satisfaction of the first criterion partially satisfies the second as well. As suggested earlier, use of the vehicle of language imposes standards and restrictions upon the individual which must be met by all those who use the language. These standards, however, are necessary, not sufficient, conditions of "reason." Utterances that do not satisfy the basic rules of the language in which they are expressed would not be called reasoned, but many utterances that do satisfy those standards would nevertheless be called unreasoned.

Both criteria are relevant to the notion that the roots of the individual's interests are lodged so deeply in his "psyche" that he cannot understand or describe, much less alter, them. He may be able to know and to state what he has an interest in, but the cause of his having that interest is beyond the ken of his understanding. Since he cannot understand the matter himself, he cannot state it in language and cannot make it available to others. If this is true, the source of interests cannot be a public matter and could not be reasoned about or controlled by trans-subjective standards.[2] If it is also true that interest is a basic source of political activity, it is analytic to say that those interests and the political behavior to which they lead contain an arational or subrational component. To say that interests are private and uncontrollable by public processes is the same as saying that they are arational or subrational. This argument does not go to the heart of present problems, but it is important in connection with policy decisions which do not involve value ranking. Our strategy in examining it will be to look at two of the more systematic and influential formulations, those of Hobbes and Hume.

". . . The thoughts are to the desires, as scouts, and spies, to range abroad, and find the way to the thing desired." [3] "Reason is, and ought only to be the slave of the passions, and may never pretend to any other office than to serve and obey them." [4] The ends of political activity, from this view, are given by the passions, and cannot be altered, modified, or controlled by the entirely distinct faculty of reason. With the exception of a few specialized usages, "ought" implies

[2] Interesting questions arise here with regard to psychoanalysis. Through analysis the therapist claims to gain access to the sources of emotions and attitudes which are inaccessible (without the assistance of the therapist) to the individual whose attitudes and emotions they are. The object of this process is to make the source of the attitudes accessible to the individual and thereby allow him to bring them under control of reason. This conflicts with the above formulation insofar as that formulation places the burden of exposing the source of attitudes and interests on the person whose attitudes and interests they are. But it supports the above analysis in that it equates "reasoned" with "public." Furthermore, given the practical limits upon the practice of psychoanalysis, it is obvious that the political process must rely primarily upon self-revelation. See John Ladd, *op. cit.*, especially pp. 333–4.

[3] *Leviathan*, Part I, Chapter VIII, Michael Oakeshott, editor (Oxford: Basil Blackwell, 1955), p. 46.

[4] David Hume, *A Treatise of Human Nature*, Book II, Part III, Section III, L. A. Selby-Bigge, editor (London: Oxford University Press, 1888), p. 415.

"can." Therefore, if it is true that reason can only be the scout or the slave of the passions, it would be absurd to argue that men have a duty to control their passions by reason or to find rational grounds on which to mediate conflicts of passion and interest. If the logic of "public interest" reflected such a demand, it would reflect a philosophical mistake on the part of those using the language.

This conclusion is an extremely depressing one—how then would such conflicts be mediated?—and the thinkers mentioned were not prepared to embrace it without reservation. Let us look first at the case of Hobbes, who went farther in following out the political implications of the position than any other thinker.

It was largely because Hobbes believed that men are incapable of finding neutral ground between their individual desires that he insisted so strongly that there be an authority no one could question. The Hobbesean sovereign plays a part of the role assigned to reason in Part 1. He is a neutral agent who establishes public rules that control relationships between men and prevent their conflicts from becoming destructive. The sovereign, of course, is himself a creature of passion, and the rules he establishes may be unjustifiable if viewed simply as imperatives enunciated by a private individual. But the fact that these rules are universal in application means that they provide a kind of common ground among all individuals. They acquire some of the characteristics of reasons from the standpoint of the system. Hobbes's philosophy is one of the first of a number of attempts to achieve a rational system despite individual behavior which is arational in crucial respects. This argument has the seductive feature of promising morally satisfactory results while minimizing the need for moral effort on the part of the individuals involved.

But when we examine Hobbes more closely, we see that he was unwilling to hold consistently to this view. Consider how Hobbes gets passionate, self-interested men out of the state of nature. This transition requires the covenant in which I "give up my right of governing myself to this man . . . on this condition, that thou give up thy right to him, and authorize all his actions in like manner." [5] Given Hobbes's account of man and his passions, it is difficult to believe that the covenant could be established unless imposed by force. In order to make the covenant, the individual would have to make choices that his pas-

[5] *Leviathan*, Part II, Chapter XVII, Oakeshott, p. 112.

sions militate against and take risks that he would be imprudent to take. How then can Hobbes urge men to act contrary to their passions and establish the covenant?

In part, the covenant is possible owing to the negative passion of fear of violent death and the consequent desire for peace. In the absence of this passion, which establishes the end of a whole set of actions, civil society would not be possible.[6] But the fear of death is not enough. The covenant must be made in the state of nature, and hence it involves risks which the fear of death itself would militate against taking. Furthermore, the desire for peace produced by the fear of death conflicts with those other passions which Hobbes summarizes as passions for power. In Hobbes's account, as long as the passions alone are operative the state of war continues. It is at this point that reason, which had been assigned a secondary role, begins to become important. "And reason suggesteth," as Hobbes puts it, "convenient articles of peace, upon which men may be drawn to agreement." [7] These "articles of peace" are called the laws of nature; as "rules of reason" they provide grounds on which men can agree to establish authority and civil society. Reason intervenes in the conflict of passions and desires and finds arrangements and modes of behavior that allow the greatest possible satisfaction of the passions and desires. The ends, it is true, are given by the passions, and reason can be said to be "scouting" for them. But the scout is apparently able to alter most radically the plans of the leader of the party. Some behaviors which the passions had induced in the state of nature are now entirely proscribed, and many others significantly modified. The passions do not disappear, but reason, acting as the scout, is able to control and redirect them.

Hobbes is prescribing, not describing, and he explicitly says that in practice men do not heed the voice of reason.[8] This is why he insists that authority must do a large part of the job which reason would do under more ideal circumstances. But the fact that he is willing to prescribe, together with his entire argument concerning the covenant, requires a belief that reason can exercise control over passion. Once this admission has been made, behavior which is not modified by the voice of reason becomes legitimately subject to criticism.

[6] *Ibid.*, Part I, Chapter XIII, p. 84.
[7] *Ibid.*, Part I, Chapter XIII, p. 84.
[8] *Ibid.*, Part II, Chapter XVIII, p. 120.

The "slave" metaphor used by Hume suggests that he minimized the efficacy of reason in a manner even more radical than Hobbes. And it is no accident that Hume is famous for his skepticism of the efficacy of reason. Yet examination of his theory regarding the point of present concern leads to the same conclusion reached in the examination of Hobbes's theory.

The "will," Hume says, is influenced or moved only by the passions.

> A passion is an original existence or, if you will, modification of existence, and contains not any representative quality, which renders it a copy of any other existence or modification. When I am angry I am actually possest with the passion, and in that emotion have no more a reference to any other object, than when I am thirsty, sick, or more than five feet high.[9]

The passions, in short, are simple, unanalyzable, and incomparable. Reason, on the other hand, is the discovery of truth or falsehood. Truth or falsehood consists

> . . . in an agreement or disagreement either as to the *real* relations of ideas, or to *real* existence and matter of fact. Whatever, therefore, is not susceptible of this agreement or disagreement [e.g., "passions, volitions, and actions"] is incapable of being true or false, and can never be an object of our reason.[10]

Reason can never contradict passion, and " 'Tis not contrary to reason to prefer the destruction of the world to the scratching of my finger." [11] There is simply no confrontation between reason and passion,[12] and it would appear that there is no possibility of one influencing or controlling the other.

But Hume qualifies this position in respects which are very important for present purposes. The typical merchant is said to use "abstract or demonstrative reasoning" to calculate his accounts and thereby to discover the effects of various possible courses of action. Similarly, when an individual has "the prospect of pain or pleasure from any object," he experiences an emotion of "aversion or propensity" to that object, and then "reasoning takes place" to discover the cause and effect relationship between the object and the emotion. Hume insists

[9] Hume, *op. cit.*, Book II, Part III, Section III, Selby-Bigge, p. 415.

[10] *Ibid.*, Book III, Part I, Section I, p. 458.

[11] *Ibid.*, Book III, Part II, Section III, p. 416.

[12] "We speak not strictly and philosophically when we talk of the combat of passion and of reason." *Ibid.*, p. 415.

that the "impulse" or emotion "arises not from reason." But he concedes that the emotion "is . . . directed by" reason, and "according as our reason varies our actions receive a subsequent variation." [13] Even if reason and passion do not confront one another directly, their concerns and functions intersect in a manner which allows the former to influence the latter. Therefore, it is possible to accept Hume's restrictive definition of reason and his rigid dichotomization of human faculties, and yet avoid the conclusion that political behavior is immune to the influence and even the control of reason.[14]

The theories of Hobbes and Hume are paradigmatic of a type of argument that minimizes the role reason is able to play in political life. The point of our discussion of them has been an exceedingly simple one: if we grant the fundamental tenet of these theories, that the ends of individual political behavior result from nonrational or subrational processes, the behavior chosen to implement and satisfy those ends can nevertheless be made to depend upon calculations of a rational sort. This conclusion means that the imperative "consider the consequences" is not ruled out by the maxim "ought implies can," which, in turn, makes available that whole set of devices and principles—for example the universalizability principle—developed to discover and point up the consequences of an action. These devices place logical restrictions or limitations upon the behaviors an individual can choose in order to satisfy a passion or an interest. Some behaviors would be inconsistent with satisfying an interest—for example, destroying the world in Hume's aphorism. Finally, this conclusion opens the way for discourse with other men concerning the means chosen to satisfy an interest or passion. The interest or passion itself might be wholly unanalyzable and incomparable, but the consequences of various ways of satisfying it would be subject to investigation and discussion. There would be grounds on which a second party could dissuade an individual from an action. Much discourse concerning public policy takes exactly this form. For these reasons, it is possible to concede a good deal to the view that political behavior is motivated by unanalyzable interests and passions and yet reject the conclusion that reason has no significant place in those aspects of political life of concern here.

[13] *Ibid.*, Book III, Part II, Section III, p. 414.

[14] Hence I would agree with Henry Aiken's view that "in speaking of reason as 'slave,' Hume was overstating his own position." Henry D. Aiken, editor, *Hume's Moral and Political Philosophy* (New York: Hafner, 1948), p. XXV.

II. INTEREST AND MORALITY

The utility of the position reached so far is severely limited. As long as the individual remains convinced that the effects of his contemplated behavior will be consistent with his interests and passions, the argument provides no rational grounds on which to object to that behavior. Whatever the evidence or argument offered, the individual is always free to reply, "But you don't really understand what I am after. My intended behavior may appear inconsistent to you, but that is only because you are not me." On the position as it has been sketched, there is no possibility of a reasoned reply to such a statement.

There are situations in which the limitations of the argument are not disturbing. Self-determination continues to be highly valued in Western societies, and often we do not care to probe into the grounds of individual desires and behaviors. Furthermore, for reasons which Hume in particular emphasized, the subjectivism of the position is not as anarchistic in consequence as its abstract formulation might suggest. The fact that the individual alone can know his interests and passions does not require that there be great differences between the interests and passions of the members of a society. Independence of judgment does not exclude a relatively homogeneous result. Hume was correct in emphasizing that such a result obtains to a marked degree, and that no society could hold together if it did not.[15] From the standpoint of present concerns, homogeneity of interest expands the potential utility of the means-end type of rational argument by enhancing the capacity of the members of society to understand one another's demands and what is necessary to satisfy them.[16]

But these observations underscore the fact that the discussion in this chapter has not been concerned with what Baier aptly calls the "moral point of view." Because attempts to satisfy interests and pas-

[15] He emphasized, however, that societies nurture homogeneity of interests and passions through exposing their members to common customs, traditions, and mores. The consensus is not purely natural.

[16] Compare Jouvenel's suggestive remark from a somewhat different context: "If Jesus had not entirely assumed man's nature, if he was merely God in disguise, it would follow that human nature would be powerless to imitate him." Bertrand de Jouvenel, *Sovereignty*, (Chicago: University of Chicago Press, 1957) p. 113n.

sions affect other men, interests and passions readily come to have moral significance. Moral significance and other-regarding consequences are not identical—for instance in the case of manners—and to make them so would be moralism of an extreme kind. Because there are situations in which interests and passions can be served without raising moral questions, there is an area within which the individual's judgment is acceptable. But interests and passions can have moral significance, and when they do the Hobbes-Hume position becomes untenable.

It is the very essence of morality that the content and range of applicability of moral principles and rules does not depend upon purely subjective judgment. If Mr. Bobble has a passion to murder his mother-in-law, satisfaction of that passion is immoral whether Bobble thinks so—whether Bobble thinks it is in his interest to murder his mother-in-law despite the consequences to himself. We simply do not say,

> Well, Bobble, it seems to me that the decision to murder your mother-in-law is based on a faulty calculation of means-end relationships. But if you understand the consequences and are nevertheless sure that the decision accords with your interests and passions, of which you must be the final judge, far be it from me to question your decision.

If Bobble claimed the right to judge his own interests in this matter, we would reply, "You don't understand. This is not a matter of interest and passion at all, but one of right and wrong—and you happen to be wrong." We are prepared, in other words, to claim trans-subjective status for our moral judgments. (And if we wish to explain the genesis of immoral behavior, assuming we consider the agent in question to be sane, we do not analyze his interests and passions but his values and the reasons he can offer in defense of them.) The fact that we are prepared to do so means that, in contrast with the situation regarding interests and passions, we believe we have trans-subjective grounds for determining the moral standing of actions and of the values which prompt or permit such actions.[17] It is this view that must be defended.

[17] If this were not the case, replies of the type suggested in connection with Bobble would never be attempted. If Bobble should say, "I have examined the consequences of murdering my mother-in-law, and by my values it is the thing to do," we could only reply, "It is unfortunate that we disagree. My values happen to suggest a different conclusion, but it is impossible to adjudicate between values, and far be it from me to insist that yours are wrong. I won't murder my mother-in-law, but neither shall I pretend that my moral code is demonstrably

Two preliminary points: the position in question, the position that reason is relevant to value selection and adjudication, has the support of the overwhelming majority of contemporary writers in the fields of ethics and value theory. This alone, of course, proves nothing concerning the validity or defensibility of the argument. It does mean that a considerable body of supporting analysis and argumentation is available. Those who wish to reject the position are obliged to rebut this considerable body of analysis. These facts are worthy of mention only because a sharp reason-value dichotomy continues to hold sway in political and social science. An appropriate first response on encountering the view that "value choices are arbitrary" or "value statements are emotive expressions and are not fit subjects of rational examination" is to say, "Go read some ethics."

Two questions must be distinguished at the outset. The first or practical question is, "Can reason play a significant and useful role in solving the problems distinctive of value selection and adjudication?" The second, which is very difficult to formulate intelligibly, is, "Can values and value choices, or moral principles and rules, be justified in some ultimate or final or utterly conclusive sense by reason or by rational discourse?" Something will be said about the latter question (or pseudoquestion), but our central concern will be the practical question. As Aristotle said, ethics is a practical science. This is more than a slogan.

---

superior to yours." Note that I might still urge that Bobble be arrested and even punished, but I could not claim a moral warrant for such a demand.

Chapter Seven

THE STRUCTURE OF MORAL DISCOURSE: A PRELIMINARY VIEW

I

This is the question before us: Are there logical or other philosophical difficulties with the argument that reason is relevant to moral decisions? A possible strategy for approaching this question is known as the argument from the "paradigm case." This strategy consists in examining attempts to answer moral questions in order to learn whether individuals faced with such questions use what they regard to be reason to answer them. If we learn that what is generally regarded as reason is generally used in answering such questions, the proper conclusion is that it is nonsensical to dispute the possibility of using reason for that purpose. The allegation that there are philosophical difficulties which prevent what is known to occur reflects faulty philosophizing. If nothing more, this approach will provide an overview of the problems before us.

Imagine a discussion of race relations in which *A* asserts that he is opposed to segregation in public schools. If the conversation is a serious one, his assertion is apt to prompt some form of a "Why." *A* might reply in morally neutral terms.

The evidence is that segregation in public schools serves to discourage new industry and depress the economy, increase the costs of education and hence raise taxes, and foment disturbances destructive of property. As a businessman, a taxpayer, and a property owner, these consequences are contrary to my interests.

The previous chapter is intended to demonstrate that a reasoned exchange could follow such a response. But suppose that *A* responded to the challenge as follows.

A. Well, it seems to me that it is morally wrong to treat Negroes in that way.

B. Why?

A. Just think of the consequences for the Negroes and for everybody who shares a society with them.

B. I don't see that they are so bad. It seems to me that the "separate but equal" formula makes a good deal of sense.

A. We've had a long experience with the operation of that particular doctrine, and the facts are pretty well established. We know that the schools are rarely if ever equal in either material or more intangible respects, and we know that by almost any measure the lives of the graduates of Negro schools (hence the quality of the society in which those graduates live) are poorer than graduates of integrated schools. There are other variables involved, but the evidence concerning the importance of education in these respects is overwhelming. You don't have to take my word on these matters. Go read . . . and . . . etc. To diminish the quality of life, to deny opportunity, and to cause human waste and suffering are to act immorally. Especially when we deliberately use the power of the state to do it.

B. You have a considerable array of evidence there. I'm dubious about some of it, but I admit I haven't looked into the matter as deeply as I might.

A. I think you should. And don't forget that these consequences are imposed in an unequal manner. The conditions segregation imposes upon and the opportunities it denies to Negroes are not ordinarily imposed upon or denied to whites.

B. The last point carries no weight. We treat people unequally in a host of ways, and nobody thinks it morally wrong. This equality business is the most dubious part of the entire controversy about the treatment of Negroes in this country.

A. Of course we treat people unequally—our whole system depends upon it. For example, some have political authority which others don't. But we don't do it just arbitrarily.

B. What do you mean, "just arbitrarily?"

A. I mean for no reason. If we treat people differently in significant respects it is because there is something different about them which justifies such treatment. For example, we put some men in jail because they have broken the law and we let others go free because they haven't. And we give aid to some people because they are unable to work and don't provide it for others who are able to work.

B. I hope you won't deny that Negroes are different from whites.

A. Hardly. But I don't see that the differences have anything to do with receiving an education. Surely having dark skin is irrelevant.

B. I agree that it's not the color of their skin. They just aren't as intelligent as whites. They don't profit from the schooling, and they drag down the others. Of course we should give them the best education they can handle, but mixing them with whites is no way to do it.

A. These are matters of fact. Just the other day I was reading that . . .

B. You certainly have made a study of the matter.

A. It's important to have the facts.

B. I can scarcely disagree with that.

A. You agree, then, that if the facts are as I believe them to be, there are no differences between Negroes and whites which provide a valid justification for segregated education.

B. I suppose I must. But I still don't agree with the moral position that you started with. I still don't agree that a policy of segregation in schools is a morally unacceptable policy. I'm no philosopher, but I know that there is a difference between a statement of fact and a moral judgment.

A. Of course there is. But let me ask you a question or two. Let us say that Jones did an act *X*, and you examined that act and determined that it was a morally right act. Later you discovered that Smith did an act *Y* which was identical in every respect to *X* except that it was done by Smith and not Jones. Would you feel obliged to say that *Y* was a morally right act?

B. What a silly question! If the two acts are identical, and the one is morally right, the other must be morally right as well.

A. Identical in relevant respects you mean.

B. Why so?

A. If one act was done by Jones and the other by Smith, they weren't identical. You are saying that the acts were identical in all respects relevant to deciding whether or not they are morally right.

B. True.

A. We agreed, as a matter of fact, that there are no differences between Negroes and whites which are relevant to receiving an education.

It would seem to follow that treating Negroes and whites differently in this regard would be to violate the principle which we discovered in discussing Jones and Smith. Since we also agreed, again as a matter of fact, that to give separate educations to Negroes and whites is to give different educations with very different consequences, such a policy would violate the rule and would be unacceptable. So far as I can see, then, unless you reject our evaluation of the consequences as undesirable, you are logically required to accept the conclusion that segregation in public education is a morally unacceptable policy.

The point of the example is to suggest that a moral problem can be dealt with in a rational manner. The reader is not requested to ask himself, "Is this a conclusive argument against segregation?" but rather, "Do I regard this as an example of meaningful reasoned argument?" If it is agreed that the label "reasoned argument" properly applies to the dialogue, the individual who persists in the assertion that reasoned argument concerning value problems is logically impossible can be accused of not understanding the concept "reasoned argument."[1]

It will surely be objected, however, that the paradigm case argument cannot resolve disputes as complex as the controversy concerning the place of reason in moral discourse. This objection has considerable force, but it must be handled with great care, for it can lead to a failure to take ordinary language seriously and to philosophical legislation which creates a disjunction between the language of the philosopher and the ordinary language in which the problems of concern to the philosopher arise and are expressed. Hume's discussion of "reason" illustrates the danger. On the present argument, Hume is in the position of instructing mankind that it cannot do something which it knows it has been doing all along. This instruction rests upon the warrant that David Hume has chosen to define "reason" in a manner which conflicts with the manner in which men ordinarily use it. This does not carry the earmarks of an enormous philosophical advance.

The difficulty with the paradigm case argument does not trace to the appeal to general usage regarding the application of "reasoned discourse." It is traced to the extreme generality of our presentation of

[1] The validity of this line of argument has received considerable discussion. See especially the exchange between Benson Mates and Stanley Cavell in *Inquiry*, Vol. I (1958). Both papers are reprinted in V. C. Chappell, editor, *Ordinary Language* (Englewood Cliffs, N. J.: Prentice-Hall, Inc. 1964), the Cavell paper in an expanded version. See also the literature cited in Chappell's Bibliography.

the elements and features of moral argument. We have asked the reader to make a judgment concerning the character of a type of argument on the basis of the presentation of an example of such an argument. We must present a detailed analysis of the elements of the type of argument in question and the problems which arise in connection with them. When this has been done we will be in a position to reach conclusions concerning the general category into which the type of argument can appropriately be placed. Our strategy will be to continue to assume the basically unproblematical character of "reason" and "reasoned discourse" [2] and concentrate upon discovering and clarifying the elements of moral thought and discourse. Taking the hypothetical dialogue concerning segregation as typical of moral arguments, our task will be to isolate the major components which that model exhibits.[3]

If we separate out the basic components of the above dialogue we arrive at the following inventory. (1) Factual statements (or alleged factual statements). For example, "Negroes just aren't as intelligent as whites." (2) Statements concerning the consequences of a particular behavior or policy. "Segregation in schools results in . . . " (These may be statements of fact concerning the consequences of a policy in the past, or predictions of the anticipated consequences of any future employment of the policy.) (3) Statements of formal principles. "If two acts are identical (in all relevant respects), and the one is morally right, the other must be morally right as well." (4*a*) Statements of substantive moral rules expressing an evaluation of a type of action. "To diminish human opportunity is morally wrong." (*b*) Particular moral judgments of examples of such types of action. "Segregation in these public schools is morally wrong." (5*a*) General imperatives. "Don't segregate in public schools." (*b*) Particular imperatives.

[2] The assumption rests upon a truism about ordinary language. It assumes that there is a general understanding of what the concept "reasoned argument" refers to, an understanding which is sufficiently clear to allow individuals who know the English language to discriminate between reasoned arguments and other kinds of arguments. If there were no such understanding, the concept could not be used to communicate, and "reason" and its cognates could not be part of ordinary language. We would then be in the position of creating a technical concept or category as a home for the type of argument we are examining. To proceed to prove that moral discourse and arguments fit into the category we had created would be something less than a spectacular achievement.

[3] The basic purposes of the dialogue should now be clear.

"Don't segregate in these public schools at this time." We will examine these elements in the order in which they have just been listed. In all cases we shall try to discover the important features of the components and to determine whether those features are such as to render them, or aspects of them, inaccessible to reasoned analysis and discourse. Our criterion will be the very general one which we have described. Is it possible to analyze and discuss the component in a manner that is public in the two senses identified?[4]

II

The first two components, factual statements and statements concerning consequences, are at once least and most problematical with regard to reasoned discourse. Of the components identified, they are the two which would most indisputably be termed cognitive in character. It is for this reason that thinkers whose aim it has been to establish a "scientific" basis for moral decisions have emphasized the significance of facts and consequences in such decisions. There are, of course, epistemological problems of ancient and honorable standing (especially regarding consequences, i.e., cause and effect relations), difficult borderline cases, and enormous practical complexities.[5] But however great these difficulties might be, the ascertainment of facts and consequences is the paradigm case of a process amenable to discipline by the canons and criteria of reason, and it is the contrasting case usually cited

[4] This criterion does not require that private experiences be dismissed as irrelevant. Private experiences may be valued very highly by the individual who undergoes them, and they may be extremely important in the development of the knowledge and understanding on which he rests his public behavior. But until the individual can translate his private experiences into public terms, those experiences can never provide a valid warrant for behavior which affects other people. This is because, by definition, the individuals affected by the behavior can have no means of assessing the merits of the experience in question. Consider an analogous case. The theories of an Einstein might begin with "hunches" or "feelings" or "intuitions." Perhaps no scientific theory would ever develop without such hunches. But until the hunches and feelings can be stated in public form, they can have no scientific standing.

[5] For discussions especially relevant to present concerns, see J. L. Austin's treatment of the notion "real" in his *Sense and Sensibilia*, G. J. Warnock, editor (London: Oxford University Press, 1962); concerning the concepts of causation, consequences, and related notions, see especially H. L. A. Hart and A. M. Honoré, *Causation and the Law*, especially Part I (London: Oxford University Press, 1959).

to show that moral discourse is not amenable to such discipline. Investigators in the field of ethics are justified in assuming that the presence of these components in moral discourse creates no insurmountable problems for the argument that such judgments can be made in a reasoned manner.

From other standpoints, however, the importance of facts and consequences to moral judgments is a source of the greatest possible difficulties. For it raises the hoary question of the exact place of these components in moral judgments. On this issue, moral philosophers have argued positions ranging from the view that facts and consequences are irrelevant to moral judgments to the view that they are the sole components of moral discourse. Both of these views have been rejected here. But it is impossible to deal adequately with the place of facts and consequences when so little has been said concerning the other components to which they relate. We shall proceed to examine the other components and deal with the significance of facts and consequences as the question arises in the course of that examination.

Chapter Eight

MORAL PRINCIPLES

The central problem of a rationalistic ethics is to account for the possibility of providing reasoned justification for the conclusions of moral arguments. Facts and consequences are parts of moral argument, and they pose no insurmountable problems of verification in a rational manner. But Hume, G. E. Moore, and many others have argued powerfully that no arrangement of the facts and consequences, taken alone, can ever generate normative force, and this conclusion is widely accepted by philosophers.[1] If moral arguments are to have such force and if those arguments are to rest upon reasoned grounds, whence is that force to be derived?

Many philosophers have thought that normative force might be derived from principles. This is not surprising because we regularly turn to principles to provide conclusive force for various types of arguments. Indeed, principles are *defined* as force or warrant-giving agents. The *OED* defines a "principle" as "A general statement or tenet forming the (or a) ground of, or held to be essential to, a system of thought or belief; a fundamental assumption forming the basis of a chain of reasoning"; or more narrowly concerning "practical" discourse, "A general law or rule adopted or professed as a guide to action; a settled ground or basis of conduct or practice; a fundamental motive or reason of action, especially one consciously recognized and followed." A number of recent writers, including Toulmin, Nowell-Smith, Singer, and Hare, have presented arguments to the effect that principles pro-

[1] See especially the works of R. M. Hare, who returns to this question again and again.

vide the value-infusing "major premise" of moral arguments, that facts and consequences provide the minor premise(s), and that the two together warrant imperative conclusions of a normative kind.

This use of principles is consistent with there being a place for facts and consequences in moral discourse, and it holds promise with respect to the logical gap which has long been believed to separate the "is" and the "ought." The argument is also attractive in that it accounts for an important feature of our discourse *about* moral matters. We regularly say that a moral decision is a "principled" decision, and that a moral man is a man who acts "on principle." This usage of the word principle does not exclude the consideration of contextual facts and consequences, although Kant and others thought that it did. It does require that moral decisions be *more than* mere descriptions of the features of an action and its consequences.

There are also a number of objections to heavy reliance upon principle. Those objections which concern the relationship between principles and the other elements of a moral argument will be considered. But there are prior questions such as "What, precisely, are principles?"; "Can they be established in a rational manner?"; "How, in establishing them, can we overcome the 'is-ought' gap?"

The first mistake to avoid is the *unum nomen unum nominatum* fallacy. There are at least two basic types of moral principles (to say nothing of nonmoral uses), and they are established and justified in quite different ways. The distinction between them has been discussed somewhat in the literature, but no consensus has developed concerning terminology. Primary and secondary, fundamental and derivative, indefeasible and defeasible, principles and rules, are among the formulas which have been utilized. Following Singer,[2] we will differentiate between principles and rules, treating the former as fundamental and indefeasible, the latter as secondary and subject to modification under various circumstances. This chapter will present examples of such principles, analyze their characteristics, and discuss the manner in which they can be established. Rules will be considered in Chapters 9 and 10.

Singer distinguishes principles from moral rules by the following characteristics. "They hold in all circumstances and do not admit of

[2] Marcus G. Singer, *Generalization in Ethics* (New York: Alfred Knopf, Inc., 1960), especially pp. 96–110, 327–8.

exceptions"; "they are always relevant" to all moral decisions; they are "invariant"; and "it is impossible for [them] . . . to conflict with each other." In his view, principles provide the essential basis for moral thinking and moral decisions, and if the "arguments [for these principles] are sound, . . . we have established the rational basis of morality. . . ." [3] These are heady claims, and some of them have been vigorously disputed in the extensive critical literature concerning Singer's book. But the bulk of the criticism has been directed at one of Singer's principles, what he calls the Generalization Argument, and there have been few challenges to the contention that principles provide the foundation for a rational ethics. We will deal with two principles, one of which, we will argue, is fundamental to morality. We will attempt to show that these two principles can be established or justified in a rational manner. If this can be shown and if it can be shown later that these principles, along with the use of rules and the knowledge of facts and consequences, account for the possibility of making moral decisions in a rational manner, a major objection to the arguments of Part 1 will have been met.

I. THE PRINCIPLE OF CONSEQUENCES (PC)

"If the consequences of *A*'s doing *X* would be undesirable, then *A* ought not to do *X*." Or in its positive formulation, "If the consequences of *A*'s not doing *X* would be undesirable, then *A* ought to do *X*." [4] Singer contends that PC is a necessary ethical or moral principle and that "once it is properly understood, there could be no reasonable question about it." [5] There are a number of features of the principle which must be examined before passing judgment on these contentions. As formulated, the principle is elliptical in important respects. As

[3] *Ibid.*, p. 339.

[4] Singer rejects as invalid the statement: "If the consequences of *A*'s doing *X* would be desirable, *A* ought to do X." *Ibid.*, and pp. 179 ff. This is proper insofar as the aim is to produce a conclusion which properly uses "ought." There is no moral imperative to do that which is morally good. But if PC as stated in the text is valid, there is no difficulty with the statement, "If the consequences of *A*'s doing *X* would be desirable, it would be good if *A* did X." The "ought" formulation is more difficult to validate, and we will concentrate upon it in the present chapter. But the formulation using "good" is of great importance to discourse about the public interest.

[5] *Ibid.*, pp. 64, 337.

Singer himself notes, it is elliptical for "If the consequences of *A*'s doing *X* would be undesirable, then *A* ought not to do *X without a reason or justification.*" [6] We are sometimes right to act in a manner which has undesirable consequences. In some cases, this is because the action has some desirable and some undesirable consequences, and the former "outweigh" the latter. In such a case, we could say either that the consequences of the action "as a whole" were desirable or that the desirable consequences of the action provided a reason or a justification for the action despite its undesirable consequences. There might also be cases in which all of the consequences of *X*, taken alone, are undesirable, but *X* is justified because some action must be taken and the consequences of *X* are less undesirable than all other alternatives.

Because PC is a moral principle, the above formulation must also be elliptical for the statement, "If the consequences of *A*'s doing *X* would be *morally* undesirable, it would be *morally* wrong for *A* to do *X*." If this expansion is not understood, PC would institute moral duties to avoid consequences undesirable on grounds having no relationship to moral issues. If the consequences of *A*'s leaving his manuscript on his desk overnight are that dust gathers on the manuscript, and if dust gathering on the manuscript is undesirable, *A* would be obligated not to leave his manuscript on his desk overnight. The importance of this emendation lies in its connection with the is-ought relationship. If valid, PC establishes a formal bridge between a type of fact about the world, the consequences of doing *X*, and moral imperatives. But the emendation in question shows that this bridge provides only a partial solution to the is-ought problem. The facts about the world become relevant to PC only *after* they have been provided with moral standing. PC does not assist us in assigning such moral standing.

Finally, the above formulation is elliptical for the statement, "If the consequences of *A*'s doing *X* would be justifiably regarded as undesirable, *A* ought not to do *X*." The principle itself does not determine the content of the word "undesirable." But if the principle established no criteria for making that determination, "undesirable" could be construed in a frivolous or adventitious manner. For reasons already indicated in part, "justifiably" means "defended in a reasoned manner." [7]

Combining these emendations, a complete statement of PC follows:

[6] *Ibid.*, p. 65.

[7] See chapter 10 for further discussion.

"If the consequences of *A*'s doing *X* would be justifiably regarded as morally undesirable, *A* has a moral duty not to do *X* without a reason or justification." All subsequent uses of the principle are to be read as elliptical for this formulation.

A second feature of the principle is now apparent, namely its "formal" or "neutral" character. By this is meant that the principle itself will never determine whether an action is undesirable or not. Nor will it, with the exception of requiring that the undesirability be established in a reasoned way, provide guidance as to how to determine whether the consequences of an action are desirable or not. Assessment of the desirability of an action is an independent step to which the principle is irrelevant. The principle does one and only one thing: if the consequences of *A*'s doing *X* are undesirable, the principle establishes that *A* ought not to do *X*.

Is Singer right in contending that there can be "no reasonable question" concerning PC? What can be done to validate the principle? PC establishes a union between a moral judgment, the undesirable consequences of *X*, and a moral imperative: the duty not to do *X*. When "undesirable" is interpreted to mean "morally undesirable" and when the other emendations have been entered, the principle appears to be analytic; that is, it is a statement which is valid because of the relationship between the uses of its words; one could deny its validity only if he misunderstand the uses of these words. This interpretation asserts that the concepts "duty to do or not to do" are contained in the concepts "morally desirable or undesirable" in the same way as "unmarried" is contained in "bachelor." In this view, when we say "*X* has morally undesirable consequences," one of the things we *mean* is that it is morally wrong to do *X*. If this is true, the principle cannot be questioned, and Singer is justified in offering no arguments for it.

This interpretation can be defended, but there are complexities that must be analyzed. It does not violate the uses of moral words to admit that *A*'s doing *X* will have undesirable consequences and yet to hold that it would be right (or morally permissible) for *A* to do *X*. We could say that it would be right for *A* to do *X* if his motive was morally good. Smith says, "I am aware that my refusal to steal will mean that my family will starve. However undesirable that would be, I regard stealing to be morally wrong under any and all circumstances. Since my motive in not stealing is to uphold a moral principle, my refusal to steal is morally right." At the very least, validating PC requires support for the view that consideration of consequences is a necessary part of moral reasoning and decision making. This issue was involved in the discussion of contextual considerations in Part 1. The arguments presented there, together with the discussion in Chapter 9, are intended to provide the requisite support. Moral reasoning which does not consider consequences can always be forced to do so or be shown to be inadequate.

This consideration supports PC, but it does not show that PC is analytic. If I say, "Jones is a bachelor, and he and his wife live in Cherryville," the only evidence needed to upset my statement is linguistic evidence. But the foregoing statement concerning stealing cannot be upset so easily. Smith's reasoning is faulty, but his English is perfectly correct. To upset his statement we must attack his reasoning. But the fact, if it is a fact, that we are always able to do so, is relevant to establishing the analyticity of PC. For it shows that "the consequences of *X* are morally undesirable" is logically although not linguistically equivalent to "*X* is morally wrong or undesirable." Hence PC is equivalent to "if it is morally wrong to do *X*, *A* ought not to do *X*," which is analytic.

There is an important sense in which this argument validates PC. To say that the principle is analytic means that it satisfies the recognized criteria for the validity of a class of statements. When these criteria have been satisfied, the principle or statement is, by hypothesis, valid. This means that PC provides the major premise of an argument which, with the addition of a defensible minor premise, will produce an impeccable imperative conclusion. (If the consequences of *A*'s doing *X* are undesirable, *A* ought not to do *X*; the consequences of *A*'s doing *X* are undesirable; therefore *A* ought not to do *X*.)

In the moral realm, however, discomfort can remain when the analyticity of moral statements has been established. As noted, analytic statements are statements the truth value of which derives from the relations between the words used in the the statement. PC concerns the manner in which we use the words "morally undesirable"; it asserts that we use those words to describe things that it is wrong to do. Knowing this usage, we are able to show that the structure of discourse is such that certain types of logically sound arguments can be constructed. But to the extent that such arguments rest on analytic statements, they seem to rest moral conclusions on facts about our language. Faced with an argument grounded in this manner, Smith might reply, "I understand that the English expression 'action *X* has morally undesirable consequences,' is equivalent to 'action *X* ought not to be done.' I agree that when I admit that action *X* has morally undesirable consequences and yet say 'I may do *X*,' I am departing from accepted usage. But departing from usage and acting in a morally wrong way are different things. I plead guilty to the first, but I will not admit guilt to the second until I am shown why the words *ought* to be used in that way." In the case of purely descriptive language, this objection would make no sense. If Smith were to say, "I know everyone uses the word 'knife' to stand for a specific type of object, but I want to know why I should," we would regard the question as a jest or as an indication of mental disturbance. We could give reasons for general uniformity in the use of words, and we could explain the genesis of the particular uses in question. But there is nothing more to explain or justify—nor is there anything arbitrary or unjustified.

J. O. Urmson has shown, however, that Smith's objection can be appropriate in the case of moral words.[8] The case of PC demonstrates that matters of moral substance hinge upon using moral words in a particular way. This suggests that the uses are not arbitrary, and that if pressed we ought to be able give reasons for them.[9] What can be said in defense of the uses that make the principle of consequences analytic?

There is an intimate connection between the analyticity of the principle and its formal or neutral status. It is neutral because the language of which it consists describes no particular and uses no proper names. The force of the principle derives from the generic terms "undesirable" and "wrong." The moment we assign specific content to these generic terms the principle is no longer neutral and no longer analytic. If we say, "The consequences of *A*'s doing *X* will be monetary loss for *Y*," "*A* ought not to do *X*" does not follow analytically. For it is not clear that such consequences are morally undesirable or wrong.

[8] See "Some Questions Concerning Validity," in Antony Flew, editor, *Essays in Conceptual Analysis* (London: Macmillan Co., 1960).

[9] It is true that constant questioning of our uses of moral words, as with any part of our language, would make discourse impossible. This is perhaps why we are inclined to be impatient with Smith's objection. But the generalization that constant questioning would be destructive does not warrant indifference to the importance of being able to justify moral uses if necessary.

Yet whenever we can establish that the consequences *are* morally wrong, the principle becomes analytic again. This suggests the reason or justification for the uses in question and hence for the principle. "Wrong" and "undesirable" are generic terms used to describe the whole array of characteristics and properties which it is the purpose of morality to eliminate or minimize. "Wrong" means, according to *OED*, "unjust, unfair, amiss"; "evil or damage inflicted"; "perverse." The latter terms are used to refer to yet more specific phenomena which men have come, through experience, to seek to avoid. The justification for PC, then, is that it prohibits a whole array of consequences of which men disapprove sufficiently to regard as immoral. Entering any particular consequence under the heading "morally wrong" requires independent justification. But once it has been properly entered, it is perfectly clear that the consequences should be prohibited. The answer to the question "Why ought the words to be used that way?" is simply "Because using them that way serves the very purpose for which morality and moral words exist." Could a better reason be imagined?

II. THE UNIVERSALIZABILITY PRINCIPLE

The universalizability or generalization principle has received very extensive discussion in recent philosophical literature, and several basic controversies have emerged. Singer, who calls it the generalization principle (GP) states it as follows: "What is right (or wrong) for one person must be right (or wrong) for any similar person in similar circumstances." [10] This formulation is elliptical for a more inclusive version which amends the final clause to read "for every relevantly similar person in relevantly similar circumstances." [11] If *A* claims that it is right for him to do or have *X*, he must agree that it is right for *BCD* . . . *N* to do or have *X* unless he can show that he or his circumstances are different from *BCD* . . . *N* or their circumstances in a manner relevant to the justification of his being an exception. In political terms, if government *A* treats *BCD* in fashion *X*, it is obligated to treat *EFG* in the same way unless it can show differences between *BCD* and *EFG* which justify different treatment.

[10] Marcus George Singer, *Generalization in Ethics* (New York: Alfred A. Knopf, Inc., 1960), p. 5.

[11] *Ibid.*, pp. 19–20. For a number of alternative formulations see p. 31.

The most important controversy over the principle hinges on whether it is a formal rule of logic which has no moral force, or a moral principle which can provide grounding for moral imperatives. R. M. Hare is the leading proponent of the former position,[12] and Singer has urged the latter.[13] In Hare's view, to violate the universalizability principle (U) is simply to contradict oneself—to make a logical mistake. In Singer's view, to violate the principle is to commit a moral wrong. This controversy, leading into the most significant questions which arise about the principle, hinges upon the relationship between GP, U, and PC.

There is at least one sense in which the principle is formal or neutral, namely, the same sense that we said PC is formal or neutral. Just as PC does not inform us concerning the content of "morally undesirable" or "wrong," so GP provides no help in giving substance to the first and second of its particular premises, namely that "this *X* is right for this *A*" and "this *B* is, vis-à-vis this *A*, a relevantly similar person in relevantly similar circumstances." Establishing these particular premises is an independent step, and the principle can be activated only after they have been established. GP does one and only one thing; when it has been established that *ABC* and *DEF* are relevantly similar persons in relevantly similar circumstances, the principle requires that for *ABC* to act or to be treated differently in a moral matter is morally wrong.[14]

Hare argues that the principle is morally neutral in a more inclusive sense. It is a logical thesis that applies to all statements with descriptive dimensions, whether they are moral statements or not. Whenever we attribute specific predicates to a person, object, or action (whether "good," "right," "eight-sided," or "oily"), we are logically required to attribute the same predicates to any other person, object, or action sim-

[12] *Freedom and Reason*, (London: Oxford Univ. Press, 1963) pp. 10–13, 30–35. See also Charles E. Caton, "In What Sense and Why 'Ought'—Judgments are Universalizable," *The Philosophical Quarterly*, Vol. 13, No. 50 (January, 1963).

[13] Singer, *op. cit.*, especially pp. 46–51. See also, Dorothy Emmet, "Universalizability and Moral Judgment," *The Philosophical Quarterly*, Vol. 13, No. 52 (July, 1963).

[14] This statement highlights the differences between Singer and Hare. In Singer's view the above formulation is appropriate. But for Hare, U alone allows us to say only that an inconsistency or logical error has been committed. The logical error may coincide with a moral wrong, but the moral wrong must be determined independently of U.

ilar in relevant respects. Every descriptive statement is implicitly a universal statement, and failure to recognize this leads to contradiction. Since universalizing is a logical requirement that must be met by all descriptive statements, there is no warrant for imputing other than logical force to it in the case of the specific kind of descriptive statement (or statement with descriptive dimensions) we call a moral statement. To do so is to risk the accusation "that a moral principle has been smuggled in disguised as a logical doctrine." [15]

In Hare's view, then, U does not establish the particular premises in any instance, and it carries no moral force once they have been established. Yet he holds that U "has momentous consequences for ethics" [16] and "great potency in moral arguments." [17] The individual who advocates or engages in behavior with deleterious effects for others will want to make an exception of himself; U shows that he can do this only at the price of commiting a logical contradiction.[18] This is to say that the individual can be shown that his position will not stand rational examination. It is worth emphasizing, however, that so far as U is concerned the individual has been caught in a logical error, not in a moral wrong. We will see that Hare is right on this question, but that his acuteness in dealing with U exposes a basic incompleteness in his ethical theory.[19]

As far as it goes, Hare's argument is incontrovertible. Once the difficulty of establishing the particular premises is overcome, the logical requirements are those which Hare suggests. Furthermore, the fact that the thesis is a logical one simplifies the task of validating the prin-

[15] R. M. Hare, *op. cit,* p. 31.

[16] *Ibid.,* p. 13.

[17] *Ibid.,* p. 31.

[18] Hence the requirement of universalizability does not reach what Hare calls fanatics, that is, people who genuinely will apply their immoral decisions against themselves. An example would be the fanatic antisemite who is willing to go to the gas chamber if he discovers that he has Jewish blood.

[19] The thesis can criticize the antisemite who will not go to the gas chamber if he discovers he is a Jew, but has nothing to say to the fanatic who will. Their positions on the moral question, antisemitism or not, are identical, but one is a better logician than the other. This is not to suggest that the fanatic antisemite is not immoral in Hare's view. But Hare regards U as one of the three foundation stones of his ethic. (*Ibid.,* p. 17.) Whatever moral judgments he may choose to make, questions arise as to whether his ethical theory can account for the rational basis of such judgments.

ciple. Nor is the principle trivial; no one interested in a rational foundation for moral discourse should forgo a principle that allows him to expose adventitious and discriminatory arguments and behavior as logically untenable.

Yet Hare's treatment of U, together with his heavy reliance upon it, creates serious problems. As Hare interprets it, U does not help us to find normative principles that allow us to move to a conclusion which has moral force. Since U is devoid of moral or normative content, an argument grounded on it alone has no means of overcoming the gap between moral judgments and moral imperatives. Arguments constructed with U as the major premise and particular moral judgments as minor premises can never generate moral imperatives. This, of course, is simply to point out what Hare himself insists upon. But U is held to be a foundation of rational discourse about moral issues, and it fails to touch a fundamental problem of such discourse.

Second, discomfort is created by the similarity between Hare's logical thesis and what has long and widely been regarded as a moral principle. Hare's thesis can be formulated. If *X* is a predicate of *Y* and *Y* and Z are identical in relevant respects, *X* is a predicate of Z. Singer states GP as follows: What is right (or wrong) for one person [i.e., in Hare's language, what is a predicate of an action which is taken by or which affects one person] must be right (or wrong) [i.e., must be a moral predicate of. . .] for any similar person in similar circumstances. The differences in form are trivial. Singer regards GP as a moral principle, as have many other philosophers, for example, Kant and Sidgwick. The principle provides an adequate statement of what is widely regarded by philosophers and nonphilosophers alike as a principle of justice or fairness. If *A* agrees that there are no relevant differences between Negroes and whites with regard to their capacity to profit from an education, and yet advocates or engages in segregation, we say not simply that *A* has contradicted himself, but that *A* favors acting in an immoral manner. We are consequently prepared to treat *A* in a fashion, or adopt attitudes toward *A*, which we would regard as unwarranted if *A* had simply made a logical mistake. We have already said that Hare is right about U; our problem is to find other means of accounting for these important facts of moral life.

Let us consider further a problem which is raised by Hare's position. Despite his view that U is one of the three foundation stones of his ethics,[20] Hare concedes that there is a class or type of individual whose behavior appears to be objectionable but who is not affected by the logical restrictions which the thesis establishes. Hare calls such individuals fanatics, a fanatic being a person who pursues an "ideal" [21] so relentlessly as to run roughshod not only over the interests of others but over all of his own interests as well (with the exception of his interest in satisfying his ideal). Hare's prototypical fanatic is the Nazi who believes so strongly in a society free of Jews that he will prescribe his own death if he discovers himself to be a Jew. This man's behavior cannot be criticized under U. But neither can it be criticized under GP alone à la Singer.[22] This provides an important clue to the solution of the problem.

In the case of Hare's system, as he admits, this conclusion means that there is no rational ground on which to object to the Nazi's behavior. U is a foundation of the system of ethics; the Nazi does not violate it, hence the system cannot account for condemnation of the Nazi. This is a paradoxical situation. Few of us would regard the Nazi who satisfies the demands of U as significantly less culpable than the one who draws back from prescribing his own death.

Hare is untroubled by the situation, but the reasons he offers for his equanimity involve a confusion of two issues. Hare argues that the paradox of the fanatic is "no scandal" because solving it makes demands which no ethical theory could be expected to meet.

> If somebody wants to send himself and his whole family to the gas-chamber simply on the ground that they are descended from people with hooked noses, is there, or could there possibly be, any moral philosophy that could argue with him? [23]

If the issue was whether moral philosophy could successfully dissuade the Nazi from his view, we could accept Hare's argument without qualm. Unfortunately, that is not the issue. The fact that our moral arguments will not "stop [the Nazi] from wanting to do this" [24] is

[20] He does consider the possibility that there are types of moral questions which his account cannot handle, but, with the exception of the point presently to be considered, he leaves this open. (*Ibid.*, pp. 137–9.)

[21] See *Ibid.*, Chapters 8 to 9 for Hare's use of this term.

[22] The ground of this assertion will emerge as the argument proceeds.

[23] *Ibid.*, p. 172.

[24] *Ibid.*, p. 172.

scarcely the end of the moral problem. Indeed, the fact that the Nazi persists in his behavior is the beginning of the moral problem *for us.* If the Nazi persists in his behavior, *we* as moral agents must do something about it. If his behavior is the behavior of a nation, we fight a horrible war to put an end to it. If he behaves this way within our nation, we use the force of government to lock him up and prevent him from continuing. This is where the paradox becomes a first-order moral dilemma. If we cannot adduce rational considerations in justification of our use of violence against the Nazi (as opposed to pasting labels, for example, "The man is mad"), in what sense is our position preferable to his? Indeed, in Hare's view the fanatic Nazi is in a superior position to those who attack him. His behavior cannot be criticized, whereas that of his attackers involves an unwarranted and unwarrantable use of violence.

Hare would undoubtedly consider the Nazi (fanatic or not) depraved and would support the actions necessary to halt his behavior. But he admits that his ethics cannot account for the possibility of offering more than the possession of authority or power or self-interest as a justification for taking action. Given the centrality of the case under discussion, this is a sufficient demonstration that Hare's ethical theory is incomplete. But a system that regards GP as an adequate foundation for moral discourse is equally incomplete.[25]

[25] The point here is essentially the same as the one involved in the hypothetical dialogue with Bobble in Chapter 6. A second and more general difficulty with Hare's argument is that it treats moral arguments as equivalent to a force or restraint brought to bear upon the individual to whom they are addressed. Note the following language. "Should it disturb us, as moral philosophers, that no argument can *stop him* [the Nazi] wanting to do this, if his desire is sufficiently intense and unshakable? Should we not rather say 'Well, at any rate, thank goodness not many people feel like that'?" (p. 172) "The distinguishing characteristic of the ideals of [fanatics] is that they are made by their holders to override all considerations of people's interests, even the holders' own. . . . This is what made golden-rule arguments seem *powerless* against [them]." (p. 175) "In his *war* with the fanatic, the best strategy for the liberal . . . is one of persistent *attrition.* For there are . . . certain *weapons* available to him, in the nature of moral thought, which . . . will *cause all* but a small hard core of fanatics to relent." (p. 180) The true fanatics "will remain *unshaken* by any argument I have been able to discover." (p. 184, italics mine throughout.) This approach is incomplete because it ignores the requirement that the nonfanatics be able to justify action against the fanatics. It ignores the problem of the hangman. But the entire set of physical metaphors Hare employs is misleading. A moral argument, or any other rational argument, is neither a club with which to beat an opponent into submission nor a drug de-

There is a sense in which the example is an unfortunate one. The evil of the Nazis' action (whether fanatic or not) is so gross, so horrendous, that it is inconceivable there could be any moral dilemma for those who must deal with it. It is simply obvious that the fanatic Nazi is morally depraved if not insane, and no elaborate apparatus of justification is necessary to prove that society ought to do whatever is necessary to control him. But this is an extremely dangerous position in that the warrant for an action is exclusively "what is obvious to the community." When we note that it was "obvious" to many that the Nazis were saving the human race from degradation, or when we observe that there are communities for whom it is "obvious" that Negroes are subhuman and ought to be treated accordingly, the dangers of this view are manifest.

Indeed, the extreme character of the example serves to call attention to the real issue raised by Hare's position. However we might reach the conclusion, most of us would agree that both fanatic and nonfanatic Nazis are morally depraved. It would appear that the problem is not that we are unable to deal with the fanatic, but that U and GP are insignificant. For the Nazi is to be condemned whether he lives up to them or not. There is a sense in which this is the case; there is a sense in which GP and U are subordinate to PC.

The difficulties we have been discussing obtain in the case of GP as well as U. The problem is particularly acute for Hare owing to his extremely heavy reliance upon U, but any ethical theory that hopes to account for the moral arguments of practical men must go beyond U and/or GP. Since it has already been suggested that PC is a fundamental moral principle, it is appropriate to examine more systematically the relationship between PC and GP or U. This should also allow us to find support for our conclusion concerning the GP–U controversy.

Let us look more formally at the situation just discussed. The posi-

signed to alter the functioning of his central nervous system. It is an attempt to demonstrate, by the best criteria we can construct, the validity, verifiability, or justifiability of a position. The question of whether particular individuals are somehow moved by the demonstration is entirely independent. If this distinction, between the justifiability and the persuasiveness of an argument is not drawn *and maintained*, moral argument is readily confused with propaganda. Hence the fact that fanatic Nazis will not be moved by rational moral arguments is scarcely grounds for concluding that moral arguments cannot be or should not be made against Nazis, or that ethical theories ought not to attempt to account for the possibility of making such moral arguments.

tion to be examined is that of the Nazi (*A*) who holds that all Jews (*B*) ought to be killed (*X*). His argument is: All *B*'s ought to be *X; Y* is a *B;* therefore *Y* ought to be X. Assume that *A* is a fanatic and hence invulnerable to U. To object to his argument we must attack the major premise, "All *B*'s ought to be *X*." If we cannot do so on the basis of U or GP, to what do we turn? An obvious candidate is PC. If we can show that the major premise violates PC, the rest of the argument falls. The problem, then, would be to adduce grounds for thinking that the consequences of all *B*'s being *X* would be undersirable. Let us assume for the moment (not really such a difficult assumption) that such grounds can be adduced (remembering that the question whether *A* is convinced or whether he alters his behavior is independent of whether the argument is valid). If so, and if our earlier arguments for PC are valid, we have an impeccable demonstration that *A* ought not to do X namely: If the consequences of all *B*'s being *X* are undesirable, no action ought to be taken such that all *B*'s are *X;* The consequences of all *B*'s being *X* are undesirable; Therefore, *A* ought not to act such that all *B*'s become X.

Do GP or U have a role to play here? If PC makes it wrong for *A* to do X, and if *D* is (vis-à-vis *A*) a similar person similarly situated, GP shows *D* that it would be wrong for him to do X. In the same circumstances, U shows *D* that if he agrees that PC makes X wrong for *B*, it would be inconsistent for him to claim that it was right (or permissible) for him to do X. If *D* wishes to make an exception of himself, in other words, GP shows him that he ought not and U that he logically cannot do so. In this sense, PC's relation to GP or U is such that it establishes the first of the particular premises in GP and U. But GP and U are logically unnecessary. For *D* can discover the wrongness of X directly from PC. From the standpoint of the persuasiveness of the argument, of course, GP and U are anything but trivial. They catch *D* when he attempts to make himself an exception to the rule of PC. The important point, however, is that PC accounts for the condemnation of the fanatic whereas GP or U are of no help. If we accept Singer's criteria of fundamental moral principles, neither GP nor U qualifies.

Are there situations in which GP allows us to adduce valid reasons for condemning an action or position independent of PC? This type of case would be crucial for the GP–U controversy. Consider the recurrent political problem concerning the proper distribution of representation. Is it right for *ABC* to have representation X whereas *DEF* have representation *Y?* GP prohibits this if *ABCDEF* are similar persons similarly situated. Is this conclusion independent of PC? Its independence is suggested if we consider the possibility that X might be right for *ABC* under PC when *DEF* are not a part of the system. But the moment *DEF* enter the system, what is right for *ABC* must be right for *DEF* as well (assuming that the second particular premise has been established), and to deny it to *DEF* and to continue to grant it to *ABC* would be wrong under GP.

But this is misleading. PC governs because the entrance of *DEF* makes X wrong for *ABC* owing to the fact that the consequences of *ABC* having X are now different and are now undesirable. If the consequences were not undesirable, it would not be wrong to treat *ABC* and *DEF* differently. In political or legal language, we would say that we had discovered a permissible classification.

This conclusion means that GP is subsidiary to PC. If PC did not make it wrong to treat either or both *ABC* or *DEF* in manner X, GP could not make it wrong to treat them differently. The fact of difference of treatment, in other words, is not sufficient to show undesirable consequences. GP accommodates this through the two particular premises. This conclusion is obvious in the case of "this *X* is right (or wrong) for this *A*." A moment's reflection shows it to be true of "similar persons similarly situated" as well. The point of examining "persons and circumstances" is to determine whether they make a moral difference. But this determination depends upon PC, and GP or U are of no help. Neither particular premise of GP can be established without use of PC. From a moral standpoint, GP generates the imperative, "Don't treat people in a manner that violates PC."

GP states a logical relationship between two (or more) applications of PC. If we apply PC to all of the parties involved in or affected by any decision or action, and if we obtain the same results in each case, it follows, by hypothesis, that the action or decision is right (or wrong) for all, and that all are, for purposes of the decision, relevantly similar persons in relevantly similar circumstances. If different results are obtained, the specific premises are not established.[26]

[26] There are complications involved in his argument which will not be considered here. We have attempted to deal with them in a forthcoming article, "Equality, Generalization, and Apportionment, a Formal Analysis."

GP and U are not moral principles in the same sense as PC. GP and U can never have moral force if PC has not been satisfied. These conclusions also seem to support the charge that GP and U teach us nothing which we cannot learn from PC, and hence that GP and U are trivial. This is not correct. If I say that X is red, I do so because of certain properties of X. When I do so, I commit myself to saying that any other object with the same properties is red. If *Y* has the properties that led me to say X is red, I must say *Y* is red as well (or retract my statement concerning X). To deny that *Y* is red is to contradict myself. There is a logical relationship between the statements "X is red" and "*Y* is red." [27]

If the foregoing interpretation is correct, GP states the same logical relationship between two (or more) moral judgments that obtains between "X is red" and "*Y* is red." The first particular premise of GP is of the form "This X is right for this *A*." We establish this premise by applying PC. We say, "X is right (or wrong) for *A* by virtue of the desirability (or undesirability) of the consequences of X for *A*." The second specific premise is established in the same manner. We determine the relevant similarity of *A* and *B* by examining the consequences of X for *B*. Having applied PC we say, "X is right (or wrong) for *B* by virtue of the desirability (or undesirability) of the consequences of X for *B*." Between the two specific premises of GP stands "must be right for." "Must be right for" has exactly the standing of the logical rule requiring that we say "*Y* is red" if *Y* has the same properties which led us to say "X is red." Therefore, GP states a logical relationship between the conclusions reached through two (or more) applications of PC. A logical relationship between two conclusions is not the same thing as the two conclusions themselves, and hence GP is not the same as two (or more) applications of PC.

If this interpretation is correct, GP tells us nothing concerning the moral status of any action. But it does not follow that GP, that is, the rule of logic which GP states, has no utility in discourse concerning morals. If X has properties (*P*) such that we call it red, and if *Y* has *P*, we do not need a rule of logic to tell us that *Y* is red. When we see that *Y* has properties *P*, we say *Y* is red simply because it has the properties to which we apply the word "red." But moral matters are more complicated. To say that X is right by virtue of its having *P* (desirable

[27] This argument is taken from Hare, *op. cit.*, especially pp. 10–16.

consequences) is not merely to describe *X*. It is also to evaluate or commend *X*. We commend in order to guide conduct, that is, to convince people, including ourselves, to act in a manner that might be contrary to our inclinations. Therefore to say "*X* is right for *A* because *P*" is not simply to describe *X*; it is to say that *A* ought to do X. Under the logical rule of GP, it is to say that every *A* ought to do X. If I say, "Jones ought to give $1000 to charity because *P*," and if my giving $1000 dollars to charity produces *P*, I must give $1000 to charity (or retract my statement concerning Jones). But giving $1000 to charity is apt to conflict with my inclinations in a manner that saying "*Y* is red" is not likely to; I am apt to try to avoid giving $1000 to charity. But if I have GP in mind, or if a moral adviser reminds me of it, I have a logical principle, neutral to the moral question, that can discipline my thinking in a salutary manner. "Didn't you say Jones ought to give $1000 to charity?" "Yes." "How does his case differ from yours?" If I am unable to show a relevant difference, if I am unable to show that for *A* to do X produces *P* whereas for me to do *X* produces Q it will be inconsistent for me to refuse to do X.

Stated less formally, GP and U function to condemn unwarranted exceptions and to force the individual to think of himself not as an isolated agent but as related to and comparable with other men. It also provides a valuable instrument for dealing with the large-scale distribution problems which are characteristic of public policy decisions. We decide such questions by predicting and evaluating the consequences of the policy for those affected by it. This involves examination of the characteristics or properties of those affected. Since we are dealing with large numbers, we must employ comprehensive classifications. GP is useful here because its second particular premise directs attention to the characteristics and properties of those affected as an appropriate consideration in making a *general* judgment of the kind required. If we know that *A* has properties *Y*—for example, is under 26, unmarried, and with no physical disabilities—and if we know that the consequences of *X* for him are not undesirable, we can predict that X will not have undesirable consequences for other individuals who have properties *Y*. The better the evidence on which this prediction rests, the better the justification for using "possession of properties *Y*" as a classification. Since GP explicitly calls attention to the distributive character of the problem, it is sometimes a more useful manner of stating the basic principle such decisions ought to satisfy than is PC. This is why GP rather than PC was emphasized in parts of Chapters 3 to 5. (It should be evident that the discussion in Chapters 3 to 5 is misleading if the relationship between PC and GP, as described in the present chapter, is not understood.)

What do these conclusions imply for the Hare-Singer controversy? Hare is right in urging that U establishes a logical requirement, and we now see that GP does the same. There is an important sense in which that is all they do. Any moral force that GP or U has stems from and depends upon PC, not GP or U. GP and U state a logical relationship between two or more applications of PC. Yet, whenever GP or U are violated *in the realm of moral discourse*, it is true by hypothesis that a moral principle has been violated. Strictly speaking, the violation of PC is the moral wrong, the violation of GP or U is the logical error, and the two coincide when GP or U is invoked in a moral case. The important thing is to be clear concerning the relationship between PC and GP or U and to understand that, taken together, they account for the possibility of satisfying a necessary condition of the production of valid moral arguments.

III

We conclude that the utilitarian principle PC is the fundamental moral principle at the root of all moral decisions. It is a formal principle which, taken alone, will never provide answers to particular moral questions. But if properly combined with facts, consequences, and moral rules, it accounts for a part of our view that moral decisions are principled decisions, and it provides a bridge between moral rules or evaluations and moral imperatives.

PC also contributes to overcoming the "is-ought" gap. Consequences are facts about the world, and PC establishes that such facts about the world are necessary to moral judgments. Those facts must be given moral standing (must be assigned the status "morally desirable" or "morally undesirable") before they become relevant to moral judgments. PC does not assist us in assigning that standing. Hence PC itself does not bridge the is-ought gap in any substantive sense in any individual case. But without PC we would not be directed toward the evaluation of facts about the world as an absolutely necessary step in any moral argument. In this sense PC is a formal principle that must stand behind any argument in the moral realm. The next question is whether there are rational means of assigning moral standing to specific consequences. If so, the particular premise of PC would be established and a logically impeccable moral imperative generated.

GP is a valuable logical adjunct to PC which, although depending upon PC for its moral force, states a relationship between applications of PC which is useful to bear in mind in moral discourse. Owing to its explicit emphasis upon the distributive aspects of moral decisions, it is particularly valuable in connection with the evaluation and justification of public policy, with giving discriptive meaning to "public interest."

Chapter Nine

MORAL RULES (I)

The utilitarian premises from which we have been working suggest that consideration of contextual facts and consequences occupy an important place in the process of establishing the particular premises of formal principles. But there are excellent reasons for thinking that examination of facts and consequences is not enough. Our starting point is the fact that ordinary moral discourse contains statements of a type not accounted for so far. Nothing has been said concerning the type of statement found in the Decalogue and other moral codes—statements we will call moral rules. It is possible that such rules do not play an important role in moral reasoning. Given their prominence in our discourse and our history, however, a theory that attempts to account for the logical structure of moral reasoning must begin with the hypothesis that moral rules are significant and their significance can be discovered and stated. Very little thought arouses the suspicion that rules such as "Stealing is wrong," "Thou shall not kill," and "Never say what is false" serve as aids in establishing the particular premises of moral principles.

I

The concept of "rule" has a variety of uses which must be kept distinct. Max Black has developed the following fourfold classification. (1) Uses for which "regulation" is an approximate synonym. Laws, traffic rules, and rules of games would be examples. (2) Uses for which "instruction" or "direction" would be approximate synonyms.

Black's examples are, "In solving quartic equations, first eliminate the cubic term," and, "Do not plant tomatoes until after the last frost." (3) Precept or maxim sense of rule. "It is a sound rule to pay one's debts"; "Put charity ahead of justice." (4) Uses for which "general truth" or "perceived uniformity" would be approximate synonyms. "People who smoke heavily suffer more bronchial and pulmonary disorders." Black admits that these distinctions are not sharp, but he argues persuasively for their utility. The breakdown will be sufficient for present purposes.[1] We will deal with rules in the sense of regularities first.

It has been suggested that a moral decision is one which attempts to take account of consequences. This provides the key to understanding the function of regularity-type rules in moral reasoning and discourse.[2] Hare contends that such rules are important for three reasons: (1) to make predictions concerning the consequences of behavior; (2) to make moral teaching possible; (3) to make nonarbitrary moral choices.

To take account of the consequences of prospective decisions we must make predictions. Unless we are clairvoyant, predictions can only rest upon experience. Where we have had no relevant experience, we can only guess, flip a coin, or, as we say, "act blindly." Whenever we do not act blindly, there is an important sense in which we act on the basis of a rule, on the basis of a regularity perceived in the course of our experience. The rule may be extremely ill-defined and informal in character. This is likely to be the case where we have had very little experience or where the matter at hand is complex and despite a considerable amount of experience we have yet to uncover significant reg-

[1] The discussion is to be found in Max Black, *Models and Metaphors* (Ithaca: Cornell University Press, 1962), especially pp. 109–15. It was originally published in an article entitled "Notes on the Meaning of 'Rule,'" in *Theoria*, Vol. 24, pp. 107–36, 139–61 (1958). For a very similar analysis see Kurt Baier, *The Moral Point of View* (Ithaca: Cornell University Press, 1958), especially pp. 122–7.

[2] Hare has dealt with this topic with great skill, and I will follow the main lines of his argument. It should be noted, however, that Hare does not distinguish between rules and principles. In the terminology of the present essay, the one *principle* which Hare discusses is U—which he calls a "thesis." He uses "principle" in a manner identical with the present use of "rule" in the sense of regularity. (He does not distinguish between different uses of either "principle" or "rule.") Hence the reader should make the appropriate translations in reading the quotations in the following discussion.

ularities. Some of our rules, on the other hand, are very precise, as is the case with scientific laws. The greater the precision of the rule, the more it will assist us in making predictions and decisions based on those predictions. We predict with great confidence in matters covered by scientific laws. In political and moral matters, our experience speaks more equivocally, prediction is hazardous, and our decisions are correspondingly more difficult. However ambiguous or indeterminate our experience and hence our rules, they are the only source of guidance we have concerning the consequences of our behavior. If it is true that a moral decision is one which considers consequences, moral decisions require rules.

The first point is the key to the relationship between rules and moral teaching. Just as the individual, in surveying his own experience, searches for regularities that will aid him in dealing with later cases, so the teacher seeks to pass on generalizations or rules that will aid the learner when he is no longer under tutelage, not descriptions of idiosyncratic or isolated facts. This is particularly the case when, as in moral life, the individual is learning to *do* something. As Hare says:

> . . . to learn to do anything is never to learn to do an individual act; it is always to learn to do acts of a certain kind in a certain situation; and this is to learn a principle. Thus, in learning to drive, I learn, not to change gear *now*, but to change gear when my engine makes a certain kind of noise. If this were not so, instruction would be of no use at all; for if all an instructor could do were to tell us to change gear *now*, he would have to sit beside us for the rest of our lives in order to tell us just when, on each occasion, to change gear.
>
> Thus without principles we could not learn anything whatever from our elders. This would mean that every generation would have to start from scratch and teach itself. But even if each generation were able to teach itself, it could not do so without principles; for self-teaching, like all other teaching, is the teaching of principles.[3]

The third point, that rules make nonarbitrary choices possible, summarizes the arguments concerning prediction and teaching. If *A* does X and we ask, "Why did you do that?", knowledge of a rule allows *A* to reply, "Because X leads to *Y* and I wanted to accomplish *Y*." The rule allows *A* to give a reason for doing what he did. To be

[3] R. M. Hare, *The Language of Morals* (London: Oxford University Press, 1952), pp. 60–61.

able to give a reason is one of the things we mean by nonarbitrary decisions.

II

Regularity-type rules account for only one of the respects in which we expect moral decisions to be nonarbitrary. In defending moral decisions, we must be able to say not only that the decision will lead to certain results, but that those results will be morally right or good. If rules are to offer further assistance in making nonarbitrary moral decisions, they must help us in evaluating as well as describing or predicting the consequences of those decisions. Rules of Type 1, regulations or laws, go farthest in this respect. In many circumstances, regulations are intended to provide a sufficient answer to the question of what we ought to do. Where a law or rule, passed or promulgated by a proper authority, has been established, we often regard it as a satisfactory reason for acting according to the rule. "Why did you do that?" "Because the law commands it." Between the commands of the state and the regulations of various subsidiary associations to which we belong (unions, churches, business organizations), a substantial share of our behavior is determined and justified in this way.

Despite their significance for behavior, regulation-type rules involve special considerations which limit their importance in the present context. To the extent that we justify obedience to a particular rule *on the ground that* it is promulgated by authority, the element of reflection about the consequences of the action, which is a part of moral decisions generally, is reduced. The point is not that it is entirely inappropriate to consider the consequences of actions commanded by law. This is the position of Hobbes, and it excludes the possibility of morally justifiable disobedience (except, in Hobbes's view, in the case of a command to submit to one's own death). Nor are we suggesting that the decision to establish or place oneself under authority is something other than a moral decision properly made by reflecting about consequences.

But one of the purposes of establishing a system of authority is to maximize uniformity of behavior. Individual decision on the basis of an assessment of consequences often reduces uniformity, and we buttress authoritative decisions with sanctions which discourage such assessment. The individual is free to consider consequences, but if his decision leads him to violate a regulation he must face the application of the consequences. For these reasons, laws and regulations play a distinctive role in moral discourse and do not enlighten us concerning the aspects of that discourse which is of central concern in this context.[4] We hasten to add, however, that these remarks do *not* apply to a decision to support or oppose measures proposed for adoption as laws or regulations. Such decisions—decisions as to whether measure *X* is in the public interest—are typical moral decisions, but rules of the law or regulation-type rules do not play an important part in making them.[5]

Rules in the "instruction sense" are also peripheral to the discourse of moral decision. They are best thought of as regularities that have been stated in the form of hypothetical imperatives. "Don't plant tomatoes until after the last frost," is a short way of saying "Whenever tomato plants undergo a frost they are damaged; therefore, if you don't want your tomato plants damaged, don't plant them until after the last frost of the season." As with any stated regularity, verification of the rule depends upon its being true that tomatoes are damaged by frost. But even where the regularity is verified, instruction-type rules are useful only if the hypothetical applies to the individual in question. If I don't care whether my tomato plants are damaged or not, if I am planting them solely because I like the feel and the smell of moist spring earth, I am untouched by the imperative that the rule generates. Because the fate of my tomato plants is ordinarily my affair, it makes

[4] Despite these remarks, we do not agree with the view, argued by Kant and T. H. Green, that attempts to "legislate morality" will be self-defeating. Individuals who are legally subject to the commands of a government might choose to conform to them for reasons other than their authoritative source. The fact that a specific behavior is required or prohibited by law does not mean that everyone subject to the law behaves in the required manner because it is required. This is obvious in the case of *dis*obedience, but it is possible in the case of behavior which accords with the law as well. Furthermore, as Aristotle said, a man might first behave in a certain manner owing to the commands of the state, but over time such behavior might become a part of his character so that he continues to behave that way for moral reasons—whether the law remains. See *Nicomachean Ethics*, esp. II, 1.

[5] The foregoing discussion will be taken up again when consideration is given to the controversy between "act utilitarians" and "rule utilitarians." We will argue that the apparent strengths of the rule-utilitarian position depend upon a failure to distinguish between regulation-type rules and precept-type rules. Or more precisely, upon improperly placing some precept-type rules into the regulation-type category.

no sense to speak of legal or moral obligations to live up to the rule. Hence instruction-type rules do not contribute to finding reasoned answers to the question, "What, morally speaking, ought I to do in this case?"

III

Many of the reasons given for the importance of regularity-type rules in moral thinking apply to precept-type rules as well. Just as it is valuable to have past experience of consequences codified into easily applied rules, so it is useful to have such rules with respect to the moral character of recurrent types of consequences. To have the rule, "Lying regularly diminishes faith in one's word," allows the prediction that such lying will continue to do so in the future; it facilitates the task of anticipating the consequences of any prospective lie. To have the further rule, "The moral consequences of lying are bad, and therefore lying is wrong," facilitates reaching a decision not to lie on many of the countless occasions when lying is a possible form of behavior. If we try to imagine a moral life in which literally every moral decision has to be thought through from start to finish, we can readily appreciate the utility of such rules.

John Stuart Mill has a passage, akin to a remark of Hare's quoted above, which applies specifically to precept-type rules.

> . . . defenders of utility often find themselves called upon to reply to such objections as this—that there is not time, previous to action, for calculating and weighing the effects of any line of conduct on the general happiness. This is exactly as if any one were to say that it is impossible to guide our conduct by Christianity, because there is not time, on every occasion on which anything has to be done, to read through the Old and New Testaments. The answer to the objection is, that there has been ample time, namely, the whole past duration of the human species. During all that time, mankind have been learning by experience the tendencies of actions; on which experience all the prudence, as well as all the morality of life, are dependent. People talk as if the commencement of this course of experience had been put off, and as if at the moment when some man feels tempted to meddle with the property or life of another, he had to begin considering for the first time whether murder and theft are injurious to human happiness.[6]

[6] *Utilitarianism* (New York: Everyman's Library, 1951), pp. 28–9.

In addition to freeing the individual for more difficult and less recurrent decisions, rules provide reasons for actions and decisions which help to render the latter nonarbitrary. There are difficulties involved with this point. How are precept-type rules distinguished from regulations, and why do decisions made in accordance with them not cease to be moral decisions? But it is a fact that we sometimes regard the citation of a rule as an adequate answer to the question "Why did you behave that way?" "Why didn't you avoid embarrassment all around by telling a lie?" "Because lying is wrong." Rules also introduce an element of consistency, continuity, and predictability in moral life. This in turn, as conservative theorists have always emphasized, makes possible the development of intricate patterns of expectation in society; without such patterns social life itself, and certainly a developed moral life, would be impossible.

IV

The evidence concerning the significance of rules in moral discourse is so weighty that a number of philosophers have argued that rules are the dominant ingredient or component in moral practice. The most important version of this argument is known as "rule utilitarianism."[7] Rule utilitarianism attempts to save utilitarian ethical theory from the long-standing charge that it cannot account for, indeed is in flagrant conflict with, the importance of rules and obedience to rules in our moral practice. By insisting that the moral character of an action depends upon the consequences of that action, its critics have long maintained, utilitarianism has undercut moral obligations and fostered opportunism. Rule utilitarians are inclined to disagree with this interpretation of "classical" utilitarian theory.[8] Whatever the historical facts, they insist that utilitarianism is compatible with full recognition of the significance of moral rules. We will argue that rule utilitarianism over-

[7] The basic writings produced by this school of thought are listed in the bibliographies of Richard Brandt, *Ethical Theory* (Englewood Cliffs, N. J.: Prentice-Hall, Inc., 1959), and Singer. See also the notes in J. J. C. Smart, "Extreme and Restricted Utilitarianism," *Philosophical Quarterly* (1956), and Smart's later *An Outline of a System of Utilitarian Ethics* (Adelaide: Melbourne University Press, 1961).

[8] See especially J. O. Urmson, "The Interpretation of the Philosophy of J. S. Mill," *Philosophical Quarterly*, Vol. III, p. 33 (1953).

estimates the difficulties in "act utilitarianism" and that its attempted improvement upon utilitarian theory rests upon confusions and leads to more serious difficulties than those which it seeks to resolve.

The question at issue in the following discussion will be whether an aphorism of Wittgenstein, "When I obey a rule, I do not choose. I obey it blindly," is applicable to precept-type rules. But that aphorism suggests two very different questions which must be distinguished. The first is, "Do men, as a matter of behavioral fact, act blindly or without reflection when they act in accord with precept-type rules?" The second is, "Does the logical structure of precept-type rules require that men act blindly or without reflection when they act in accord with such rules?" The following discussion will be concerned exclusively with the latter question.

A leading statement of the rule-utilitarian position is presented by John Rawls in his paper, "Two Concepts of Rules." [9] Rawls's position conflicts much less sharply with the present argument than do other formulations available.[10] He does not contend that all obedience to moral rules is "blind" or "without reflection," but attempts to delimit a certain type of moral rule with a logic that severely restricts the grounds on which the moral agent can choose to conform with it or not. If it is possible to demonstrate fatal difficulties in his position, we will have disposed of the less circumscribed theories as well.

The basis of Rawls's position is a distinction between two concepts of rules, the "summary" concept and the "practice" concept.[11] These two concepts correspond to two types of rules found in legal and moral practice, but Rawls contends that the summary concept dominates philosophical discussion of rules and is regularly and improperly used in analyzing practice-type rules. This confusion lies at the bottom of many of the standard criticisms of utilitarianism, and when it is eliminated those criticisms lose their force.

Rawls's summary concept of rules corresponds closely to the conception we have used in discussing precept-type moral rules. Rules are summations of experience that provide guides or aids to decision making and action. They depend upon regularities in the consequences and

[9] *Philosophical Review*, Vol. 64, No. 3 (1955).

[10] See, for example, A. I. Melden, "Action," *Philosophical Review*, Vol. 65, No. 1 (1956).

[11] He defines a "practice" at *op. cit.*, p. 3.

evaluation of particular classes of action. The obligation to obey them stems from the fact that the consequences of obeying them are preferable to the consequences of any alternative action. Where this is not so, the rule is either inapplicable or "defeated" by the special circumstances.[12] Hence it is open to the individual to depart from the rule whenever following it does not meet the utilitarian test.[13] Rawls thinks that this is a perfectly valid conception which accounts for a familiar type of rule.

The practice concept corresponds closely to regulations. Practice-type rules are not summations of experience, rather, they establish the conditions prerequisite to having certain kinds of experience. The contention is not that experience plays no part in establishing practice-type rules. Rawls insists that utilitarian considerations are relevant to establishing and/or defending a practice (as practice), and utilitarian considerations necessarily depend upon experience. But the rules defining the practice are prior to any experience of the type defined by the practice: "There cannot be a particular case of an action falling under a rule of a practice unless there is the practice." An individual cannot strike out in a baseball game without the prior existence of the rules which define the practice of playing baseball. Most important, the logic of the practice concept prohibits appeal to general utilitarian considerations in justifying or attacking specific actions taken under the practice. If we ask a baseball player why he retired from the batter's box after the third strike was called, the only answer available to him is that the rules under which the game is played require that he do so. For him to recite and evaluate the consequences of retiring or not would demonstrate that he had ceased playing baseball and had taken up something else—probably philosophy.

Rawls does not argue that the practice concept of rules demands or allows unreflective conformity to the rules of a practice. There are recognized exceptions to and defenses against most rules ("The catcher dropped the third strike"), and applying them is often difficult ("Was it fouled off or not?"). He goes so far as to agree (or at least to appear to agree) with what he describes as the utilitarian view "that

[12] I borrow the latter term from H. L. A. Hart's "The Ascription of Responsibility and Rights," Antony Flew, editor, *Logic and Language*, First Series (Oxford: Basil Blackwell, 1951). I will discuss the notion in detail below.

[13] See Rawls, *op. cit.*, pp. 22–4, for a description of the summary concept.

every practice should admit the defense that the consequences of abiding by it would have been extremely severe."[14] But he insists that such defenses "cannot be [regarded as] an exception to a rule of a practice. An exception is rather a qualification or a further specification of the rule."[15] Hence, the presence of exceptions "must not be confused with the general option to weigh each particular case on utilitarian grounds which critics of utilitarianism have thought it necessarily to involve."[16]

The similarities between rules defining a practice (and the practice concept of rules derived from them) and regulation-type rules are obvious. Rawls himself suggests the close correspondence between the two. Virtually all of his illustrations are taken from situations involving regulations—for example, games—and in the final footnote of the paper he says:

> As I have already stated, it is not always easy to say where the [practice] conception is appropriate. Nor do I care to discuss at this point the general sorts of cases to which it does apply except to say that one should not take it for granted that it applies to many so-called "moral rules." It is my feeling that relatively few actions of the moral life are defined by practices and that the practice conception is more relevant to understanding legal and legal-like arguments than it is to the more complex sort of moral arguments.[17]

To the extent that practice-type rules are identical with regulation-type rules, the differences between Rawls's argument and the present position are primarily terminological.[18] But Rawls does contend that a fundamental moral rule, the rule that promises ought to be kept, is a practice-type rule, and that its logic must be understood in the manner summarized above. Since the rule concerning promises is clearly a moral rule, this contention creates difficulties for the present argument.

That promising is a practice, Rawls says, "is beyond question . . .

[14] *Ibid.*, p. 17.
[15] *Ibid.*, p. 27.
[16] *Ibid.*, p. 18.
[17] *Ibid.*, p. 32.
[18] I have two substantive disagreements: The first is that Rawls's handling of the question of defenses and exceptions ignores the points which Hart makes about "defeasibility" in his paper, "The Ascription of Responsibility and Rights." The second is that his view would require qualification in order to deal with the problem of justifiable disobedience to the law.

[T]his is shown by the fact that the form of words, I promise, is a performative utterance which presupposes the stage-setting of the practice and proprieties defined by it."[19] This argument begs the question at issue. It is true that such an utterance requires a "stage-setting" or general pattern of usage which gives it meaning for other agents. (This is one of the major contentions of the Melden article cited above.) But the need for a stage-setting scarcely proves that the setting can only be supplied by a practice as Rawls has defined it. A setting is required for the use of words such as lying, stealing, and many others, but this hardly shows that the rules providing the setting are practices in Rawls's sense.[20] This argument sits poorly with Rawls's view that few moral rules fall under the practice concept. What Rawls must show is that the setting which makes "I promise" meaningful can be provided only by a practice-type rule. This he has not done.

Rawls attempts to buttress his first contention with a second although closely related argument.

> It would be absurd to interpret the rules about promising in accordance with the summary conception. It is absurd to say, for example, that the rule that promises should be kept could have arisen from its being found in past cases to be best on the whole to keep one's promises; for unless there were already the understanding that one keeps one's promises as part of the practice itself there couldn't have been any cases of promising.[21]

This appears to be a purely logical point—and one of considerable force. But it makes a crucial and dubious assumption about the history or genesis of the rule. The key words are "unless there were already." We can readily concede that it is impossible to test the wisdom of a rule until the rule has come into effect. But this leaves open the question of how it came into effect.

[19] Rawls, *op. cit.*, p. 70. The notion "performative utterance" stems from the work of the late J. L. Austin. See the paper of that title in his *Philosophical Papers, loc. cit.* But see also his *How To Do Things with Words*, J. O. Urmson, editor (London: Oxford University Press, 1962). In the latter work he abandons the terminology and modifies the thought which it represented.

[20] In discussing the same point, Austin used the word "convention"; a convention is necessary for a performative to be successfully uttered. Some of Austin's examples involve regulations—for example, marriage—and some precepts—for example, insulting. See *Philosophical Papers*, pp. 224–5, and *How To Do Things with Words*, pp. 14, 26 ff.

[21] Rawls, *op. cit.*, p. 30.

Rawls's practice concept involves rules that are "laid down" or "promulgated." (Recall his words "legal or legal-like.") Such rules are "*set up* for various reasons, but one of them is that in many areas of conduct each person's deciding what to do on utilitarian grounds case by case leads to confusion . . . As an alternative one realizes that what is required is the *establishment* of a practice, the *specification* of a *new* form of activity." [22] What is there in the logic of Rawls's second argument that requires the rule to be "*set up*" in this way? The logical requirement would be satisfied if the notion of a promise had evolved slowly over time and out of individual behaviors, gradually obtained prominence and significance as an important instrument in social life, and then progressively attained the status of generating a moral obligation. On purely logical grounds, Rawls's arguments for the practice status of the moral rule against breaking promises are not convincing.

Let us apply some of the tests Black has taught us for differentiating regulations from other types of rules. If the rule is of the regulation-type, we should be able to ask of it, "Who made it and on what authority?"; "Who punishes violations?"; "Who has the authority to amend the rule?" If asked these questions regarding certain legal analogues to the rule about promises, such as the law of contract, we could provide a precise answer. We could point to legislative acts or court cases or decisions of administrative tribunals, and we could describe what we mean when we say that such bodies are authoritative. But we could scarcely say the same of the moral rule against breaking promises. Is it appropriate, then, to speak of the rule as being *set up*, or as involving the *specification* of a *new* form of activity? Surely these words are inappropriate.[23]

[22] *Ibid.*, p. 24. Italics supplied.

[23] Note Rawls's admission that the "rules defining promising are not codified, and that one's conception of what they are necessarily depends on one's moral training." (*Ibid.*, pp. 30–31.) Compare this with his requirement that "It is the mark of a practice that being taught how to engage in it involves being instructed in the rules which define it, and that appeal is made to those rules to correct the behavior of those engaged in it. Those engaged in a practice recognize the rules as defining it. The rules cannot be taken as simply describing how those engaged in the practice in fact behave; it is not simply that they act as if they were obeying the rules. Thus it is essential to the notion of a practice that the rules are publicly known and understood as definitive; and it is essential also that the rules of a practice can be taught and can be acted upon to yield a coherent practice." (*Ibid.*,

It is apparent that the rule about promises meets few if any of the requirements of a practice-type rule. There is nothing in the logic of this rule prohibiting use of the general utilitarian defense as an excuse against or justification for conforming to it in specific cases. Rather, there is much in the logic of the rule, and of moral rules in general, that requires the utilitarian defense to be available. This point is of considerable relevance to the rule-utilitarian—act-utilitarian controversy and to the more general question of the role of consequences in moral decisions.

It will be helpful to make use of an argument developed by H. L. A. Hart in his paper, "The Ascription of Responsibility and Rights." [24] Hart shows that many of the concepts and rules that are the basis of legal claims are "defeasible" concepts. We can understand or explain their operation in a legal system only if we understand not only the conditions which must be satisfied if a judge is to sustain a claim based upon them (set of conditions *A*), but also the set of conditions (*B*) which, despite the presence of *A*, may defeat or weaken the claim. Hart illustrates this notion with the example of contract. The set of conditions (*A*) required for the existence of a valid contract are "at least two *parties*, an *offer* by one, *acceptance* by the other, a *memorandum* in writing in some cases and *consideration* . . ." [25] But the presence of these conditions does not guarantee the existence of a valid contract; it does not guarantee that it will be proper for a court to sustain a claim based upon that contract. "For these conditions, although necessary, are not always sufficient . . . [and the student] has still to learn what can defeat a claim that there is a valid contract, even though all these conditions are satisfied." [26] The key words are "even though all these conditions [*A*] are satisfied." Hart is contending against the view that concepts, such as "contract," can be reduced to a set of necessary and sufficient conditions so that whenever a claim under that concept is valid it is because those conditions are present and whenever one or more of them is absent, the claim is therefore invalid. The judge cannot simply test the facts against a pre-established list of conditions. He

p. 24.) On the points just covered see H. L. A. Hart's excellent analysis in his "Legal and Moral Obligation," in A. I. Melden, editor, *Essays in Moral Philosophy* (Seattle: University of Washington Press, 1958), pp. 102–103.

[24] *Op. cit.*, pp. 102–3.

[25] *Ibid.*, p. 148. Italics Hart's.

[26] *Ibid.*, p. 148.

must also determine whether, *in the case at hand*, there are any circumstances or conditions that will serve to defeat or weaken the claim despite the presence of *A*.[27]

Hart argues that a number of nonlegal concepts operate in a manner similar to "contract." When we "ascribe" responsibility or rights to individuals, or when we describe a behavior as an "action," we do not simply examine the facts to determine whether a set of positive conditions is present. Even where such conditions are present, we must make a judgment whether other conditions obtain that serve to defeat the claim of a right or nullify the ascription of responsibility or action. In some types of cases, especially in the law, the available defenses are well worked out and carefully catalogued. In others, little codification or systematization is available. In the latter, the only generalization we can make is that the concept is defeasible and we must make a judgment as to whether, despite the presence of *A*, there are other factors present which modify or render inappropriate the ascription in question.

The notion of defeasibility is illuminating when applied to moral rules.[28] Moral rules function in much the same manner as legal concepts or concepts such as "responsibility" and "rights." Not only do they stamp an act or a set of conditions with an evaluation or designation; they also serve as a guide in deciding whether it is appropriate to designate an act or set of conditions in a particular manner. The concept of contract is both a classification to set a phenomenon apart from others and a set of criteria developed to determine whether X falls into that classification. Similarly, a moral rule both designates a type of behavior "right" or "wrong" and provides criteria for deciding whether *X* falls under that designation. (Or, more accurately perhaps, a set of criteria develop around and in connection with the concept.)

[27] Note the similarities between Hart's notion of defeasibility and the earlier arguments regarding the contextual dimensions of the descriptive meaning of "public interest."

[28] Consider the following sentences from Hart's "Legal and Moral Obligation," *op. cit.*, p. 102. "Morals, like law, may have principles of 'public policy' and render 'void' a promise that from the start involved doing something patently immoral; but we should distinguish from such cases those where we subsequently discover moral reasons (perhaps in changed circumstances) against doing what we have promised to do. In these latter cases we have a moral obligation arising from the promise, but one that we consider in the light of other principles we ought not to carry out."

Thinking of rules in this way is suggestive concerning the thesis that they must be obeyed "blindly." [29] If we are to follow a rule "without reflection," the rule must be well enough defined so that it is clear when it is applicable and when it is not. Some legal concepts satisfy this requirement. Hart presents well-defined criteria for a valid contract. This is possible because the law is a highly organized system that keeps records, communicates extensively internally, and is subject to comment and criticism. Yet even in a legal system the application of concepts such as contract is not always a simple matter that can be carried out in a mechanical, unreflective manner. That it is often a relatively mechanical matter is one of the great achievements of legal systems. But we would not say that it is only when it is simple and mechanical that a rule is being followed; difficulty, complexity, and need for "judgment" do not indicate that the court is not following a rule or is acting in an arbitrary manner. Creative application of the criteria developed in the past to a ceaseless flow of new situations and problems is the essence of judging, the essence of the paradigm case of deciding on the basis of established rules. To suggest that it can be done "without reflection" is to misunderstand one of the impressive achievements of our civilization.

If reflection, judgment, and creativity are required in applying legal concepts and rules, how much more must this be the case in following the comparatively unorganized, unsystematized, recordless body of moral rules. Have any of our moral rules been codified and systematized to the degree that centuries of decisions have codified "contract"? That there has been some "codification" (notice that the language is obviously metaphorical) is a precondition of saying that there is a rule. There is regularly no doubt that we are, let us say, telling a lie and telling it under conditions such that the moral rule against lying condemns us. Similarly, moral rules are often applied with a rigidity and lack of reflection that could not be justified in the light of the clarity of the rule or its relationship to the situation at hand. But these are not the only situations in which a rule has been violated or followed.

[29] The discussion of this point is not intended as a criticism of Rawls. His position does not create the following difficulties. I present these considerations because they are applicable to less restricted forms of rule utilitarianism and because they are enlightening about the notion of applying and following a rule.

Where the rule and its exceptions are not clear, the *only* available alternative is to examine the *consequences* of the actions. We praise the individual whose moral behavior accords with moral rules, who acts in a "principled" manner, but we are critical of the person who does so mechanically (slavishly?) or without reflection. Although no man, to paraphrase Burke, can draw a stroke between the confines of moralism, principled behavior, and opportunism, the fact that we have these distinctions is weighty evidence that moral rules cannot properly be followed without reflection—any more than they can be ignored.

The defeasible character of moral rules reinforces these conclusions.[30] The rule that lying is wrong is ordinarily defeated when a lie is genuinely necessary to save a life. The rule against taking lives is defeated when taking a life is necessary to save other lives or to avoid widespread and intense human suffering. Rawls views these departures as part of the rule itself; as exceptions which serve to specify the rule in greater detail. This is exactly the mistake Hart has attacked, especially if we subsume the exceptions under *A*. It is attractive to do so because certain exceptions are well established and come to mind whenever we reflect upon the rule. But Rawls's position obscures the basic point involved in saying that the rule is defeasible, the point that rules cannot be reduced to a list of necessary and sufficient conditions. This is dangerous because it blinds us to the fact that the rule may be properly defeated in other circumstances which are uncommon and not recognized as part of the rule. Thinking in terms of the defeasibility of the rule allows us to account for the well-established exceptions and to remain open to the possibility that new types of defeating circumstances will arise. In general, it instructs about what is involved in the notion of following a moral rule.

The argument against Rawls's version of rule utilitarianism has been made in abstract terms. The discussion will conclude with an attempt to illustrate the above points with an example. The example is contrived, but we hope not unrealistic.

My close friend Max is not feeling well, and I promise to take him to see a doctor. Max is to see a specialist who has a very heavy schedule of appointments, and missing the appointment will mean a long wait before another can be obtained. As I drive to Max's house to fulfill my promise, a dog, the cherished pet of another close friend Jones, runs in

[30] The following points are applicable to Rawls's position.

front of my car and is injured. I examine the dog and conclude that it will die if it does not receive immediate attention from a veterinarian. There is no one around to aid me. I know that there is a veterinarian's office close by, but I also know that if I take the dog there I will be unable to fulfill my promise to Max. What is relevant to deciding what to do?

If Rawls is correct, the one thing I cannot do (without acting immorally) is to consider the consequences of the alternative available to me and decide which is best given the circumstances. Having placed myself under the practice-type rule concerning promises, my only recourse is to determine what the rule requires and do that. Later, when either of my friends asks me why I chose as I did, I can only reply, "Because that is what the rule required me to do." If I choose to abandon the dog, and Jones asks me why I left the poor beast on the roadside to die, the only reply permitted me is that the rule concerning promises required that I do so. As Rawls says, "One doesn't so much justify one's particular action as explain, or show, that it is in accordance with the practice." [31]

Rawls does not suggest that "following the rule" is always a simple matter. Determination whether giving aid to dogs under such circumstances is an established exception to the rule will be complex business. Simply to state a specific problem in some detail, of course, is to bring home the significance of the practical problems discussed above.[32] Waiving practical difficulties, the point to be emphasized is that the decision must be based upon and explained in terms of decisions made in the past. Only those decisions, and not any independent weighing of the circumstances at hand, can provide morally adequate grounds for a conclusion.

It would contradict much of what has been said to suggest that we should, or even that we could, ignore the experience and decisions of

[31] Rawls, *op. cit.*, p. 27.

[32] In this case, where would one go to learn the rule? In the case of a regulation, one would go to an authoritative body which, if the point had not been covered previously, would make a ruling. But Rawls admits that there is no authoritative body which has jurisdiction over the moral rule against breaking promises. One must decide for himself. This is one of the things we mean when we say that keeping promises is a *moral* rule. The importance of this is obvious when we consider the reponse of our interrogator. If there is no accepted authority in the matter, why should he regard my appeal to precedent as valid? What is there to convince him that my reading of the rule is superior to his if the two happen to conflict?

the past. But it is one thing to look upon them as the only adequate ground for decision and quite another to look to them for *guidance* as to what to do now. The rule would teach us that breaking promises ordinarily has the effect of undermining confidence and that such results are disapproved because they hamper a number of important human activities. Knowing this, a presumption is created that similar consequences and concomitant disapproval would follow from breaking the promise in this case. In the absence of strong evidence to rebut this presumption, the rule would provide grounds for a decision. But it would be our duty to discover whether such rebutting evidence exists in *this* case.

Suppose I choose to aid the dog and explain the breaking of my promise to Max.

> I knew you were counting on me, but there was that dog . . . and I can't tell you how much Jones loves that dog. If I had left Rover he would have been dead in no time. I know that I promised you, but Jake next door has a car, and if worst came to worst you could have called a cab; you said it wasn't an emergency. I'm sorry to have let you down, but it just seemed the thing to do.

Would it be the case that the breaking of my promise would undermine confidence? We cannot deny the possibility. Max might never trust me again, and he might head straight for the local saloon complaining bitterly about my conduct. "Don't ever trust Smith; he'd rather help a dog than keep his promise." And this might lead Max and his cronies to conclude that you can't trust anyone any more, which might lead to . . . etc. (Even if this were the case, it would be necessary to weigh the consequences of this breakdown in confidence against the pain and death of the dog and the unhappiness suffered by Jones. This is a good example of how values intersect and have to be referred one to the other in the process of moral decision making.)

But surely we would not expect such a result. Max and many others might disagree with my decision. But it would be difficult for them to say, on the basis of this incident, that I did not take promises seriously or that I disregard them on purely arbitrary or self-serving grounds. It would be the plausibility of the latter charges, not the breaking of the promise, that we would expect to undermine confidence in my promises in general.

Consider the case in which I decide to keep the promise. "Terribly sorry about Rover," I say on meeting Jones returning from the animal cemetery. "I just couldn't take time to help him because I had promised to pick up Max at ten o'clock." In Rawls's view this is where we stop. Or at best we go into a general dissertation about why keeping promises is a moral rule. But unless Jones is a confirmed rule utilitarian of the Rawls ilk (or perhaps a Rossian or a Kantian), he is not likely to find this very satisfying. After all, Rover is in his grave. "I guess Max had something pretty important up?" we can imagine him saying. "Well, he had an appointment with a doctor." (What if it were a dentist? a barber? a shoemaker?) "Max is pretty sick?" "Well, not so bad, but the doctor is hard to see. If you miss an appointment you wait at least a month for another." "Oh," says Jones, fingering Rover's collar. We can imagine the discussion continuing through ambulances, neighbors, and perhaps on to the respective weight to be assigned to human inconvenience and risk as against pain and death to dogs and sorrow to their owners.

The point of the example can be summarized by noting the strangeness of Rawls's view that one "doesn't so much justify . . . as explain" a decision to conform to certain moral rules. What is wanted, whether by Max or Jones, is a justification. Their position is that Smith has made a moral choice and one of the characteristics of moral choices is that they affect others and hence must be justifiable to others. They hold further that justification involves presenting reasoned grounds for the decision, that presenting reasoned grounds requires consideration of the consequences of the action in question, and that this is impossible without examination of the facts and circumstances in the case at hand. In their view, it is *this* decision that has been made and requires justification.

Everything said about following a moral rule stems from the fundamental proposition that the moral character of an act depends first and foremost upon its consequences. Rules have a place in moral reasoning because there are discoverable regularities in the consequences of our actions and in our evaluation of those consequences. Rules are defeasible and cannot be applied without reflection about consequences, because in moral life our regularities are imperfect, and we must be alert to morally significant departures from regularities, and imaginative and creative in adapting our conduct to the departures. These considerations provide a case against the notion that the logic of following a moral rule requires that we follow such rules blindly or without reflection. They also constitute a case for the fundamental point that consideration of consequences is a necessary part of moral reasoning and moral decision making.

V

Emphasizing *this* decision and *these* facts and circumstances inevitably suggests a crude kind of opportunistic ethic. It raises the spectre of the traditional objection that utilitarianism is unable to account for and in fact serves to undermine the obligation which in practice is generated by promises. (This is exactly the objection against which Rawls sought to guard utilitarianism.) It is impossible to deny the force of these objections entirely. Emphasis upon circumstances and particulars *is intended to* diminish the sanctity of rules and *is intended to* give the individual agent freedom and flexibility in applying and adapting rules to particular cases. We have tried to show, however, that even mildly formalistic theories such as Rawls's cannot account for the contextual character of moral decisions and the particular nature of the requirement that we be able to justify the decisions we make. Therefore, our first reply to these objections is that the distortion (if it be such) created by the present theory is much less serious than that produced by theories which impute greater sanctity to rules. But there are other replies at our disposal as well.

The present account is consistent with the demand that moral decisions be "principled" in the sense demanded by the generalization or universalization principle. Whenever the second particular premise of that principle is satisfied with regard to two persons or situations, a previous decision is binding upon a later one.

In addition, a number of replies traditional to nonrule utilitarianism are available. The most prominent of these argues that one of the factors to be considered in any decision is the effect of that decision upon the general pattern of obedience to rules. Will breaking this promise undermine the general practice of keeping promises? If so even if there are grounds for thinking that the consequences, in this case in its narrower dimensions, will be better if the promise is broken, it ought not to be broken. This argument obtains enormous weight because of the very great importance of stability, continuity, and a consistent pattern of satisfaction of expectations in human affairs generally and moral life in particular. But the argument must be handled very carefully. It cannot be *assumed* that breaking *this* promise will undermine promise-keeping in general. There is a presumption that such will be the case. If there were not, we could not say that we had a rule covering the matter. But if, given the circumstances of the case, there is weighty evidence for thinking that it will have no such effect, this consideration ceases to be relevant.

The last point leads directly to another reason for keeping promises and for cultivating a general habit of conforming to existing moral rules, a reason which stems directly from the fundamental fact that a moral decision is a decision which considers consequences. It might be called the "wisdom of the species" argument. Moral rules derive much of their force from the fact that they are *not* promulgated at a given moment to meet a specific problem; they are a summation or gathering together of the fruits of the experience of generations of men in countless types of situations. It would not be unreasonable to believe that this vast experience uncovered the consequences of a type of action with a thoroughness difficult for the individual to equal or surpass on his own. Faced with a judgment regarding the consequences of an action, the individual must ask himself whether, recognizing the complexity of human affairs and the limits of his personal resources, he is justified in acting contrary to a rule that rests upon so much more vast an experience than his own. We have argued that the possibility can never be eliminated, that moral rules, in Baier's language, are only "presumptively" binding,[33] that they are defeasible or rebuttable in specific cases. The alternative is to adopt a rule-worshiping conformism that would commit us to moral stagnation. But to insist upon the defeasibility of moral rules is scarcely to deny their relevance or to concede that the utilitarian is bound by his theory to treat them with less than the enormous respect they deserve.[34]

[33] See Kurt Baier, *op. cit.*, p. 193.

[34] There is an analogy (but only that!) between moral rules and scientific laws. Both can be thought of as summations of previous experience. As such, both provide the best single source of guidance for further activity. But both are rebuttable or defeasible when new evidence arises which contradicts them. To ignore moral rules in making moral decisions would be analogous to starting anew on every occasion on which we wanted to understand nature. But to suggest that moral rules are indefeasible, or that we can depart from a moral rule only if we are prepared to overthrow the rule, would be analogous to suggesting that we ought to rest content with the scientific principles we have, or that we can alter or modify a scientific principle only if we are prepared to abandon it.

Chapter Ten

MORAL RULES (II)

I

Precept-type moral rules are summations of experience, statements of regularities in our experience. But they involve two types of regularities, only one of which is of concern in this chapter. First, they involve regularities of the type, "Whenever X, Y: whenever a lie is told, confidence is undermined." These are matters of fact, and we speak of verifying, not justifying, them. Second, precept-type moral rules involve a regularity in the sense that they ordinarily receive a specific evaluation. "Undermining confidence is ordinarily undesirable," "lying is ordinarily wrong." This too can be a matter of fact. "Is it the case that men ordinarily regard undermining confidence as undesirable?" "Is it true that men ordinarily regard lying as wrong?" Here again we speak of verification, not justification, but we might speak of justification as well. Having answered the question of descriptive ethics just stated we might ask: "Are men justified in thinking that undermining confidence is undesirable?" "Are men justified in regarding lying as wrong?" [1] These questions are not questions of fact, but questions of

[1] We might also ask, "Should men regard lying as wrong?" whether men so regard it. It is possible to ask questions of justification independent of questions of behavior. Note, however, that it would be impossible to ask questions of justification without having first answered questions of the first type mentioned, that is, questions about consequences. We cannot evaluate an action until we know what its consequences are. This applies both to evaluations of particular actions and the more general evaluations which we call moral rules.

evaluation and justification. The issue now before us is whether, or to what extent, it is possible to provide reasoned answers to such questions.

The category "precept-type moral rules" contains a variety of subtypes, and the problem of justification varies somewhat from one type to the next. Singer distinguishes between (1) fundamental moral rules, (2) local rules, and (3) neutral rules or norms.[2] Fundamental rules are comprehensive, general, not dependent upon specific contexts, and so important that "without them no civilized society would survive and few goods could be achieved." [3] Examples are the rules against breaking promises, lying, stealing, and killing. Local rules apply fundamental rules to specialized contexts or regulate aspects of specialized situations, for example, business or professional communities.[4] Neutral rules are of the "drive on the right" variety. They occur where behavior must be regularized but where there is little or nothing to choose between various possible rules. (It would be just as well to drive on the left as long as everyone did.)

The basic question is whether reasoned justifications can be provided for fundamental moral rules. If this is possible, justifications for local or neutral rules would be relatively simple. Our procedure will be to take a particular rule and see what can be said in defense of regarding it as morally obligatory. Singer offers a two-sentence defense of the rule against lying that will provide a starting point. "Lying is wrong because of what would happen if everyone lied. It would be nothing short of disastrous if everyone were to lie whenever he wished, if lying became the rule and truth-telling the exception . . ." [5] This statement would profit from specification and amplification. In

[2] As one of several other systems of classification, see Nowell-Smith's distinctions between "superior" and "subordinate" rules, with the former category further divided into rules creating "duties of beneficence" and those creating "duties of justice." P. H. Nowell-Smith, *Ethics* (Baltimore, Md.: Penguin Books Inc., 1954) pp. 230–32.

[3] The quotation is from J. D. Mabbot, "Moral Rules," *Proceedings of the British Academy* (London: Oxford University Press, 1953), Vol. 39, pp. 109–10. Quoted with approval by Singer, *op. cit.*, p. 113.

[4] For a good account of local rules (without using that terminology) see H. L. A. Hart, "Legal and Moral Obligation," in A. I. Melden, editor, *Essays In Moral Philosophy* (Seattle: University of Washington Press, 1958), pp. 103–4.

[5] Marcus George Singer, *Generalization in Ethics* (New York: Alfred A. Knopf, Inc., 1960), p. 121.

particular, the consequences regarded as disastrous could be discussed in greater detail. But the consequences of lying are widely appreciated, and most of us would agree that they could fairly be termed "disastrous"; therefore, Singer's brevity seems to pose no serious problems.[6] But even if Singer's formulation is adequate for everyday purposes, its lack of specificity immediately lands us in philosophical hot water. He points to certain facts and then applies an evaluative adjective. But the issue in question is exactly whether he is justified in applying that adjective.[7]

This is the point at which the proponent of the "moral decisions and choices are ultimately arbitrary" school of thought is apt to leap triumphantly into the fray. "After pages and pages of skirting the issue," he is likely to say, "we have finally reached a real moral question: is lying good or evil? Now by your own admission, a moral 'ought' can never be validly derived from an 'is.' Also on your own admission, consequences are a necessary part of moral decisions, and

[6] This example points to one of the reasons that moral rules can readily be thought to be self-evident. Such rules generally refer to familiar aspects of human behavior, and societies tend to instill and human beings to adopt common attitudes toward recurrent phenomena. Hence the rules seldom require or receive detailed analysis or justification, and a request for such an analysis seems strange and unnecessary, thus readily prompting the view that the rules are self-evident. But Singer's formulation is correct. If a rule is justifiable, it is justifiable because of the consequences of the behavior which it commands or forbids. See David Hume, *Enquiry Concerning the Principles of Morals,* III, II (Henry D. Aiken, editor, Hume's *Moral and Political Philosophy,* p. 201. (New York: Hafner, 1948). However strange the request may seem, we must always be able to adduce and evaluate the consequences of the behavior when the rule is challenged. We are forced to do this in periods of rapid social change when accepted rules are called into question. But if we are properly fulfilling our duties as moral teachers, we also do so when we pass our moral rules on to our children. This is one reason that consideration of the probems of moral teaching is one of the most effective ways to advance our understanding of both morals and ethics. See Hare, *The Language of Morals,* (London: Oxford University Press, 1952), pp. 74–78. See also Hare's excellent discussion of why moral principles cannot be self-evident. (*Ibid.,* pp. 38–44.)

[7] Singer emphasizes that the rule cannot be valid if it is not consistent with GP. But GP is a formal principle that provides a logical test which any substantive rule must satisfy but which cannot determine whether a particular set of consequences is to be regarded as morally desirable. Hence GP, or any other formal principle, will never help us with the question we now face, namely, how can we justify evaluating a specific set of consequences in a specific manner? The reader will note the relationship between the question now under consideration and the argument of Chapter 5.

moral rules and decisions cannot be intuited or regarded as self-evident. I agree with you on these points, and between them they require my view that moral evaluations are merely expressions of personal attitudes, emotions, or preferences for which anything that would properly be called reasons cannot be given." However, our opponent has claimed a far more decisive victory than he will be able to win.

An important argument against lying is that it has the consequence of breaking down the fabric of confidence and trust in society. To the extent that lying becomes prevalent, one person cannot rely upon the statements, assurances, and representations of others. This breeds suspicion and distrust and creates the need for constant surveillance and watchfulness, which in turn divert human and material resources that could otherwise be devoted to more positive and constructive ends. Since such surveillance can never be wholly successful, lying regularly leads to the injury of the person or persons to whom the lie is told. If *A* commits himself or his resources on the basis of false information received from *B*, he is likely to suffer injury, and the injury will be in part a consequence of *B*'s lie.

If we are asked why lying is wrong, we reply that it is wrong because it breaks down confidence, breeds suspicion and distrust, wastes resources, frustrates human purposes, and leads to avoidable injuries. "But this reply," our interrogator might counter, "is really no improvement on the shorter answer that the consequences of lying are disastrous. You have simply recited in greater detail the *facts* concerning what happens when lying becomes a general practice. It is true that you have smuggled in evaluative expressions, such as "breaks down," "suspicion and distrust," "waste," and "injury," and these appear to give support to your summary evaluation that lying is wrong. But this is a mere rhetorical trick which at best pushes the question back a step. I am fully aware that waste and injury are ordinarily regarded as undesirable, and that actions which produce them are ordinarily regarded as wrong. But I would still like to see a reasoned justification for thinking that they ought to be regarded as undesirable and wrong. If I choose to regard a hostile, suspicious, wasteful, and injury-ridden society as the best possible society, and hence choose to think that lying is good, what sort of trans-subjective, public considerations can you possibly adduce against me?"

Before attacking the substance of this objection, it will be useful to pause briefly to note that only the most persistent philosophical axe-grinder is likely to press it. For most of us, sentences of the type with which we began the previous paragraph would be regarded as constituting good reasons for thinking that lying is wrong. This suggests that we might reflect again concerning the "practical" (in the Aristotelian sense) character of moral discourse. That sentence is a substantial improvement upon "lying is wrong," accompanied by a threatening facial expression, a bang on the table, or a stamp of the foot. Surely recommendations for public policy accompanied by such statements are preferable to "I think it ought to be done!" or "if you don't do it I won't support your campaign!!" A theory that cannot distinguish between these replies is inadequate, and our opponent has no ground on which to prefer one to the other.[8] Finally, the nature of the objection begins to create suspicions about what our opponent would consider a reasoned justification for a moral rule. But we are not yet in a position to pursue these suspicions to their source.

Use has already been made of Hare's distinction between the commendatory and descriptive meanings of the moral word "good." This distinction provides a useful way of restating the problem now before us. Consider the case of the preceding summary of the reasons why lying is wrong. At the expense of considerable circumlocution, the consequences of lying could have been presented without the use of evaluative words. "Breaks down confidence" and "creates suspicion and distrust" would be replaced by a description of the many actions which individuals take in order to protect themselves in the face of widespread dishonesty; "waste" would be eschewed, and we would simply tabulate the manner in which resources were expended.

Such an account, in addition to being clumsy and drawn out, would undoubtedly seem odd, because we ordinarily tote up the consequences of behavior for the purposes of deciding whether to engage in it. To do the latter we must evaluate. Therefore, omitting evaluations would make the account seem incomplete and distorted. Yet the fact that such an account is possible indicates that there is a difference be-

[8] Note that "What if I should choose to regard waste and injury as good?" has the paradoxical consequence of reversing the very firm connotations of common words. Apart from its other difficulties, a theory that leads to such results is likely to have gone wrong somewhere.

tween commending or evaluating and stating facts. Hence it is not true that those sentences simply state the facts about what happens when lying is prevented. It is clear that the evaluations would make no sense without the facts and consequences—for what would we be evaluating—but it is equally clear that evaluations are more than statements of facts.

The question, then, is how to justify that "something more" which evaluations add to statements of fact. Hare says that we do so by applying "criteria" of good. This of course is true, but it is no help here since our problem is exactly how we justify the criteria we utilize. Let us recur to what we might, in Hare's terminology, call the criteria employed in deciding that lying is wrong. When our interrogator asks us to justify using these criteria, what can we say? We might reply,

> Well, think for a moment about situations in which confidence obtains and compare them with situations marked by suspicion and distrust. Take for example two scholarly communities characterized in these ways. In the former, when we analyze a scholarly article, the fact that we can assume the honesty of the writer allows us to concentrate our attentions upon the significance of the findings, the correctness of the interpretations, and in general the degree to which the article advances our understanding of the subject matter. We must be alert to the possibility of misstatement and factual errors, and we have an elaborate apparatus of scholarly procedure to assist us in so doing. But consider the problems of the second community. Literally every phrase would have to be scrutinized and unmasked. Given the enormous potential for lying, members of that community could never be confident of having discovered all of the falsehoods in a particular piece of work. If afflicted with the general practice of lying, scholarship would be impossible.

Two types of objections might be entered here. The first is that the example is unfair because of the nature of the activity in question. Scholarship is defined as the search for truth, and hence the general practice of lying would necessarily render the activity impossible. But this will not do. The argument is particularly easy to make in the case of scholarship, but it is relevant to any form of activity which has a cooperative dimension. How would the construction industry fare if carpenters and masons regularly lied to one another concerning measurement? Could banking go forward if bankers made a practice of lying to depositors, investors, and borrowers? Lying takes place in these activities, and the activities survive. But what if it became the general practice? When we consider the range of human activities to which some degree of cooperation and mutual confidence is necessary, the view that the rule against lying is a fundamental moral rule is easily understood.

The second objection is somewhat weightier. It might be contended that the arguments presented above are not moral arguments but simply hypotheticals or instructions of the "if . . . then . . ." type. *If* you want to engage in cooperative activities, *then* do not lie. Lying is simply a form of self-defeating behavior and hence is irrational. Naturally enough, good reasons can be marshaled against lying, but these reasons are not moral reasons. This objection is tricky because it leads into the murky waters of the means-end relationship. Without attempting a general clearing of those waters, let us make the following points.

1. It is decidedly odd to speak of a rule that is necessary to so wide a range of man's activities as a "means to an end." For this designation to ring true, it must make sense to consider rejecting the "end" and hence to be freed from the obligation established by the rules about "means." But man cannot seriously consider permanently rejecting cooperative activities. This is *not* to concede that man has no choice but to accept and seek to live up to rules such as the rule against lying. Rather, it is the fact that man is able to, and often does, reject the behavior most appropriate to his condition, which leads him to construct moral rules and seek to live up to them. Also, there are circumstances in which we mindfully and properly choose to behave in ways that hamper cooperative activities. But it is the fact that regular violation of such rules interferes with basic human activities which makes the case for fundamental moral rules so powerful.

2. Many of the activities and conditions that we value highly and that moral rules are designed to protect could be eschewed if we so decided. This does not mean that the objection in question is valid. Moral discourse involves working between values, referring one to the other in concrete circumstances, and assigning priorities for the purposes of those circumstances. It is often difficult and misleading to assign any one of the values the status of means to some other end.

Consider the case of suspicion and distrust. Let us say we argued that lying is wrong because it creates suspicion and distrust. We are then asked why suspicion and distrust are undesirable. We might respond that they are undesirable because they hamper cooperative activities. It could then be said that the rule against creating suspicion and distrust is a "means" to the end of facilitating cooperative activities. But we might also argue that to be forced to be suspicious and distrustful is to be forced into an unpleasant, unhappy, or debilitating condition, and that one of the purposes of morality is to minimize the occurrence of such conditions. In this case, avoiding suspicion and distrust would not be a means to cooperative activities at all. Notice also that if pressed as to why cooperative activities are to be valued, we might respond that such activities are valuable because they minimize suspicion and distrust. In this case minimizing suspicion and distrust would appear to be an end. Similarly, consider the argument that the rule against wasting resources is a means to facilitating cooperative activities or, perhaps, to maximizing the possibility for satisfaction and development on the part of individuals. I have no quarrel with these contentions, and it would be useful to draw the connections. But it also makes sense to argue that wasting resources is itself an evil which it is a basic purpose of morality to minimize. This sounds slightly odd when we think in terms of material resources, but consider expressions such as "the tragedy that is a wasted life."

These reflections suggest that assigning the status of "means" and "ends" to the considerations we adduce in justifying fundamental moral rules will often be a perilous enterprise. Therefore, the facts that a single rule serves a number of values and that we often relate one value to another in reaching and justifying moral decisions do not necessarily serve to subordinate either (or any) of the values so related.

II

The substance of the considerations relevant to justifying other fundamental moral rules would of course differ from those just presented. This would be true of justifications for the application of a moral rule in particular circumstances as well. This is because consequences are central to moral decisions and vary from one type of action to another and from one situation to another. But there is no reason to believe that the form or structure of the reasoning would vary significantly. Hence it is possible that we have now made some headway with our interrogator. He might agree that saying that lying is wrong because it breaks down confidence, together with saying that breaking down confidence is wrong because it hampers cooperative activity, is to give something we would ordinarily call reasons for thinking that lying is wrong. He might agree, for example, that this kind of reason is distinguishable from and perhaps even preferable to mere assertions, shouts, threats, stamping of the feet, and related kinds of behavior. He might also agree that the account presented bears some resemblance to the way moral discourse is in fact conducted. If these contentions are true, we have accomplished a good deal. We have shown that practical men can, at least within some limits, rest their commitment to moral rules and their evaluations of particular consequences on rational considerations, and can discourse concerning them in a reasoned manner.

These are not insignificant conclusions. Even if it should prove that certain philosophic doubts cannot be eliminated, combining the arguments about facts, consequences, and principles with those just presented about rules and evaluations, it is clear that there is a significant place for reason in the consideration and decision of moral questions.

But it would be naive to expect that our interrogator will now be silenced. Even if he agrees to the propositions just summarized, he will surely respond that his basic contention, that moral choices are *ultimately* arbitrary, stands untouched. It might not be possible to dispose of this contention entirely, but perhaps we are now approaching a position from which we can discover some of the things that such a contention could involve.

An objection that is almost certain to be brought against the preceding account is that it involves us in an infinite regress. If we justify the rule against lying because it breaks down confidence, and the rule against breaking down confidence in terms of maintaining cooperative activities, and maintaining cooperative activities in terms of basic human needs, and so on, but do nothing by way of specifying some fundamental value the reaching of which will stop the chain of referrals, how can the chain ever stop? Will we not go on indefinitely relating one set of consequences to the other? If there is no point at which we can stop the chain of referrals, how can we ever make a firmly based decision? This objection is fair in that we have not attempted to specify a hierarchy of values culminating in one or a small number of fundamental values which are somehow self-justifying and in which all other values somehow, perhaps as with the structure of a system of geometry, culminate. The view that such an ultimate value is necessary to a conclusive argument has a long history of respectable adherents.

The first and most important answer to this objection is that it is impossible to discover such a hierarchy or such an ultimate value in moral life as we know it. Some hierarchy there is. The distinction between fundamental, local, and neutral rules is a recognition of a kind of hierarchy, and it is obvious that the loss of life is ordinarily thought more serious than the loss of money, that causing suffering is considered more heinous than causing inconvenience. But we search in vain for a single value or even a small number of values that everywhere and at all times are considered inviolable. As highly as we value life, we often think it our duty to sacrifice it to justice. Injustice is sometimes deliberately done in order to save lives or obtain peace and stability; despite our abhorrence of suffering, we regularly inflict it with a clear conscience. As basic as order and stability are agreed to be, we often conclude that we are obliged to disrupt them.[9] These facts might be regarded as evidence of the immaturity or inadequacy of our moral life and practice, but it would be difficult to deny that the situation is as described. To the extent that the aim of this essay is to ascertain the structure of moral discourse, the omission of an "ultimate" value or values is appropriate.

It might also be useful to speculate about the gains and losses that would be incurred if such a hierarchical moral code could somehow be created and brought into operation. The gains would be in the area of greater certitude and stability of decision and, perhaps, increased confidence in and willingness to abide by the conclusions reached in the analysis of moral problems and issues. The establishment of a "fundamental" or "ultimate" value or set of values would not reduce decisions

[9] Consider the outcry over Senator Goldwater's statement that extremism in defense of liberty is no vice. The statement suggests that liberty is an ultimate or indefeasible value and that anything done in its defense is legitimate. Those who objected to the statement ought not, for that reason, be accused of indifference to liberty. The point, rather, is that liberty is one of a considerable number of basic values and that to assign it special or inviolable status is to threaten other values regarded as of great importance. We do decide among liberty, equality, security, harmony. But we do so in concrete circumstances and in the light of the consequences in specific cases, not abstractly or in a once-for-all-time manner.

and problems to simple proportions or eliminate all controversy from moral life. There would still be the complex problems of determining facts and consequences and specifying their relationship to the values or norms. Also, as we know from subject matters in which we have something analogous to such a moral code, for example geometry, the existence of unquestioned propositions does not preclude enormous complexity and the need for great imagination and ingenuity in working out the implications and applications of the basic propositions. If morality were analogous to geometry, however, we could, in principle, say that there was always a right answer to moral questions—however difficult it might be to discover it. It is perhaps the fact that our moral practice does not allow us to say this that leads to the view of moral decisions as ultimately arbitrary.[10]

A useful way to think about the losses that would be incurred or the price that would be paid if a rigidly hierarchical moral code were established is to note that there would be at least some indefeasible moral rules.[11] There would be a set of conditions *A* that would constitute the necessary and sufficient conditions of the application of the rule, and when those conditions were present, the rule would be applied and the issue would be decided—entirely without regard to the presence of circumstances other than those comprising *A*. Such a moral code would reduce if not eliminate the possibility of the individual adapting the rule to special or unforeseen circumstances. It would

[10] It should be noted, however, that one regularly hears the view expressed that systems of geometry are "ultimately arbitrary." I cannot claim to understand fully what is involved in this statement, but it reinforces my view that there are few words used more loosely in academic circles than "ultimately" and "arbitrary."

This is perhaps the appropriate point to comment about a general strategy of this book. We have not challenged the view that there is a very sharp difference between the degree of rigor and certainty attainable in moral as opposed to mathematical or scientific reasoning. Our strategy has been to concede that there is an important difference and yet to argue that moral discourse can be reasoned. In part, this strategy is required by the facts. There *are* significant differences between moral and mathematical or scientific reasoning, but we have conceded more than is necessary. Scientific and mathematical reasoning share some of the problems of moral reasoning, and the degree of rigor and certainty they attain is an extremely complex question.

[11] Another useful way to think about it is to read the works of the man who above all others thought about it systematically and with great power. We refer of course to Plato. Whether one agrees or disagrees with Plato's conclusions, his work, and especially *The Republic*, has more to teach us on this subject than any other.

turn moral rules into regulations and place the moral agent in a position analogous to that with which he is faced when in a situation covered by a law of the state. There are many instances in which this kind of limitation upon the agent's freedom is desirable. But general and prospective legislation rarely achieves great sensitivity and discrimination in its classifications. To impose rigidity of this kind upon the entire sphere of moral life *might* render morality a more powerful instrument; it would surely render it a blunter one.

But a rigidly hierarchical moral code which culminated in absolute or indefeasible rules *would not have* the flexibility of a code of laws. Utilitarian considerations are relevant to justifying practice-type rules, and changed conditions might require changes in the rules. An absolute rule, by contrast, would not be subject to *any* kind of change under any circumstances. There could *never* be any other value or consideration to which appeal could be made to justify a change.

Taken together with earlier arguments, these points are sufficient to show that the demand for a morality founded upon indefeasible or absolute rules or values, which sometimes appears as a plea for rationalism in moral life, is in fact a plea for a morality grounded in arational or subrational (or perhaps suprarational) commitments. Owing to the very special status of such rules or values, we would not be permitted to consider their relationship to circumstances. If it is impossible for new circumstances to alter the rule or its application, it is impossible that the rule could have been arrived at through experience in a number of circumstances concluding in the view that the rule was a good and an especially important one. Furthermore, if the rule is absolute in the sense that all other rules derive from it, we cannot justify the rule by relating it to other rules and to the consequences of following any one of those rules in various contexts. This seems to leave only the option of justifying the rule on the grounds that it is self-evident. But arguments for self-evident principles are always either logically defective or simply an appeal to a psychological fact concerning a particular person or set of persons.[12] What remains as a strategy for justifying the claim that X is an absolute or indefeasible moral rule? A variety of such "strategies" can be imagined (revelation, faith, intuition), but they all share at least one characteristic, the characteristic of being nonrational. This means that when disagreement arises concerning

[12] See Hare, *The Language of Morals, op. cit.*, I. 3., and especially pp. 38–44.

them, it can be resolved only by resort to some nonrational agency. Historically, this agent has often been violence. (In fact, of course, these are not strategies of justification at all but devices for obviating justification.)

III

It will not have escaped the reader that the strategy of the previous section was less to answer the objection to the present account than to discredit the alternative which that objection seemed to offer. We argued that (1) there are no absolute or indefeasible rules in moral discourse as we know it, (2) the establishment of such rules would eliminate valued features of our present moral discourse, and (3) rational justification could not be provided for regarding any particular rules as absolute or indefeasible. But to discredit the alternative associated with an objection is not necessarily to answer the objection. We are still faced with the contention that the present account leads to an infinite regress and hence either to an arbitary interruption of that regress (which is what our countercharge alleged of any attempt to establish indefeasible rules) or to a paralysis of moral decision making.

Our strategy was selected because the notion of indefeasible or absolute rules had to be dealt with, and because that notion is a plausible solution to the problem of infinite regress. Moreover, the present account of justification could readily be thought to involve the problem of infinite regress. But a much more plausible charge against the present account is that it involves a bootless if not a logically vicious circularity. Infinite regress suggests a hierarchy without a top or bottom that one can ascend or descend without end. The above account suggests that justificatory discourse orbits from consideration to consideration until it returns fruitlessly to the point at which it began. If there is no sharply defined hierarchy differentiating or defining the significance of the values and disvalues utilized in the process of justification, what do we gain by moving from one to the other, from "breaks down confidence" to "creates suspicion and distrust," to "hampers cooperative activities," to "wastes resources," to "causes injuries," and so forth. Can we genuinely say that we have a stronger or more "reasoned" justification for the rule against lying when we reach "causes injuries" than we had when we were at "breaks down confidence?"

Will we not simply exhaust the relevant considerations and work our way back to the consideration with which we chanced to begin?

Let us consider first the possibility that there is a logically vicious circularity or *petitio principii* in the argument. The point of the argument is to demonstrate that reasoned justification can be provided for the moral rule "lying is wrong." One of the reasons given in justification of the rule is that lying "breaks down confidence." The reader might be tempted to treat "breaks down confidence" as a major premise and to write the argument as follows:

It is wrong to break down confidence.
Lying breaks down confidence.
Lying is wrong.

If he yields to this temptation and then reads the rest of the argument, he might well conclude that the argument is circular. For he soon discovers that "breaks down confidence" is not treated as an established premise but is said to be wrong because it "creates suspicion and distrust." As he prepares to write a new syllogism beginning with "It is wrong to create suspicion and distrust," his eye catches the next sentence which tells him that to "create suspicion and distrust" is wrong because it "hampers cooperative activities." Puzzled and by now rather suspicious, he thinks the argument through and finds that, if it leads anywhere, it eventually leads back to "breaks down confidence." Since "breaks down confidence" has simply been referred to other considerations none of which are able to stand alone, it is as much in need of proof as ever. "A gross and palpable *petitio principii,*" he exclaims, and, with considerable satisfaction in the poetic justice of the act, hurls the book into the wastebasket.

But our hypothetical reader has gone wrong. (No accident that!) He has imposed upon the argument a logical model (and its attendant criteria) which it was never intended to satisfy. The logic of that aspect of justificatory discourse now under discussion is not formal deductive logic. The considerations adduced in justification of moral rules and decisions cannot be treated as the established premise of deductive syllogisms. (This, of course, is not to suggest that induction and deduction have no place in moral decisions. They are entirely relevant to uncovering and integrating facts and consequences and to validating formal principles.) If they could be so treated, justification would be easy, at least in form. But these remarks are painfully arbitrary. To improve upon them we must step back from the logical objection and attempt to explain more fully what is involved in our argument in support of the rule against lying.

The purpose of referring one consideration or consequence to another is not to provide "proof" for either. By no system of logical inference does the fact that "breaking down confidence" serves to "create suspicion and distrust" entail that the former therefore constitutes a justification for regarding lying as wrong. Nor will the addition of any number of further such considerations strengthen the case in this respect. When we are attempting to justify a moral rule, one of the things we must do is gain the fullest possible understanding of the impact of the action covered by the rule upon those multitudinous and complex aspects of life that morality is established to protect and facilitate. The type of reasoning described above is intended to foster such an understanding. It depends, of course, upon it being true that "breaking down confidence" tends to "create suspicion and distrust." It seeks to call attention to that fact and to the relationship between that fact and other facts about the type of action in question. It cannot be said, therefore, that it is a logically untenable argument simply because this would be an irrelevant thing to say.

It will perhaps be admitted that we cannot justify a rule if we do not understand the consequences of the action the rule covers. Hence it might also be admitted that, when understood as it has just been described, the reasoning process we have been considering is relevant, indeed indispensable, to justifying moral rules. But a gap seems to remain. When we understand all there is to be understood about lying and its impact upon man and society, we still want to ask, "What justifies regarding it as wrong?" Unless we are now to adopt the naturalistic position we have avoided throughout, we must admit that the predicate (morally) "wrong" is not a part of, does not come along with, any of the facts, consequences, or relationships we can adduce. Whence, then, does it come?

The answer to this question is extraordinarily simple to state, but, as centuries of moral philosophy testify, painfully difficult to accept. Value predicates, moral and otherwise, are *assigned to* actions, consequences, and natural objects by man. "Goodness," "badness," "desirable," and "undesirable" do not inhere in saying what is untrue or in the set of behaviors and attitudes which we designate suspicion and distrust. They are conventional predicates (in the sense of the ancient distinction between nature and convention) which man, reflecting upon what he has learned to be the consequences of such behaviors and their relationship to his needs, desires, and the facts of his existence, has chosen to assign such behaviors. The realm of moral value, in the language of Hobbes, is the realm of "artifice." It is unique to man among the creatures of the earth, and it exists not by "nature" but because man chooses that it should exist. The shape that it takes, the things that are right, wrong, good, and bad, depends upon man's designation. These conclusions (if not the language in which they are stated here) follow necessarily from the rejection of naturalism in any and all of its forms.

But these conclusions do not lead necessarily to the view that moral discourse and decision making must be arbitrary or nonrational. The fact that man is free to establish and maintain a moral realm and free to construct that realm as he sees fit, leaves it open to him to construct it in a nonrational manner; it does not require that he do so, which brings us back to the type of moral discourse we have been discussing for some time. Discourse of this kind will never relieve men of the necessity to *choose* to designate lying as wrong. Understanding those features of lying described does not prove or "establish" that lying is wrong in the strong sense in which we can "prove" or "establish" the laws of science or the propositions and theorems of mathematics. But it will provide him with *reasons* for the choices that he makes. The fact that lying breaks down confidence and creates suspicion and distrust does not *make* lying morally wrong. But knowing that it has these consequences gives men *reasons* for designating it morally wrong. Take away the decision to designate in a particular way and you have a statement about the world; eliminate the account of facts, consequences, and relationships, and you have a mere emotive or subjective expression which is not discourse at all [13] and with which it would be impossible either to agree or disagree; combine the two and you have an exercise of moral choice about which reasoned discourse is not only possible but uniquely appropriate.

[13] The failure to draw this distinction is responsible for much of the plausibility of the so-called emotivist ethical theory.

IV

It is time to take stock. Have we made additional headway in showing that reasoned justifications can be provided for moral rules and decisions?

It is clear by now that the controversy over the place of reason in moral discourse is in part a terminological controversy. It has been conceded that moral rules and other value decisions cannot be proven or verified in the sense in which we use those words in mathematics and science. The justification we have offered for the rule against lying would never satisfy the criteria of deductive logic or inductive proof. If we hold, as Hume held, that only arguments or demonstrations which meet these criteria are to be called "reasoned" arguments, crucial aspects of justificatory discourse will never deserve that designation. If we are prepared to adopt a more inclusive use of "reason" and its cognates, it is fair to claim that the above arguments demonstrate the relevance of these terms to moral discourse.[14]

But the issue is not purely terminological. We noticed earlier that Hume's position violated ordinary usage. It should be clear by now that Hume paid a high price for this violation. Our justification of the rule against lying falls within the ordinary boundaries of the concept "reasoned argument." Hence ordinary usage provides no additional general category in which to place such arguments. The philosophers who have wanted to narrow the ordinary boundaries of "reasoned argument" have not developed new categories under which to classify the types of arguments that they have excluded from the category "reasoned." Rather, they have maintained the dichotomy "reasoned-unreasoned." Since moral arguments have been banished from the former category, they have fallen inevitably into the latter, with con-

[14] This point has received considerable discussion in contemporary philosophy. In addition to literature already cited (especially Ladd, *loc. cit.*), see the extremely relevant remarks of John Wisdom in his paper, "Gods," especially VI ff, *Proceedings of the Aristotelian Society* (1944–45), Reprinted in Antony Flew, editor, *Essays in Logic and Language*, First Series (Oxford: Basil Blackwell, 1963). For a more extended discussion see Stephen Toulmin, *The Uses of Argument* (Cambridge: Cambridge University Press, 1958). For a related argument applied to political problems, see Thomas L. Thomson, *The Logic of Democracy* (New York: Holt, Rinehart and Winston, 1962).

sequences that have been of anything but purely terminological significance.

This is an egregious error. Just as it is essential to recognize the differences between the logic of justificatory discourse and the logic of deductive or inductive reasoning, so it is essential to recognize the differences between arguments such as those we have been considering and unsupported assertions, exclamations, grunts, or threatening gestures; essential, first, in the fundamental sense that a theory which does not recognize those differences cannot do other than hopelessly distort the subject matter it purports to clarify; essential, second, because our understanding of moral discourse affects our practice of moral discourse, and failure to recognize these differences serves to reduce our moral practice to the impoverished level of our ethical theory.

But what of our old friend "ultimately"? Perhaps it will be conceded that there is an area in which reasons can meaningfully be exchanged about moral rules and decisions. Perhaps it will even be conceded that our moral life will be better or more adequate or more satisfactory if we endeavor to present and exchange such reasons when we make moral choices. But the fact still remains, it might be contended, that the theory presented fails to disprove, indeed offers evidence in support of, the view that "ultimately," or "in the final analysis," or "when all is said and done," moral choices and decisions rest upon subjective or arbitrary preferences in support of which (as opposed to in explanation of which) reasons cannot be given.

Stated at this juncture in the discussion, the objection sounds suspiciously like a demand for a morality that satisfies the canons of deductive logic in all respects. But it is possible that it focuses upon what we have called the element of freedom or choice (or, more broadly, the conventional character of morality) involved in moral decisions. To the extent that this is the case, we will be forced to concede an element of truth to the objection, albeit one which requires very careful handling. Before doing so, we must draw a further distinction.

The distinction can be stated in several ways: between the genesis of a moral decision and a justification for that decision; between a private mental or psychological state and a public defense of a position or decision which reflects or corresponds to that private state; between a behavioral explanation for a decision and moral discourse in support of that decision. If X urges the undergraduate college at which he teaches to initiate graduate instruction, his position might be "explained" in terms of various features of his psyche or private life; his frustration at never having been hired by a school offering advanced work; desire for greater freedom for research; or increased personal prestige. This explanation might be entirely accurate, and in some contexts it might be relevant and appropriate—for example, the context of a session with *X*'s analyst or of an investigation by any one of several kinds of behavioral scientist. There is at least one type of context in which it would be totally irrelevant (and probably impertinent), namely the context of deciding whether the college ought to initiate graduate programs. Here the only relevant question would be, "What sorts of public considerations can *X* offer in support of this proposal?"

This very common distinction is important in connection with the question of "ultimate" justification. It is perhaps true, as a matter of behavioral fact, that some of our inclinations in the realm of value stem in part from highly personal, internal, or subjective factors and that, when they are viewed in this perspective, we can only explain their genesis, never justify them. But this is not the question with which we are dealing, and if this is the sense in which value decisions are ultimately arbitrary, it may or may not be true but it is irrelevant to ethics.

We are concerned not with the genesis of moral positions but with their *justification.* We want to know whether the logic of moral decisions makes it possible for the individual to refine the impulses and emotions that might lie behind his moral judgments and find reasoned grounds for justifying them publicly. The reasoned grounds might be "rationalizations" in the sense that they are not the "true" or the "real" *explanation* for his conduct. It is of course one of the purposes of moral training to bring the two to coincide, for we would expect, as a behavioral matter, that our moral practice would be affected if they did not coincide. But there is one important sense in which ethical theory can afford to be indifferent to (if not encouraged by) the existence or even the prevalence of rationalization of this kind. Such rationalization testifies to the possibility of giving reasons for moral choices and gives other parties, for whom my private life is no concern at all, interpersonal grounds on which to judge the position in question. (Indeed, the presence of rationalization supports the argument in that it is testimony to the prevalence of the view that there are areas in which it is improper to choose or act on the basis of subjective considerations, and hence to the prevalence of the view that it is possible to avoid doing so.) If ethical theory can show that these things can be done, it will have made good its claim that there is a place for reason in moral discourse.

We have now identified three senses in which it could be charged that moral rules and decisions are ultimately arbitrary. In the case of the first two, that moral rules cannot be referred to absolute, indefeasible, or self-evident substantive rules or principles and that they cannot be proved as we prove the laws of science, we agreed they could not be so proved but argued that this did not constitute a demonstration that they are necessarily arbitrary. The third was that our moral commitments stem from and are to be explained in terms of subjective impulses; this we argued to be irrelevant to ethics. (We might add a fourth albeit somewhat different possibility; the logic of moral discourse requires that we obey moral rules blindly. Here we argued that the contention was simply false.) These are the strongest senses in which this contention of arbitrariness could be made. If they have been countered, a good deal has been gained. But there are other, less far-reaching but nevertheless important, forms which the argument might take.

The most plausible of these focuses upon the element of choice or freedom in the realm of morality. The reasons that can be given in support of a moral rule do not "establish" or "entail" the rule. They provide grounds for concluding that it is justifiable, but there is an irreducible gap between those grounds and the decision or choice to accept and act according to the rule. There is a sense in which this is true of any kind of discourse and any kind of decision, including decisions to accept the laws of science and the theorems of geometry. Evidence and logic are not clubs with which we beat one another into submission. But the language of "decision" or "choice" or "acceptance" is *odd* in the realm of scientific or mathematical investigation. We say that a conclusion is "entailed" or "established" by the evidence or the logic, or that we "infer" or "reach" or "obtain" the result from the evidence or the logic. We might "choose" to accept the canons of logic and evidence by which scientific conclusions are reached, but once we accept them, we rarely speak of "choosing" to accept the results we obtain when we utilize them. In morals, on the other hand, the verbs "choose" and "decide" are entirely fitting at crucial stages of the process.

The reasoning process available for justifying moral rules and decisions, then, does not preclude honest and well-grounded disagreement in as strong a sense as other reasoning processes regularly exclude it. Conscientious use of the best tools of moral reasoning can more readily lead to disagreement than is the case elsewhere. The extent to which this is true varies with circumstances. The justification that can be offered for the rule against lying is powerful and leaves little room for reasoned disagreement. The justification for specific applications of the rule might be less powerful and leave more room for disagreement. As one moves away from fundamental rules toward rules which are on the borderline between morality and etiquette, the room for genuine dispute and disagreement increases. This is not suprising since the consequences of actions in the latter areas are less far-reaching and relate to less central or crucial aspects of life.

Furthermore, the logical price one must pay in order to reject even the best-supported justification is lower than that exacted in science and mathematics. To reject conclusions supported by a properly conducted scientific investigation (that is one that admittedly satisfies the existing criteria of a properly conducted investigation) is to be subjected to the charge of self-contradiction. To refuse to choose to accept the conclusions of such an investigation in the moral realm is, from a logical point of view, to be charged with being unreasonable. It must be remembered, however, that to refuse might also be to subject oneself to the charge of immorality. (Again, induction and deduction are entirely relevant aspects of moral discourse.)

These facts—that the logic and the criteria which justificatory discourse allows are less rigorous, less conclusive, than those available to us in other realms, and hence that reasoned disagreement cannot be entirely eliminated from the moral realm—form the (admittedly seductive) modicum or scintilla of truth on which the "value choices are ultimately arbitrary" point of view is built. Their significance is not to be denied. There is a sense in which they constitute the basis of the distinctive features of moral life. But they do not provide a warrant for the enormous structure of conclusions that has been built upon them.

Although the relationship between moral choice and moral reasoning does not allow us to speak of entailment or inductive inference in the usual senses of those words, that relationship does allow us to adduce public, transpersonal considerations in support of moral choices. Hence we can escape the "I like it" "Well I don't" type of exchange with its destructive consequences. Adducing such considerations may not produce a single, indisputable result, but it will facilitate an understanding both of the question at hand and the bases of the disagreement about it. Sometimes this type of discourse will demonstrate that no single decision or choice is clearly superior, that two or more choices will satisfy the best criteria we can muster. In political life, where a single policy may nevertheless be required, we then turn to authority to resolve the question. If authority cannot demonstrate the final superiority of the alternative which it chooses, it can demonstrate that the alternative rests upon more than whim or caprice. In moral life, we conclude that there are two or more morally "good" policies, no single "right" policy, and the only "ought" or "duty" which is generated is the duty to choose one among the morally good alternatives.

In the absence of reasons in support of the choices we urge, such an outcome would be impossible. As long as nothing but personal preferences or inclinations are presented in support of a position, it is impossible to make any judgment concerning the relative merits of conflicting views. Alternately, sincere, disinterested use of the type of reasoning described will sometimes justify the conclusion that one among conflicting choices is superior. Whether this produces agreement or not, the advantages it offers can scarcely be minimized. When action is then taken in the face of continuing disagreement it can be justified in terms of the best criteria man is capable of developing and need not rest upon idiosyncratic inclinations or the possession of superior power. (Recall the above suggestion that we think about such problems from the standpoint of the hangman.) Use of the form of justificatory discourse which the logic of moral language makes available allows us to rest our decisions upon the most rational, the most public, the most objective grounds possible. There are limitations upon what we can achieve through justificatory discourse, but this scarcely justifies us in regarding the latter as useless or contemptible.

To summarize, these considerations suggest that it is odd to paste the label "ultimately arbitrary" upon moral decisions reached and justified in the manner we have described. Recalling again that "arbitrary" means "based on mere opinion; capricious," it is simply inappropriate to use that word to describe decisions defended in this way. Our intellectual and linguistic condition is not that impoverished.[15]

One final point. It is easy to write of the logic of justification in an apologetic tone. When contrasted with the shiny and powerful logical machinery available to the discourse of science and mathematics, it readily appears shabby and inefficacious. But logic is an instrument which must be judged according to the manner in which it performs the task for which it is designed. The element of freedom which normative discourse leaves to the moral agent is more than simply a fact about that discourse. It is also a part of our prescriptive definition of a moral action or decision. This was one of the basic points in question in the discussion of the logic of conforming to moral rules and in our speculations about a moral code modeled on a system of geometry. For the reasons presented in those discussions, and because we regard our moral freedom as an essential part of our humanity, a form of moral discourse which eliminated that freedom would serve its purpose very badly. Far from being a matter for apology, then, the moral discourse at our disposal should be numbered among the most highly prized of our possessions.

The route followed in the last two chapters has been long and somewhat circuitous, and it might be well to summarize the basic contentions that have been made. Beginning with some distinctions between types of rules, we found two of these, rules in the sense of stated regularities and precept or maxim-type rules, to be of great importance to moral discourse and decision making. We argued, however, that their importance traces to the fact that moral decisions are decisions which take account of the consequences of the action in question (or that the moral status of an action depends upon its consequences), and that rules are useful only insofar as they assist us in so doing. Hence any interpretation of moral rules that impedes, obstructs, or minimizes this basic aspect of moral discourse is untrue to our moral practice and frustrates the achievement of the basic goals of morality. We then turned to the problem of justifying the content of particular moral rules and the evaluations we place upon particular consequences in the moral realm. We found that moral discourse is unable to eliminate an

[15] Cf. Hare, *The Language of Morals*, p. 69.

element of moral choice, but that there are no logical obstacles to making such choices rest upon reasoned grounds, grounds that can be exchanged with other men in discourse properly designated "rational." Those theories which contend that such grounding and such discourse are impossible are mistaken, irrelevant, or insensitive to the purposes of morality.

Chapter Eleven

IMPERATIVES

I

The purpose of moral reasoning is, in Aristotle's sense, "practical"; its purpose is to guide conduct. Hence it must culminate in a manner appropriate to guiding conduct. We combine facts and consequences, principles, rules, and particular evaluations in order to generate a conclusion or produce a result that will be useful in deciding what to do.

Depending upon the considerations which support the conclusion, and upon our estimate of what will be efficacious in the circumstances, we use a variety of linguistic forms to express our conclusions. We provide information, offer advice, make requests, exhort, plead, and even issue commands.[1] It is a characteristic of moral discourse that we often choose forms that allow us to cast our guidance in the imperative mood. This practice reflects the urgency and significance we attach to moral decisions, but it also creates some of the thorniest problems of ethics.

"Imperative" is defined as "demanding obedience; that which must be done or performed . . . urgent; of the nature of a duty." [2] But if moral guidance "must be" acted upon, in what sense can we say that the moral realm is a realm of freedom or autonomy? The problem is nicely raised by the etymology of one of the important words of moral guidance, "obligatory." The word derives from "*ligare*," to bind. To

[1] *See* David Gauthier, *Practical Reasoning* (London: Oxford University Press, 1963), Chapter 7; R. B. Braithwaite, review of Hare's "The Language of Morals," in *Mind*, Vol. 63, p. 249 (1954).

[2] Quotations are from the *Oxford Universal Dictionary*.

be obligated is to be "bound by" an obligatory factor to do an action. Whatever it is that binds us to act upon our moral obligations, it is thought to be of sufficient power to warrant language equating it with a physical restraint. Since we use this language in guiding others as well as ourselves, it appears that one person can be bound by the guidance others provide for him—that obligations can be imposed upon us by other moral agents. Yet, if moral reasoning imposes imperatives upon us, it has often been insisted that moral imperatives are distinguished from other imperatives in that they must be self-imposed. To borrow Kant's language, moral imperatives are categorical, but a will which has been heteronomized is no longer a moral will. This dilemma is not likely to be resolved in a chapter, but it may be possible to sort out some of the elements of which it consists.

II

Setting aside temporarily the force of "must be performed" in the most rigorous of moral imperatives, much moral guidance is either not imperative at all or is imperative only in a blunted or softened sense. First, there are cases in which the most conscientious application of the tools of moral reasoning leaves room for legitimate doubt as to the morally appropriate action. In such situations, the person who is sensitive to the problems of moral life will qualify the guidance he offers with expressions such as: "I am inclined to think . . . ," "It seems to me . . . ," "Perhaps the best thing would be. . . ." These expressions reduce the force of the guidance in recognition of the possibility of legitimate disagreement. They need not indicate that the adviser lacks confidence in his own judgments. Nor need they reflect the view that there are no grounds on which a reasoned judgment can be made. The adviser might rule out certain lines of conduct as clearly inadmissible, and he might stand in judgment of the course of action the agent finally adopts. The qualifiers in his advice emphasize that reasons can be offered for several alternatives and the actor himself must choose among them. Moral guidance of this familiar kind can be called "imperative" only if we stretch the ordinary use of that term considerably.

Even further removed from imperative status are the moral judgments we express by employing the adjective "good." To say that an action is morally good is ordinarily to provide guidance for conduct.[3] Except in certain specialized circumstances, it would be inappropriate to use the word unless we are prepared to say that it would be morally desirable for the action to be taken. But to say, "*X* is (or would be) a good action," is not to utter an imperative. Although *X* is good, *Y* and *Z* might also be good, and *A* might be better. "*X* is good" eliminates doubts concerning a specific line of conduct, but it does not require that *X* be done. As Urmson has shown, there are some actions, those associated with saints and heroes, that are preeminently good but would never be required.[4]

Finally, there are circumstances in which the imperative edge of moral guidance is blunted by conditions peculiar to the agent who must act upon it or the situation in which the action must be taken. However valid the guidance may be as a general rule, the agent may be *exempted* from or held blameless for acting upon it in the circumstances. He may also be partially *excused* for the same type of reasons. Before a valid general imperative can become a specific imperative, account must be taken of the conditions peculiar to the circumstances and individual at hand. There is a considerable variety of such exemptions and excuses, and we can do no more than indicate the general character of their relationship to moral imperatives.

Perhaps the most important source of exemptions and excuses is the rule "Ought implies can." However desirable or undesirable the consequences of doing or not doing an action, if it is genuinely impossible for *X* to do it or to avoid doing it, he is exempted from all obligations (and hence from all blame) in connection with it. If it is unusually difficult or burdensome for a person to do *X*, he may be partially excused. Note, however, that we speak of *excuses* only in the case of specific persons. If it is generally the case that a specific type of action cannot be done (or cannot be avoided), no imperatives are formulated and no excuses are needed. We speak of excuses only when *X* has a specific disability or is in an unusual circumstance that makes difficult

[3] Hare, *The Language of Morals* (London: Oxford University Press, 1952), Chapter 8.

[4] See his paper, "Saints and Heroes," in A. I. Melden, editor, *Essays in Moral Philosophy* (Seattle: University of Washington Press, 1958).

an action which ordinarily can be done by those with the usual human capacities.[5] Furthermore "excuse" connotes a condition or disability of a temporary or special nature. It is odd to say that paralytics are excused from saving drowning men. No one ever expected them to save drowning men, and the question of excusing them never arises. Permanent excuses or general excuses are not excuses but recognized exceptions.

It is in part for these reasons that the topic of excuses is a difficult one. The easy cases are not excuses but exceptions. This leaves the cases in which it is difficult to be sure whether or to what extent the action (or avoidance of the action) is genuinely difficult for the individual and hence difficult to decide to what extent the imperative would be blunted. It is also for these reasons that, as Austin said, ". . . few excuses get us out of it completely." [6] (An excuse that "got us out completely" would be more properly thought of as a recognized exception.)

The foregoing considerations explain the fact that excuses are of such great interest in connection with imperatives. It is precisely the difficulty [7] of categorizing and generalizing about excuses that indicates the extent to which the imperative force of moral guidance must be adapted to individual cases. Hence the moral guide must know the distinctive features of the situation in question—both for purposes of guiding conduct prospectively and assigning praise or blame. Thus the subject of excuses provides support for utilitarianism versus formalism in general, and act utilitarianism versus rule utilitarianism in particular.

Consideration of excuses also provides a partial explanation for insistence upon a dimension of freedom or self-imposition in the moral

[5] This does not violate the universalizability principle. Anyone in the condition or with the disability will be excused. The point is that if the excuse applies widely, we cease talking about excuses and modify or abandon the requirement from which the condition or disability provides an excuse.

[6] J. L. Austin, "A Plea for Excuses," *Philosophical Papers*, J. O. Urmson and G. J. Warnock, editors (London: Oxford University Press, 1962), p. 125.

[7] The difficulty, not the impossibility. We have recognized categories of excuses, especially in the law. For example, it was "accidental," it was "involuntary," a "mistake." We also have, in some areas of the law, relatively precise rules as to the extent to which types of excuses will absolve a person. But even in the law, where there is vastly more system and precision than in morality, the courts are obliged to adjust their decisions to the special features of each case. Here again, the notion of a blind or mechanical jurisprudence is grossly misleading.

realm. Many types of excuses, especially those involving psychological disability, must be offered by the individual who wishes to be excused. To allow such excuses is to admit that there are respects in which the individual himself is peculiarly well situated to judge the special problems and conditions which confront him. It is of the essence of morality that his judgment not be regarded as sufficient or conclusive. But neither do we wish to do without it. The person must answer for his judgments, but it is his judgments for which he must answer. (Concern to maintain moral freedom is also due to the importance of motives in human action. If a person literally has no choice concerning his actions, he may not develop motives to act in a morally right way. Since most moral guidance must be self-guidance, the person without such motives is apt to act badly. Moral freedom is important to moral development and maturity.)

III

How do these considerations relate to the problem with which we began? In some respects, the relationship is straightforward and unproblematical. Some of our moral guidance is imperative—when we properly use "right" and "ought"; some of it is not—when we use "good." In some cases moral reasoning is sufficiently conclusive to warrant imperative language; in others it is not, and we leave a greater area of freedom of decision to the actor. These are not contradictory statements. The statement, "Moral reasoning sometimes generates imperatives," is true, but the statement, "Moral reasoning sometimes does not generate moral imperatives," is also true. There are also recognized exceptions to rules and requirements which are otherwise fully imperative. Here again there is no serious difficulty.

In other respects, the relationship produces a dilemma. There are circumstances in which moral reasoning generates genuine moral imperatives, in which it establishes the obligatory character of certain actions, establishes that they must be taken whatever the actor's attitude toward them, and hence justifies applying sanctions against the person who fails to take them. But in the same circumstances there is an irreducible dimension of freedom; the actor himself must assent to the imperative—he must bind himself. This suggests that one and the same action can be both right and wrong. *X* is right in holding that *Y* is morally obligated to do Z, but *Y* is right in refusing to do Z. More dramatically perhaps, *X* is right in applying moral sanctions against *Y* for not doing Z, but *Y* is wronged when *X* applies those sanctions against him.

We can narrow this dilemma somewhat further before facing it squarely. The dilemma arises only when there is a genuine moral confrontation, when *X* and *Y* rest their positions on moral grounds. If *X* has offered moral reasons for thinking that *Y* is morally obligated to do Z, and if *Y* refuses his assent on grounds of self-interest, there is no moral dilemma (and no difficulty for ethical theory), however great the practical dilemma might be. *Y* is not denying that he is morally obligated; he is not refusing his assent to a moral imperative. He is simply not participating in moral discourse at all. *X*'s proper position is not to condemn *Y* for refusing to do Z but to condemn him for the more serious failure to recognize that the question is a moral one. Until *Y* recognizes that the question is a moral one, the question of what is morally right will never arise between them. (Moral questions might arise for *X* if *Y* proceeded to act in an immoral manner.)

The difficult situation is not the one in which both *X* and *Y* can offer good moral reasons in support of their positions. In such cases, the proper inference is that the positions justify the language of "good," not "right" or "ought." Hence there is no imperative and no dilemma. (There might be serious practical problems. Both *X* and *Y* must concede that the reasons of the other are valid.)

Somewhat paradoxically, the hard case is the one in which both *X* and *Y* have sincerely held moral reasons to offer in support of their position, but *X*'s reasons are, in the view of all but *Y*, substantially more cogent and weighty than those of *Y*. We are tempted to say *X* is clearly in the right and *Y* can be held morally wrong if he refuses to assent to the imperative. To deny this would be to deny that reason has a place in moral discourse. To take this position, however, would be to deny that moral decisions are free decisions. It is perhaps tempting to say that the best policy in such cases is one of toleration; since it is *Y* who must act, it is preferable to emphasize the importance of freedom in morals and conclude that the imperative loses its force in *Y*'s case. This is difficult both on grounds of consistency and because of the other-regarding character of moral actions. To "tolerate" *Y*'s views might require that we refuse to tolerate the views or interests of those affected by *Y*'s action or refusal to act.

IV

It is now appropriate to state what cannot be the force of "must be performed." "Must" can only be a metaphor or analogy. If the individual literally has no choice but to take the recommended action, imperatives would be superfluous. Indeed, it is only when the individual is strongly inclined not to take the recommended action that it is appropriate to address imperatives to him.[8] Nor can "must be performed" be explained entirely in terms of fear of the sanctions which will be applied if the individual does not act on the imperative. We do apply sanctions to moral offenders, for example holding them in disrespect. But if the threatened sanction accounted completely for "must be performed" we could not distinguish moral imperatives from the imperatives of the highwayman.[9] This might hamper the development of moral principles and convictions on the part of the individual. One need not be a Kantian to accept the view that moral character is best developed through the free exercise of moral choice.

Hence the "must be performed" (or avoided) of moral imperatives cannot denote physical or psychological inevitability (or impossibility) and it must denote more than fear of sanctions. These are the strongest senses in which we think of imposition or "heteronomization," and they are not involved in moral imperatives. What then does "must be performed" denote? The answer lies not in the imperative itself but in the reasoning that generates and supports the imperative. "Must be performed" is best analyzed as "required by arguments that satisfy the best available criteria of a proper moral decision," which means that the action must be taken unless inclination, impulse, or some other nonrational force is to be allowed to rule the individual's action.[10]

Furthermore, if we are right that the moral life is the life of reason, it means that the action must be taken if moral life is to be maintained. Reason builds a trans-subjective bridge between individuals and

[8] On this point see Gauthier, *op. cit.*, pp. 176–9; P. H. Nowell-Smith, *Ethics* (Baltimore, Md.: Penguin Books, Inc., 1954), pp. 210–212.

[9] See H. L. A. Hart's distinction between "obliged" and "obligated" in *The Concept of Law* (London: Oxford University Press, 1961), pp. 79–88. See also T. H. Green, *Principles of Political Obligation* (London: Longmans, Green, revised edition, 1941), paragraph 118.

[10] See T. H. Green, *loc. cit.*

thereby provides a means by which one person can guide another without that guidance taking the form of imposition. One man may produce the reasons that guide other men, but the force of those reasons depends not upon their source but upon the fact that they satisfy criteria which apply to all men. The impersonality of reasons does not do away with the fact that the imperative which they support is intended to restrict the range of action available to the person to whom it is directed. But it does minimize if not eliminate the degree to which the imperative is properly thought of as imposed upon that person from the outside. To do X on the ground that there are good reasons for thinking it is morally right requires reflection upon and acceptance of the reasons which support X. We simply do not use "imposition" in talking of an action taken because of agreement with the reasons offered for taking that action.

This analysis reduces but it does not eliminate the dilemma which has been our concern. The gap between the reasons offered for a moral conclusion and acceptance of that conclusion can be closed only by an exercise of choice on the part of the individual. This proposition can be denied only at the price of adopting some form of ethical naturalism.[11] If the foregoing analysis is correct, "must be performed" cannot eliminate that gap and cannot eliminate an element of freedom from moral decision making. At the same time, recognition of this gap does not deter us from holding men blameworthy if they reject moral guid-

[11] The individual might choose once to forgo the exercise of choice in all subsequent cases—or all cases of a particular type—by commiting himself to blind obedience to the moral views of other men or groups of men, or to a particular moral rule or body of rules. But such a strategy would reduce only the incidence, not the necessity or the significance, of choice.

It is worth emphasizing that this position is not equivalent to the distinction between demonstration and persuasion, a distinction which is as important in descriptive as it is in normative discourse. Verifying Snell's law is not equivalent to persuading X to believe that it is true. The latter requires an act of assent on X's part. We hope that the assent will be based on demonstration, but we know that noncognitive processes are involved which are sometimes unamenable to the influence of demonstration. (On this point, see H. D. Aiken, "Evaluation and Obligation," especially pp. 531–3, in Sellars and Hospers, *Readings in Ethical Analysis* [New York: Appleton Century Crofts, 1952].) If the demonstration satisfies the canons of verification and validity we say that the conclusion is required or entailed; and if X rejects the conclusion we say categorically that X is in error. We cannot say these things in moral matters. The psychological problems are common to both realms, but there are cognitive problems peculiar to moral deliberation. It is to the latter that the above discussion refers.

ance which satisfies the best available criteria. We continue to believe that men are morally required to do some things and not to do others. Hence the limitations upon moral reasoning do not eliminate the "must be performed" dimension of morality.

How then do we deal with cases which create the dilemma in its most acute form? Our final conclusion will be that no general answer is possible to this question. But we have one further distinction to draw before reaching that conclusion. The distinction is between the moral status of an action and the moral character of the actor who takes (or fails to take) an action. If *X* saves a drowning child solely because he expects to receive a reward, he does not deserve to be called a morally good man.[12] Yet the consequences of his action are good. Or, to take a real case, consider the conscientious objector in World War II. A very powerful argument could be made that there was a moral (as well as a legal) obligation to participate actively in the effort to defeat the Nazis and the Japanese. Yet a substantial number of persons rejected that obligation and participated only in limited ways or not at all. Those who regarded participation as morally obligatory must hold that the position of the conscientious objectors (especially those who would do nothing but go to prison) was morally wrong. Yet few informed per-

[12] This distinction rests upon ideas about moral psychology (and raises issues in the realm of moral psychology) that we will not consider here. But the distinction creates difficulties for a utilitarian position which we should notice. If moral judgments turn upon consequences, the motives of moral actors should be of no importance. Yet no ethical or metaethical theory can deny that motives are thought to be morally significant and that moral language reflects this in a number of ways. The present distinction suggests that utilitarianism accounts for moral practice with regard to actions, whereas nonutilitarian premises would be necessary to deal with judgments about the moral character of individuals. But this is misleading if it implies that judgments about motives are made without reference to utilitarian considerations. There is nothing intrinsically wrong with desiring a reward. We criticize *X* because we know that his motive might have resulted in the death of the child if there had been no prospect of a reward. The reason that motives are morally important is that they influence conduct that has an impact upon others. Hence our judgment of what constitutes a good motive depends upon what experience teaches us to be the consequences which flow from acting upon that motive. It must be admitted, however, that the utilitarian underpinnings of concern with motive are often lost sight of, and that motives are widely thought to be significant in and of themselves. The cause of utilitarianism is not served by denying or glossing over this fact. What the utilitarian must show is that arguments that ignore consequences lead to difficulties which can only be overcome by considering them.

sons would draw the conclusion that the conscientious objectors (as a class) were morally defective in character or that they could not be trusted in moral matters generally. Rather, many (including the writer) who hold that conscientious objectors in World War II were morally wrong would regard the sincere conscientious objector as a person of well-developed moral character and as one more worthy of trust in moral matters generally than those who fought in the war without reflection about the moral issues involved.

It is difficult to generalize from these cases. It is perhaps safe to say that sincere rejection of a well-supported moral imperative is rarely if ever grounds for complete excuse. The action (or lack of action) will be morally wrong or blameworthy, and moral sanctions such as expression of moral disapproval of the act will be justified. It is perhaps also safe to say that such a rejection in a single case would not justify the conclusion that the actor is morally bad. Hence the sanctions appropriate to morally bad persons would not be fitting. But these generalizations are hazardous, and even if they are true they do not eliminate the problem completely. The gap between reasons and decisions is not overcome, and the connection between a man's character and his actions is too close to allow us to solve the problem of moral freedom in this manner. This distinction, along with the others we have noted, indicates that moral practice has developed a variety of devices for preventing the dilemma in question from excessively hampering the moral life. But these devices do not alter the fact that moral thought and practice contain both the notion that moral reasoning sometimes generates particular imperatives and the idea that moral decisions must be free decisions. Some conceptions, those called "law" conceptions of morality,[13] place special emphasis upon the imperative character of moral guidance. Others, for example Aristotle's, place greater stress on freedom. The moral practice reflected in the English language does not make a final choice between the two. It relies upon sensitivity in particular cases to maintain a fruitful *modus vivendi* between two valuable but sometimes conflicting notions (another indication of the "practical" character of moral practice). Hence if ethical theory contrives to eliminate the dilemma completely, it will simply produce misunderstanding about the moral practice it seeks to elucidate. What ethical

[13] See Gauthier, *op. cit.*, p. 174, citing G. E. M. Anscombe, *Intention*, p. 78n.

theory *can* say is that the dilemma is reduced to minimal proportions in a moral practice in which rationality is maximized.

V

The findings of this chapter serve to summarize some of the major arguments of Part 2. In the absence of reasoning in support of the conduct recommended, it would be impossible to know whether an imperative had been generated. It is the reasoning that either generates or fails to generate the imperative. Where reasoning does not produce guidance of an imperative kind, where it leaves the decision to the individual in the most complete of the senses just canvassed, it nevertheless provides the best guidance available to the individual. The fact that no obligations are created does not mean that no guidance has been provided. In the absence of reasoning, the actor would be reduced to whim or caprice. Without reasoning along the lines described above, moral imperatives would be indistinguishable from mere assertions, grunts, gestures, and exclamations. It is reasoning—that is, the facts, consequences, principles, and precepts, and the relationships between them—that gives cognitive content to, provides warrants for, and thereby establishes logical relationships between moral imperatives which in turn makes choice between them meaningful and distinguishes them from the nonrational expressions to which they had been mistakenly likened.

We receive a kind of guidance from mere assertions and emotive expressions. The question is whether we are prepared to call it moral guidance. To do so would be to return to the discredited view that the statements "X is right" and "X is wrong" are mere reports of the state of the speaker's mind or psyche, that they cannot contradict one another, and that one can choose between them only in the most subjective or capricious manner. It would be to fly in the face of the logic of moral discourse, a logic which requires that moral statements be supportable when the always pertinent "Why?" is forthcoming. No doubt "X is right" is sometimes a mere report concerning the state of mind of the speaker. But is it intelligent to elevate an abuse of language to the status of the keystone in our ethical theory? If we are not prepared to regard unsupported exclamations as proper moral imperatives, we must conclude that proper moral imperatives are impossible without moral reasoning.

Moral imperatives reflect, in an almost mirror-image manner, some of the main features of moral reasoning and discourse. The fact that moral reasoning sometimes generates imperatives reflects the trans-subjective character of that reasoning. If moral reasoning did not have such character, the guidance which it supplied could have no more obligatory force than specific individuals choose, on whatever frivolous or adventitious ground, to grant it at any moment. Moral imperatives would have no cognitive content, there would be no logical relations between them, and there would be no restrictions whatever on our moral freedom. Second, modification of the imperative force of moral guidance to allow freedom of choice, exemptions and excuses, reflects the inescapable limitations upon reasoning. Particular types of modification, for example the recognition of excuses, reflect or correspond to specific features of moral reasoning such as the importance of consequences and the shortcomings of relying exclusively upon general rules as guides to conduct. These relationships are scarcely surprising. We expect the products of a process of reasoning to bear a close relationship to the main features of that process.

PART THREE

Reason, Value, and Public Interest

Chapter Twelve

CONCLUSION

The purpose of this final chapter is threefold: to summarize by bringing together the findings of Parts 1 and 2, to deal briefly with the relationship between those findings and certain facts (or alleged facts) about the political order, and to attempt to place our conclusions in a larger perspective.

I

Because Part 2 set "public interest" aside in favor of more general categories of analysis, the vocabularies of Parts 1 and 2 differ in some respects. But the structure of the two sections, or, more precisely, the structure of Chapters 3 to 5 and Chapters 6 to 11, are roughly parallel. The components of moral discourse discussed in Chapters 6 to 11 correspond to the considerations and criteria discussed in Chapters 3 to 5. Facts and consequences correspond to contextual considerations, moral principles correspond to formal principles, substantive moral rules and evaluations correspond to community values and their "meaning" in specific cases, and imperatives correspond to commendations. The most efficient means of bringing the two sections together will be to consider each of these pairs. Only in the case of the last pair will we face new problems.

The difficulties with the first pair, facts and consequences—contextual considerations, are less with the components themselves than with the relationship between them and the other elements of discourse. In Part 1 we argued that the logic of "public interest" requires examination of contextual facts and consequences. This conclusion raised the question of the manner in which statements of fact relate to normative conclusions. A bridge between the logical categories of fact and value is provided by the Principle of Consequences. If the validation offered for PC is sound, a logically satisfactory relationship can be established between the categories. But this bridge does not eliminate the differences between the categories; it provides no alchemy for turning one into the other. It merely establishes the logical possibility that one can be relevant to the other. The relevance consists in facts and consequences being the objects or phenomena to which value is assigned, and in facts and consequences constituting a part of the grounds for assigning value to an object or phenomenon. The defensibility of such grounds depends upon the correctness of the statements about facts and consequences and upon whether the grounds satisfy formal principles including the canons of reason. If this view is tenable, a major objection to the position developed in Part 1 has been met.

The argument concerning the fact-value relationship is not all that hinges upon the validity of PC. GP would have no moral significance without PC, and together they provide formal principles that can be used to test aspects of arguments formed by relating facts and consequences to community values and moral precepts. The validation of PC turns upon the argument that the moral standing of an action depends upon its consequences. Once that is shown, PC is analytically true as long as it remains formal, and GP states a valuable but logically unproblematical relation between applications of PC. Since PC is analytic, its validity depends upon facts about language. But the linguistic uses in question are rationally defensible in terms of the most fundamental purposes of morality. Hence a challenge to PC would have to take the form of a challenge to morality as such. If the most general purposes of morality are accepted, PC and everything that depends upon it in the argument about the public interest must be taken as demonstrated.[1]

The third pair is less symmetrical than the first two. Community

[1] If those purposes are challenged, the response must be constructed not from principles taken from within morality, but from arguments that stand independent of moral principles or rules and that serve to justify not specific aspects of morality but morality as such. See William Frankena, *Ethics* (Englewood Cliffs, N. J.: Prentice-Hall, Inc., 1963), pp. 96 ff.

values and moral rules do not have the same logical status. "Value" is a more inclusive concept than "rule," values being the basis of rules. Several rules might be derived from a single value, especially if the value is a general one such as liberty, equality, or stability. But the two concepts share common ground. Both are substantive rather than formal or neutral; both indicate *what* ought to be done as opposed to providing criteria that must be satisfied by any policy or action adopted. (The "what" might be extremely general and in need of specification in specific circumstances.) Phrased somewhat differently, any value can be stated in the form of a rule, although the rule might be highly general. Conversely (precept-type moral) rules presuppose a value; they presuppose something worthy of being valued and of being served or protected by a rule. These points also apply to contextual evaluations which are rules only in the sense demanded by GP or U.

Moral rules are likely to have community standing. Few of us are sufficiently detached from or impervious to the influence of the values generally held in our society to arrive at or consistently to act upon moral rules that do not have general standing. This is especially true in the realm of public interest discourse. In such discourse the ordinary societal influences are reinforced by the practical need to win widespread agreement before a rule will be accepted as a guide to proper public policy. Yet the warrant for any specific rule is not community acceptance but the arguments that can be offered for the rule and for the value from which it derives. This raises the question of the proper modes of justification and requires that both community values and rules be defeasible. For these reasons the discussion of the place of community values in discourse about "public interest" is incomplete and must be supplemented by the more general analysis of moral rules in Part 2.

When a particular value or rule has been identified as relevant to a moral decision, the next step is to test, by PC and GP, the results of serving it in the case at hand. If the policy or action passes these tests, and if it serves a community value or accords with a moral rule, there is a prima facie case for considering it justified. It will have been shown to meet fundamental criteria of proper action. But it will remain subject to further challenge and possible defeat. The authority of community values or moral rules, which will have been the basis of establishing the specific premises of PC and GP, is always open to question.

When such questioning develops, the issue is to be decided through reasoned argument. Whether we have correctly assessed what is involved in and the limits of such argument, it is perhaps reasonable to claim that it has been shown to be more than a mere verbal solution or begging of the question. The next task would be to chart in greater detail the formal characteristics of the type of reasoning in question.

The purpose of moral reasoning is to guide conduct, and such reasoning produces a variety of types of conclusion each of which guides conduct in a different manner. The strongest result is the particular imperative, that is, a demonstration that action *X* is right (or wrong) for actor *Y* in circumstances *Z*. In such a case, *Y* ought to do (or abstain from doing) *X*, and at most we would reduce moral sanctions in recognition that refusal to do *X* was a sincere and reasoned exercise of moral freedom. The next step is particular imperatives the force of which is partially and progressively reduced by excuses, limited exceptions, and reasonable doubts about the validity of the supporting reasons. From there we move to general imperatives or moral rules that must be translated into specific imperatives and are subject to defeat in the course of translation. Finally, there is moral reasoning that produces no imperatives but guides conduct by providing moral information. The most important example is reasoning which concludes that an action or class of actions is morally good. Again, such a conclusion loses strength as it moves from particular to general and as various qualifiers are added.

How do these general findings relate to the commendations supported by discourse about the public interest? In politics, one concept does the service performed by several in moral life generally. Moral discourse distinguishes quite sharply between "good" on the one hand and "right" and "ought" on the other, but in politics one commendatory concept performs the functions of all three. This does not mean that the distinctions which lie behind "good," "right," and "ought" are of no importance in political discourse. We distinguish between policies that would be good if instituted and policies that are *the* right policy in the circumstances and therefore ought to be instituted. The fact that "public interest" does not itself draw these distinctions does not mean they are not drawn in the discourse that surrounds and provides the context in which we use the concept. In fact, the guidance which public interest discourse provides depends heavily upon these distinctions.

We must distinguish between a demonstration (*A*) that it would be in the public interest for an aspect of national life (*X*) to be regulated by public policy, and (*B*) that policy *Y* would be in the public interest in *X*. Within *A* we must further distinguish between a showing (1) that it would be *good* or desirable for *X* to be regulated by public policy, and (2) that to regulate *X* would be the *right* thing to do or that it *ought* to be done.

Justifying conclusion *A1* would require showing that the consequences of regulating *X* would be more desirable than the consequences of not regulating *X*. This would not create an obligation to regulate but would render it permissible to do so. Justifying conclusion *A2* would require showing that, in the language of the positive formulation of PC, "the consequences of not regulating *X* would be morally undesirable." Where this is shown, an obligation is created to institute regulation (the question "for whom?" and the associated problems of excuses, exceptions, etc, will be discussed below). Both *A1* and *A2* are familiar, although *A2* is less common. We know of situations in which the reasoning in support of regulating an area of political life is sufficiently powerful to generate a genuine imperative. The use of violence in society would be an example.

In *B*, we must distinguish between two possibilities: (1) The consequences of instituting *Y* would be desirable (in the public interest) and *Y* can justifiably be adopted. (2) The consequences of not instituting *Y* would be undesirable (contrary to the public interest) and *Y* ought to be instituted (in the public interest). Possibility 2 supports an imperative (subject to excuse, etc), whereas possibility 1 provides moral information but leaves considerable freedom to the moral agent or agents. Possibility 1 is the staple case of public interest discourse, whereas possibility 2, if not unknown, is certainly rare. The number of variables typically involved in public policy decisions, the broad categories which must be employed, and above all the scope and complexity of the consequences to be anticipated militate against reasoning so conclusively that they generate an imperative to institute a specific policy. It is seldom the case that only one policy will meet the criteria of the public interest. Typically, then, public interest discourse generates negative imperatives ("Don't do this or that") and offers positive guidance that allows greater freedom or flexibility ("This would be commendable or justifiable, but it is not obligatory").[2]

To whom do we properly address the guidance generated by public interest discourse? The complexities and typically collective character of decision-making processes in the public realm make this a difficult question to answer. Since action is taken for a collectivity and often collectively, it might appear that the guidance ought to be directed to the collectivity. There are respects in which this is true. The individual's obligations, for example, are limited by the restrictions the collective character of decision procedures place upon his capacity to act. Again, in assigning praise for an action in the public interest, we must take account of the diversity of contributions which made that action possible. But the complexity and collective dimensions of public action only reduce, they do not eliminate, individual capacity and responsibility. The collectivity does not act unless individuals act. However complex the practical and theoretical difficulties of sorting out and assigning individual responsibility, to give up on the task is to give up on the possibility of a politics of public interest.

In private life moral guidance is directed to individual moral agents, and the latter are responsible for acting upon that guidance. In political life something akin to this arrangement is achieved through the distribution of authority. It is the responsibility of public agents to serve the public interest in the area of their authority. As authority diminishes, responsibility diminishes as well. Where the distribution of authority is clear, responsibility for the public interest is clear as well. But we know that authority lines are often very unclear, that authority is often divided and hedged to hamper action, and that possession of the clearest possible authority is rarely a guarantee of the capacity to act effec-

[2] The distinction between *A* and *B*, although logically impeccable, is somewhat artificial as a practical matter. We would ordinarily not decide whether *X* ought to be regulated until we had given thought to the types of policies available to us; it is difficult to think about the consequences of regulation without thinking about the consequences of a specific form of regulation. Yet we do sometimes proceed in the manner suggested by the distinction. Congress has passed a statute establishing that broadcasting shall be regulated in the "public interest, convenience, and necessity." But the statute leaves it to the Federal Communications Commission to work out the content of the regulation. Congress has decided that it is in the public interest for broadcasting to be regulated, and it has separated this decision from the decision regarding the content of the regulation.

tively. Theorists who have been concerned with the public interest have noted these facts with disapproval and have urged clearer and less complex authority patterns and the development of mechanisms and institutions which facilitate effective action and the exercise of leadership. These suggestions aim at greater comparability between the position of the political leader and the position of the moral agent in private life. We are sympathetic with these recommendations, but this is a subject in itself, and not one to be treated in a brief or casual manner.[8] The present task is the simpler one of estimating the significance of the existing complexities for public interest theory.

Recall the distinction between the general duties imposed by a public interest politics and the particular duties imposed by discourse about the descriptive meaning of "public interest." It is the responsibility of those in authority to determine the descriptive meaning of "public interest" as issues arise. This is to say that they must utilize the decision criteria required by the logic of "public interest" in reaching and defending public policy decisions. This is a matter of "right" and "ought," and the reasoning that supports the imperative is rigorous and leaves little room for dispute. There might be excuses that would reduce the blameworthiness of failure to act upon the imperative in specific cases, but there are no exceptions. There will be practical difficulties in determining whether the obligation has been fulfilled, but the criteria to be used for judging are clear. The same points apply to the general duties a politics of public interest imposes upon the general citizenry.

We can also say that it is the duty of those in authority to implement or effectuate the public interest in any specific case. But there are complications with this point. The first stems from the principle "ought implies can." As one of the 100 members of the United States Senate, there are narrow limits upon X's capacity to effectuate or implement public policy. This is in part because his authority is limited. But even Charles de Gaulle at the height of his powers in the Fifth French Republic must suffer limitations on what his authority will make possible. Hence the most that can be said is that it is the obligation of the individual to make every effort to implement the public

[8] I have examined aspects of the question in my doctoral dissertation, "Leadership and Constitutionalism" (unpublished doctoral dissertation, University of California, Berkeley, 1962).

interest; the obligation to achieve implementation is limited by the extent of his authority and by practical obstacles that provide legitimate excuses. There are of course difficulties in making the judgment whether or to what degree these obligations have been fulfilled. But recognition of practical difficulties is not to be confused either with theoretical difficulties or with giving up on a difficult but important problem.

If the limits of capacity restrict obligation, they do not alter the fact that it is good if the individual overcomes those limitations and implements the public interest in spite of obstacles. Recognition of obstacles may limit the extent to which we can properly use "ought" in a particular situation, but we may nevertheless use "good" in speaking of overcoming those obstacles. This point is important to the distinction between authority and leadership or statesmanship.[4] The last point, in a slightly altered form, applies to the general citizenry as well. We would not say that it is the obligation of the citizen to implement or effectuate the public interest, but we would praise him for any contributions he might make.

The foregoing conclusions are a product of reasoning about the place of "public interest" in political life. Hence they are general duties relating to a public interest politics. They are also relevant to the question of the particular duties generated by reasoning about the descriptive meaning of "public interest," but they must be qualified in the light of the types of guidance that such reasoning is able to and ordinarily does produce. It is the obligation of those in authority to make every effort to institute regulation if failure to do so would be contrary to the public interest. These are matters of "right" or "ought," and they generate specific imperatives. The force of the imperatives is reduced if it can be shown that it is impossible for the individual, despite his best efforts, to act effectively upon the imperative. If regulation of an area of national life, or a policy, warrants use of "public interest" in the sense of "good," the individual is free to attempt to institute regulation or adopt the policy. If he succeeds, he will be deserving of praise to the degree that the accomplishment was the consequence of his efforts.

[4] There are even circumstances in which we are prepared to use "good" when the public interest is implemented in spite of obstacles created by limitations upon authority. But this is a complex matter that cannot be examined here.

In all of these cases, the formal, schematic character of the present discussion neglects very great practical complexities and problems. In passing over them, we do not intend to minimize their significance. But we could not identify, much less resolve, the practical problems of achieving a politics of public interest if we had not first sorted out the theoretical considerations just discussed. Hence if the discussion of imperatives and commendations is correct, it satisfies a necessary condition of such politics.

To summarize, the arguments of Parts 1 and 2 complement one another and together demonstrate that "public interest" performs a significant function in political discourse, that there are specifiable requirements and decision criteria associated with the concept, and that these criteria are philosophically defensible.

II

How do these findings and arguments relate to the empirical facts about political life mentioned at the outset of Part 2? Let us assume that the case has been made about the logic of "public interest" and the criteria it creates. Let us further assume that it has been demonstrated that there are no philosophical obstacles to the utilization and satisfaction of those criteria. Granting these assumptions, is it not the case that the entire book is hopelessly out of touch with or even at odds with the most salient facts about political life? However logically impeccable it may be to argue that we determine what is in the public interest by "giving reasons," can such an argument be said to contribute to our understanding of the realities of the political process?

It is important to emphasize that this book is concerned with empirical evidence concerning politics. One source of evidence, used again and again, is that humble but reliable source of data known as the dictionary. This source has been supplemented with (A) the evidence supplied by the manner in which political writers have used certain language, (B) our knowledge of the manner in which certain expressions in the English language are used, and (C) the understandings other students of ethics and politics have had of the uses of language. A involves a straightforward empirical question: Did Bentham use "interest" in manner X or not? As with all empirical matters, this evidence requires interpretation before it can be meaningful. B and C are perhaps less reliable than the dictionary, but if they even approached general unreliability, communication in the English language would be impossible.[5] It is a fact that certain words and phrases occur in political discussion, that they have a variety of uses, and that they relate to one another in various ways. The present book may be mistaken in how certain words are used or how they relate one to the other. But these are matters of fact that are as subject to verification as facts about, say, the political activities of the National Association of Manufacturers. Whatever the relation between the facts discussed here and other facts relating to politics, we have been discussing facts. We have not rested content with the facts; we have interpreted, searched for relationships, sought coherence and significance. But that is a part of the definition of a *study*.

The question, then, concerns the relationship between the set of facts examined here and other facts about politics. We have not examined this question and hence cannot answer it conclusively. But the materials examined here, together with general theories about materials of this kind, suggest some hypotheses regarding the relationship between linguistic facts and facts about other dimensions of human behavior. We have language in order to communicate about characteristics, features, and concerns of human behavior. If there were no nonlinguistic phenomena to which the linguistic uses and distinctions referred, there would be no reason to have those uses and distinctions in our language. (The hypothesis, of course, is consistent with their being residues and remnants which are no longer functional. But we would expect that these would be used very little and that in time they would appear only in historical dictionaries.) In the present case, if "public interest" and the linguistic structure which surrounds it did not correspond to nonlinguistic concerns and behavior, the concept would shift in function or fall out of ordinary usage. This is no more than a hypothesis, but it is worth testing.

There is a second point of greater importance. We have tried to demonstrate that "public interest" is a normative concept or standard, used to commend and justify, and that its logic generates a set of criteria which must be satisfied if "public interest" is to be properly applied. If our interpretation of the linguistic evidence is correct, it is a

[5] On this point, see especially Stanley Cavell, "Must We Mean What We Say," in V. C. Chappell, editor, *Ordinary Language* (Englewood Cliffs, N. J.: Prentice-Hall, Inc., 1964).

fact about politics that this standard or norm exists and can be described. The question of whether the standard is in fact met, lived up to, or widely taken seriously by the members of a political system is an independent question, the answer to which cannot upset the fact that the standard is there, enshrined in the language. We have suggested that there are reasons for thinking that the standard is taken seriously at least by some. Whether this is true would affect the significance of the linguistic facts, but it could not alter them.

It is the essence of the notion of a norm or standard that there is a tension between the norm and the phenomenon that is to be judged or evaluated according to that norm. If every example of the phenomenon in question corresponded exactly with the norm or standard, we would cease to call the latter a norm and call it a descriptive generalization. If all of mankind underwent a miraculous transformation so that they never again would lie or be tempted to lie, the norm or standard "tell the truth" or "don't say what is false" would cease to be a norm. If indeed we retained the language "tell the truth" and "lie" we would simply say "men always tell the truth" or "men never lie." Hence to trouble to examine and clarify standards despite the fact that they are seldom satisfied (if that be the case) is scarcely to be regarded as an indication of naïveté. Rather, criticism of such a procedure reflects a failure to understand the most fundamental purpose of norms and standards.

A demonstration that political behavior seldom meets the standards of "public interest," in short, is not to be taken as a refutation of a theory as to what those standards are. A theory of "public interest" will not describe all the dimensions of political behavior for the excellent reason that such is not the purpose of a theory of "public interest." (It might enlighten us about aspects of political behavior by calling attention to descrepancies between the norm and the practice.) What would damage such a theory would be a demonstration that it does not fit the relevant evidence or that it makes an indefensible interpretation of that evidence.

III

It is perhaps unnecessary to emphasize that there is a wide range of questions relevant to an analysis of the public interest but ignored or touched only lightly here. We have said virtually nothing, for example, about the institutional arrangements and political patterns and relationships called for by, or conducive to, the satisfaction of the requirements generated by "public interest." Although a good deal has been said regarding duties and obligations, we have ignored the fields of moral and political psychology and hence the entire question of the manner in which or the conditions under which individuals might be led to or would be most likely to perform those duties and meet those obligations.[6] To note these omissions is to call attention to the fact that this book offers a theory of "public interest," and only some of the rudiments of a theory of the public interest. It is also to note that a fully developed theory of the public interest, as the case of Rousseau demonstrates, would require a systematic political philosophy.

Yet the centrality of our subject matter in its largest dimensions lends significance to the particular or partial topics which fall within its scope. Insofar as we have focused upon "public interest," our concern has been the logical possibility of a reasoned exercise of state power and reasoned evaluation of the uses to which that power is put. If the foregoing arguments are tenable, there are specifiable and defensible procedures and criteria that can be employed for these purposes. The availability of such procedures and criteria, if far from a surety of their proper employment, is a necessary condition of the latter. Since the destiny of mankind is in the hands of the state, the knowledge that this condition is satisfied is perhaps not to be denigrated. If we are right that public interest discourse is a special case of moral discourse, the same conclusions apply to moral life generally, and the significance of those conclusions is extended accordingly.

[6] One of the most effective ways of appreciating the range of questions relevant to a fully developed theory of public interest is to read Rousseau's *Social Contract*, a work which is concerned with the notion throughout. Not the least of the present debt to that work is the extent to which a reading of Rousseau calls attention to the limits of the present treatment.

INDEX